Human–Computer Interaction Series

Editors-in-chief
Desney Tan, Microsoft Research, USA
Jean Vanderdonckt, Université catholique de Louvain, Belgium

HCI is a multidisciplinary field focused on human aspects of the development of computer technology. As computer-based technology becomes increasingly pervasive – not just in developed countries, but worldwide – the need to take a human-centered approach in the design and development of this technology becomes ever more important. For roughly 30 years now, researchers and practitioners in computational and behavioral sciences have worked to identify theory and practice that influences the direction of these technologies, and this diverse work makes up the field of human-computer interaction. Broadly speaking it includes the study of what technology might be able to do for people and how people might interact with the technology. The HCI series publishes books that advance the science and technology of developing systems which are both effective and satisfying for people in a wide variety of contexts. Titles focus on theoretical perspectives (such as formal approaches drawn from a variety of behavioral sciences), practical approaches (such as the techniques for effectively integrating user needs in system development), and social issues (such as the determinants of utility, usability and acceptability).

Titles published within the Human–Computer Interaction Series are included in Thomson Reuters' Book Citation Index, The DBLP Computer Science Bibliography and The HCI Bibliography.

More information about this series at http://www.springer.com/series/6033

Phil Turner • J. Tuomas Harviainen

Editors

Digital Make-Believe

Editors
Phil Turner
School of Computing
Edinburgh Napier University
Edinburgh, UK

J. Tuomas Harviainen
Management and Organization
Hanken School of Economics
Helsinki, Finland

ISSN 1571-5035
Human–Computer Interaction Series
ISBN 978-3-319-29551-0   ISBN 978-3-319-29553-4   (eBook)
DOI 10.1007/978-3-319-29553-4

Library of Congress Control Number: 2016937642

Printed on acid-free paper

This Springer imprint is published by Springer Nature
The registered company is Springer International Publishing AG Switzerland

Contents

Contributors

Luke Burrows achieved his M.Sc. in User Experience from Edinburgh Napier University and is now an independent consultant.

Lindsey Carruthers is a lecturer in the School of Life, Sport, and Social Sciences at Edinburgh Napier University. She specialises in cognitive psychology, with particular interests in creativity, attention, ADHD, memory, and pretending in adults.

Sebastian Deterding is a researcher and designer working on facilitating human flourishing through playful and gameful design. He is a reader/senior research fellow at the University of York's Digital Creativity Hub, associate of the international design agency Hubbub, founder and organizer of the Gamification Research Network, and editor (with Steffen P. Walz) of *The Gameful World: Approaches, Issues, Applications* (MIT Press, 2015). Dr. Deterding lives online at codingconduct.cc.

Tom Flint is a lecturer at the School of Computing at Edinburgh Napier University, aligned to the Make-Believe laboratory. Tom has worked in Higher Education for over 10 years, before this he has enjoyed a variety of occupations. This has included time as a BT technician, founder and publisher of cult magazines *The Lock* and *Sleaze Nation*, and a period working with urban outfitters when they first established themselves in Europe. Tom's teaching and research centre on physical computing and storytelling, particularly focusing on where these two disciplines complement each other.

J. Tuomas Harviainen is a development manager for the city of Vantaa, Finland, and a postdoctoral researcher at Hanken School of Economics. He currently focuses especially on the organizational learning aspects of games, but often ventures into service design, management, information systems, or sexology. He is also one of the three editors of the journal *Simulation & Gaming*.

Chih-Wei Huang achieved her M.Sc. in User Experience from Edinburgh Napier University and is now User Experience Designer at ZyXEL, Taiwan.

Kristine Jørgensen is as of 2015 a researcher at University of Bergen and project manager of the Games and Transgressive Aesthetic research project. She is the author of Gameworld Interfaces (MIT Press 2013) and A Comprehensive Study of Sound in Computer Games (Mellen Press 2009). She received her Ph.D. in media studies from University of Copenhagen in 2007.

Satu Luojus has a Ph.D. in Information processing science. She is a principal lecturer and head of the Master's Degree Programme in Customer-Centered Service Development at Laurea University of Applied Sciences. Her areas of expertise are user experience (UX), user-centered design (UCD), service design (SD), and user research in living lab ecosystems. Her research interests include UX, user studies, conceptualization, user-centered design, and living lab research methods. She has over 20 years working experience as a lecturer as well as over 10 years experience in conducting user-centered R&D – projects as a researcher and as a project coordinator/manager/scientific leader.

Zuzanna Rucińska is a lecturer of philosophy in Leiden University, the Netherlands. She was an early stage researcher of the Marie Curie Initial Training Network 'TESIS' at University of Hertfordshire, UK, working alongside Dan Hutto and Shaun Gallagher on the enactive account of pretence. Her research interests include pretence and imagination, embodied and enacted cognition, dynamical systems theory, sensorimotor theory, and theory of affordances. She is currently working on the application of the enactive account of pretence to the fields of sports and therapy.

Phil Turner is a reader in the School of Computing at Edinburgh Napier University and research leader of the make-believe group.

Susan Turner has 30 years experience of the human aspects of interactive systems. Her specialisms have included, in broadly chronological order: usability, user-centered design and evaluation, CSCW, presence and place, and user experience. She has recently retired from a senior lecturer post at Edinburgh Napier University.

Carina Westling based at the University of Sussex, researches interaction design with Punchdrunk theatre company, pioneers in immersive interactive theatre. Her broader research interests include digital and live interaction and experience design, in which she is also an active practitioner with The Nimbus Group, where she acts as Creative Director. Past projects include live indoors and outdoors performance events in the UK and Scandinavia with participant numbers ranging from 150 to 200,000. Carina also collaborates with human-computer interaction researchers with a particular focus on complex embodied affective states and responses during interaction.

Chapter 1
Introduction

Phil Turner and J. Tuomas Harviainen

1.1 Make-Believe: The Quest for Verisimilitude?

We occupy two worlds, maybe more. We live in the everyday world of work, family, crowded trains, mobile phones, over-priced coffee and fast food and we deal with these things with scarcely a thought, "we walk and read aloud, we get off and on street cars, we dress and undress, and do a thousand useful acts without thinking of them" (Dewey 1922). This world is public, routine and apparently primary. Wittgenstein tells us that "The world is everything that is the case", that is, the world is precisely those states of affairs which do exist, fast food and all. The other worlds are those of the imagination and of make-believe. Small children seem to spend their time fluidly moving between them and adults routinely escape to make-believe worlds by reading a novel, playing a game on their phones, or going to the movies. Take a commuter train in the evening and just see how many people have escaped into these other private worlds.

These secondary worlds are peculiarly human and may be one of the reasons our species has been so successful. This is evidenced by our ability to decouple ourselves from the primary world and to engage in make-believe which liberates us from the moment and the restrictions of the primary world. We argue that make-believe is all too frequently and mistakenly dismissed as the stuff of fairy-tales. We note that these make-believe worlds are not boundless – there are limits – and they often rely on props for their creation (Walton 1990). Donald (1991) calls these props

P. Turner (✉)
School of Computing, Edinburgh Napier University, Edinburgh, UK
e-mail: p.turner@napier.ac.uk

J.T. Harviainen
Management and Organization, Hanken School of Economics, Helsinki, Finland
e-mail: tuomas.harviainen@hanken.fi

© Springer International Publishing Switzerland 2016
P. Turner, J.T. Harviainen (eds.), *Digital Make-Believe*,
Human–Computer Interaction Series, DOI 10.1007/978-3-319-29553-4_1

"exograms" and found them in the caves of our ancient ancestors. We now encounter them as the stuff of the stories we read, or as the colourful, animated screens of a game.

The worlds are separate but interleaved. The primary is generally thought to be more important despite the scant conscious attention we pay it – operating, instead, on the basis of a kind of lightly monitored "autopilot". The secondary worlds are mistakenly treated as idle fantasy, while being apparently trivial, they demand a good deal more of our cognitive resources to create and maintain – hence their need to rely on external resources (props) to scaffold them.

We are not alone in our enthusiasm for make-believe as it has been adopted, in the form of "make.believe" (note the separating dot rather than a hyphen), as the global brand strategy for the electronics corporation Sony®. They write, "make.believe symbolizes the spirit of our brand. It stands for the power of our creativity, our ability to turn ideas into reality, and the belief that anything we can imagine, we can make real". Sony tell us that between "make" and "believe" is "where imagination and reality collide" (Sony 2009).

Corporate strategy and advertising copy aside, we all pretend and make-believe everyday. We pretend when we act *as though* or behave *as if*. Unlike pretending, make-believe relies on things to act as a prop or a trigger (such as a good book, a "light sabre" or a paper prototype) from which to spin a make-believe episode. Walton calls this the "principle of generation".

It is our contention in this book (with the occasional dissenting voice) to argue that pretending/making-believe is a form of cognition complementary to the more familiar faculties of problem solving, language and so forth which allows us to create and access these other worlds. More than this it is also provides an intuitive form of interaction and a tool for innovation.

1.2 Why Do We Make-Believe?

Cosmides and Tooby (2000) tell us that evolutionary psychology is not a specific subfield of psychology but, "It is a *way of thinking* about psychology that can be applied to any topic within it". Buss (1995, p. 2) agrees observing, "Because all behaviour depends on complex psychological mechanisms, and all psychological mechanisms, at some basic level of description, are the result of evolution by selection, then all psychological theories are implicitly evolutionary psychological theories". While evolutionary psychology is not without its critics, it is agreed that recognisably modern humans have been around for approximately 250,000 years. It has been said that if we were to take a man from that time, clean him up and dress him appropriately, he would pass more or less unnoticed amongst us. This similarity is, however, only skin deep as behaviourally and culturally he would be quite different, that is, until about 45,000 years ago when modern human behaviour appeared *almost overnight* (e.g. Klein 2002; Lewis-Williams 2004 among many more). For example, Klein (2002, p. 24) writes " ... the most recent event [in our evolution] occurred about 50,000 years ago ... it produced the fully modern ability to invent and manipulate culture". Tattersall (2006, p. 67–68) writes in a similar vein, "When the first Cro-Magnons arrived in Europe some 40,000 years ago, they evidently brought with them more or less the entire panoply of behaviors that distinguishes modern humans from every other species that has ever existed. Sculpture, engraving, painting, body ornamentation, music, notation, subtle understanding of diverse materials, elaborate burial of the dead, painstaking decoration of utilitarian objects ...". Although there is some debate about the timing, it is generally agreed that abstract thinking; planning; magick and religion; technological innovation; and symbolic behaviour witnessed a flowering about then. More recently, Mithen (2014) has added *make-believe* to this list. Mithen has proposed a number of changes to our species and to our ancestors which were needed to facilitate the emergence of what he describes as *imagination*.[1] (We won't quibble about whether this is "imagination" per se or the ability to make-believe.) These changes enabled us to acquire a theory of mind, true language, and what he calls a cognitive fluidity enabling external artefacts are treated as part of our cognition. Whether or not we agree with every detail of this, what does emerge is that make-believe is a key cognitive facility. We suggest that make-believe brings into focus abstract thought, and our abilities to plan, innovate, reason symbolically and perhaps a little magick.

In this book, we discuss the ways in which we also exploit these world as the basis of our interactions with technologies and services, as well as a vehicle for inventing new ones.

1.3 Pretending and Make-Believe

In June 2015, six scientists who had been living under a dome on the slopes of a dormant volcano in Hawaii emerged into the fresh air. It had been their intention to simulate what life might be like in Mars and it was the first time they had left their dome without donning a space suit for eight months. It was reported that crew member Jocelyn Dunn said, "When we first walked out the door, it was scary not to have a suit on – We've been pretending for so long". (Telegraph newspaper 2015)

Earlier we proposed that pretending involves acting *as though* or behaving *as if*. So, for example, I can (with varying degrees of difficulty) pretend to like sound

---

[1]Defining imagination has proved to be very difficult. A number of celebrated thinkers, such as Walton who, after listing a wide variety of different forms of imagining writes, "What is it to imagine? We have examined a number of dimensions along which imaginings can vary; shouldn't we now spell out what they have in common? – Yes, if we can: But I can't" (1990, p. 19). One of the problems with defining (much less understanding) imagination is that it might reasonable include day-dreaming, visualising, wishing and a whole host of other slippery concepts. And, of course, we are quite able to imagine without pretending and to pretend without imagining. Faced with these difficulties we will confine ourselves, in the main, to pretending and making-believe.

of bagpipes; I can pretend to be a kangaroo; I can pretend that our department's restructuring makes sense. And evidence of these forms of pretending is my behaviour towards the players of bagpipes, my hopping with both feet held together and my sitting quietly at departmental meetings respectively. It is not lying and even young children (Rakoczy et al. 2004) can tell the difference between behaving or trying for real and pretending. To pretend is to act *as though*. This emphasis on acting and behaving suggests that pretending is an expression of our embodied cognition and as such reflects the capabilities and restrictions imposed by our bodies.

Pretending is almost exclusively studied in the context of child development where it is taken to be a synonym for pretend play (e.g. Leslie 1987; Nichols and Stitch 2000; Harris 2000). The focus on pretend play relies on the generally agreed position is that it is essential to a child's cognitive, affective and social development and this ability appears quite early. Leslie (1987, p. 412) tells us that it can be observed at "the very beginning of childhood", while Harris tells us it appears later and equates it with the development of language. The importance of play is identified by Russ (2004) who tells us many of our cognitive and affective processes rely on it. Specifically, play involves the exercise of alternating cycles of divergent and convergent thinking which is the ability to generate different ideas, story themes, and so forth and then to weave them together. Pretend play also facilitates the expression of both positive and negative feelings, and the ability to integrate emotion with cognition (e.g. Jent et al. 2011; Seja and Russ 1999). When children take on different roles in pretend play it allows them to acquire and practice the skills of communication, problem solving, and empathy (Hughes 1999). However of particular interest to the current discussion are the following definitions of pretend play. We begin with Garvey (1990) who tell us that pretend play is the "voluntary transformation of the here and now, the you and me, and the this or that, along with any potential action that these components of a situation might have". While Harris (*ibid*) tells us that, "Children's pretend play is [...] an initial exploration of possible worlds" and Rutherford et al. (2007, p. 1025) suggest that pretend play is "acting as if something is when it is not". These themes of the "voluntary transformation of the here and now", "possible worlds" and acting as though "something is when it is not" are central to our argument.

Make-Believe

Props play a central role in Walton's (1990) theory of make-believe. Props enable us to create stories and episodes of make-believe. Props include everything from childhood toys to works of art. Thus a child is better able to make-believe a character from the Star Wars™ movies when armed with a "light sabre" than rushing about claiming to be an unarmed Jedi master. While these are well established concepts, we can also characterise the use of props as "thinking with things". The artefact scaffolds the pretend behaviour by, arguably, relieving some of the cognitive effort required of pretending. Here, virtual reality or a very detailed videogame, for example, must offer considerable amounts of cognitive scaffolding.

This idea has been developed to a degree within HCI by Scaife and Rogers (1996). They have observed that we often make use of external artefacts as part of our everyday problem solving and we do so by way of "interaction[s] between internal and external representations" (p. 188). They describe this as *computational offloading*, i.e. the extent to which external representations can reduce the amount of cognitive effort required to solve a problem, complete a task and (we add), make-believe which is likely to be quite demanding computationally. In their paper they suggest that different forms of representation – specifically, re-representation, can make scaffold comprehension. The use of graphs is an obvious example. Florence Nightingale, a reforming nurse working during the Crimean Wars of the nineteenth century, used graphs to communicate the extent of casualty figures to British members of parliament. She had found that significantly more casualties were being incurred from disease and poor medical treatment than from enemy action. This was poorly understood but her use of pie-charts changed that.

Indeed HCI is replete with examples such as these. We can present and re-present the same idea as a narrative description through a storyboard, low-fidelity prototypes or an interactive digital mock-up. Each has it power and its own constraint but collectively they offer their own means of thinking.

This "thinking with things" is, of course, currently the subject of sustained research in cognitive science though space prevents a thorough treatment of this subject (e.g. Clark 2008; Kirsh 1995, 2010; Malafouris 2013 among others). Kirsh (1995, 2010) who has also been very active in researching this issue has presented evidence that we make, for example, the "intelligent use of space" to simplify everything from how we prepare a salad, assemble flat-pack furniture, and complete a jigsaw by using the things themselves to help reduce the complexity of the task. For example, when confronted with a jigsaw puzzle, we tend to group the pieces with a straight edge into a single pile, or all the examples of sky.

Pretending, Make-Believe and Motor Cognition

One last thought, just how real is pretending/make-believe? We believe that pretending/make-believe rely on the self-same neural pathways and established motor cognition routines as real world behaviour, and there is a significant body of empirical work which can be used to support this position.

Decety, for example, compared real and simulated tasks from the perspective of timing, autonomic responses and cerebral blood flow. He found that when he asked people to mentally "walk" toward points placed at different distances, they found that the time it took to perform this task varied according to the actual distance of the target. Repeating this task in the real world, it was found that the times were highly correlated with the task carried out in the imagination (Decety et al. 1989). In a second round of experiments, people were asked to imagine themselves walking while carrying a variety of different loads. Again, it was found that people took longer to reach a target carrying a heavy load than when asked to imagine walking the same distance while carrying a lighter load (Decety 1996). These findings suggest that motor imagery and motor production rely the same representations. Decety went on to propose that motor images, that is, skilled motor actions – such as playing cricket, drinking tea – share the same neural mechanisms as those that are also responsible for preparation and programming of actual movements. His argument being that motor acts are represented centrally and as such are available for modification, retrieval and execution. Motor imagery and motor execution differing only in that the former is blocked prior to execution. These initial findings were subsequently developed by Jeannerod (2001) to create his "theory of neural simulation of action" which argues that real and imagined actions are mediated by the same cortical areas. Jeanerod's hypothesis is that the motor system is part of a simulation network that is activated when we intend acting or when we have observed others engaged in an activity or other. He continues that the function of this simulation not only shapes the motor system in anticipation of execution, but is also to provide information as to both the feasibility and the meaning of potential actions.

Schredl and Erlacher (2008) have extended this discussion by examining the hypothesis that REM dreams also call upon these same neural substrates. They found abundant anecdotal evidence from studies of the reported dreams of athletes – who have reported "practicing" difficult or demanding procedures in lucid dreams – and clinical evidence from people suffering from REM sleep behaviour disorder.

From this evidence we may conclude that pretending/make-believe are not just epiphenomenal but are an intrinsic part of the normal functioning of our cognition.

1.4   Introducing This Book

This volume of very diverse chapters on digital make-believe offers a glimpse at a new way of thinking about human-computer interaction. Bruner (1991, p. 4) writes that "unlike the constructions generated by logical and scientific procedures that can be weeded out by falsification, narrative constructions can only achieve 'verisimilitude'". This volume of ten chapters is not in the business of truth and falsehood: instead we seek the "appearance of truth", though we might settle for plausibility.

In A make-believe narrative for HCI Phil Turner begins by noting that HCI is a discipline with three distinct but overlapping faces. HCI as theory; HCI as practice; and HCI as experience. HCI as theory arose from the cognitive revolution of the 1950; HCI as practice, in contrast, is concerned with designing interactive; and finally, HCI as experience is concerned with, for example, how technology provides access to the virtual. This presents HCI as both a fragmented discipline and one which lacks a unifying story. Just what is HCI about? Turner argues that one such story (though there may be others) is that it relies on make-believe to create/experience and account for these digital technologies.

In Make-believing virtual realities Susan Turner and her colleagues explore how make-believe, largely through the medium of schemata, supports the experience of presence. This is illustrated by two case studies of desktop virtual environments, which despite their minimal nature, afforded a relatively high degree of sense of presence. In their discussion, they highlight intriguing evidence from neuropsychology that may suggest that similar neural features underlie all mental phenomena involving projection into locations or states other than that immediately to hand.

Tom Flint's Fiction for design considers a very familiar tool in HCI, the scenario and asks do they need a back story? Scenarios, and the many variations on them, are a ubiquitous tool in both HCI and other design rich activities. A scenario is a little story which, by default, is not so. It is make-believe. For a scenario to be credible and useful, it needs to be believable. Flint poses and answer the question as to whether a "backstory" is need to make this so. Flint draws on examples from beyond HCI to illustrate his case.

In Designing for service experiences, Satu Luojus and J. Tuomas Harviainen explain the constant presence of make-believe in service design and the usefulness that has for HCI. By introducing readers to the logics and frameworks of service design, they illustrate the ways in which designers envision new forms of service and new interfaces, how they use data to imagine both customers and user experiences, and how the users themselves later interact with first prototypes and then actual touchpoints and interfaces through a logic firmly based on make-believe. They furthermore provide three examples of tools – probes, design games and LEGO® SERIOUS PLAY® – that showcase varying types of design make-believe in action.

Gameworld interfaces as make-believe introduces us to the design of interfaces to gameworlds. Kristine Jørgensen discusses the ways in which imagination connects with types of information in the game environment and the ways in which we interact with it. Focusing on the balancing act between rules and make-believe, the chapter analyses how game-play requires the simultaneous use of two "mindsets". Using Kendall Walton's prop theory, Jørgensen then shows how the gameworld itself is a prop that enables enjoyable make-believe, as well as how different players engage in different types of imagining during play.

Blurring the line between the two worlds discussed in this introduction, Sebastian Deterding's Make-believe in gameful and playful design examines gamification and playification, the introduction of game and play-like traits into other activities, from the perspective of make-believe. By adding rules, goals and tracking systems like leaderboards into mundane tasks, people are trying to increase their level of engagement and motivation. As pointed out by Deterding, while make-believe is strongly present in gamification, it is rarely noted in design theory. To address this, the chapter provides ideas for how to both recognize that connection – and to utilize it in design.

As we have seen in the introduction to this chapter, pretending and make-believing has largely been treated as though there were the sole provenance of children. We can see children pretending and engaged in make-believe in every school playground but are these abilities lost to adults?

Lindsey Carruthers and Phil Turner report a study of professional, adult make-believers. Their chapter The role of make-believe in Foley describes the work of Foley artists who design and perform those everyday sounds in a movie. This chapter offers a perspective on the work of real life, adult pretenders. These artists act (re-enact) the actions of on-screen actors in order to create the sounds associated with them. They describe their work as hovering between the wholly real and the wholly make-believe.

Zuzanna Rucińska's, Enactive mechanism of make-belief games challenges a fundamental assumption underpinning much of the thinking in make-believe and pretending. Psychological accounts of pretending all rely on labelling make-believe content as such and maintaining the division between what is so, and what is not. Enactive accounts, in contrast, reject the notion of representation, so an enactive account of make-believe is a radical rethinking of how it might operate.

Carina Westling's, Immanent story worlds: the making of Punchdrunk's The Drowned Man – A Hollywood Fable is the final chapter of this volume. Westling illustrates just how diverse a field digital make-believe is. She discusses the work of Punchdrunk, which is a British theatre company, and which has pioneered a form of "immersive" theatre. Drawing upon practical experiences and theoretical insights she wonders how this kind of theatre can be translated into the digital.

During the peer review process, Suellen Adams, David Benyon, Lynne Hall, Richard Hetherington, Jonna Koivisto, Richard N. Landers and Olle Sköld offered their valuable critique and feedback on chapters in progress. We are very grateful for their comments, as well as those of the authors who suggested critical improvements to each other's works.

We believe that this volume of very diverse chapters on digital make-believe offers a glimpse at a new way of thinking about human-computer interaction and we very much hope you enjoy it.

References

Bruner J (1991) The narrative construction of reality. Crit Inq 18:1–21
Buss DM (1995) Evolutionary psychology, p. A new paradigm for psychological science. Psychol Inq 6(1):1–30
Clark A (2008) Supersizing the mind. Oxford University Press, Oxford
Cosmides L, Tooby J (2000) Consider the source: the evolution of adaptations for decoupling and metarepresentation. In: Sperber D (ed) Metarepresentations: a multidisciplinary perspective. OUP, Oxford

Decety J (1996) Do imagined and executed actions share the same neural substrate? Cogn Brain Res 3:87–93

Decety J, Jeannerod J, Prablanc C (1989) The timing of mentally represented actions. Behav Brain Res 34:35–42

Dewey J (1922) Human nature and conduct: an introduction to social psychology. Modern Library, New York, pp 172–180

Donald M (1991) Origins of the modern mind. Harvard University Press, Cambridge, MA

Garvey C (1990) Play. Harvard University Press, Cambridge, MA

Harris P (2000) The work of the imagination. Blackwell, London

Hughes FP (1999) Children, play, and development. Allyn & Bacon, Needham Heights

Jeannerod M (2001) Neural simulation of action: a unifying mechanism for motor cognition. Neuroimage 14:103–109

Jent JF, Niec LN, Baker SE (2011) Play and interpersonal processes. In: Russ SW, Niec LN (eds) Play in clinical practice: evidence-based approaches. Guilford Press, New York

Kirsh D (1995) The intelligent use of space. Artif Intell 73:31–68

Kirsh D (2010) Thinking with external representation. AI Soc 25:441–454

Klein RG with Edgar B. (2002) The dawn of human culture. Wiley, New York

Leslie A (1987) Pretense and representation: the origins of "Theory of Mind". Psychol Rev 94(4):412–426

Lewis-Williams D (2004) The mind in the cave. Thames & Hudson, London

Malafouris L (2013) How things shape the mind: a theory of material engagement. MIT Press, Cambridge, MA

Mithen (2014) Imagination: our greatest skill. New Scientist, September 17th edition.

Nichols S, Stich S (2000) A cognitive theory of pretense. Cognition 74:115–147

Rakoczy H, Tomasello M, Striano T (2004) Young children know that trying is not pretending: a test of the "behaving-as-if" construal of children's understanding of pretense. Dev Psychol 40:388–399

Russ SW (2004) Play in child development and psychotherapy. Earlbaum, Mahwah

Rutherford M, Young G, Hepburn S, Rogers S (2007) A longitudinal study of pretend play in autism. J Autism Dev Disord 37(6):1024–1039

Scaife M, Rogers Y (1996) External cognition: how do graphical representations work? Int J Hum Comput Stud 45:185–213

Schredl M, Erlacher D (2008) Relationship between waking sport activities, reading and dream content in sport and psychology students. J Psychol 142(3):267–276

Seja AL, Russ SW (1999) Children's fantasy play and emotional understanding. J Clin Child Psychol 28:269–277

Sony (2009) http://www.sony.net/SonyInfo/News/Press/200909/09-100E/. Last retrieved 14 Oct 2015

Tattersall I (2006) How we became human. Sci Am Spec 16(2):66–73

Telegraph Newspaper (2015) http://www.telegraph.co.uk/news/science/11673542/Mars-project-scientists-emerge-from-dome-after-8-months.html. Last retrieved 6 Oct 2015

Walton KL (1990) Mimesis as make-believe: on the foundations of the representational arts. Harvard University Press, Cambridge, MA

Chapter 2
A Make-Believe Narrative for HCI

Phil Turner

2.1 Introduction

The last 30 years have seen extraordinary and radical developments in human-computer interaction, not only in technology, but in the sheer diversity of theoretical positions which have been flirted with, examined, appropriated and adopted. Without wishing to turn this chapter into a sea of references we have seen a narrow laboratory focus, reflecting the contribution of cognitive psychology, being challenged by the adoption of anthropological perspectives (e.g. Suchman 1987; Hutchins 1995) and the appearance of Activity Theory (e.g. Engeström 1987; Bødker 1987). These have led researchers to recognise roles for context, mediation and distribution in HCI. Similarly, Sheets-Johnstone (2009) tells us that she introduced the term the "corporeal turn" in the 1980s in response to what she describes as centuries of Cartesian misrepresentation in portraying the body as the "material handmaiden of an all powerful mind". Her work "rehabilitated" the body and helped us think about the possibilities of such things as embodied interaction. The 1990s also witnessed yet another turn, this time to the social. This "turn to the social" was triggered by the emergence of computer supported cooperative working and the accompanying appropriation of sociological theory and practice (e.g. Dourish 2001). Cognitive science has made its contribution too by suggesting that our cognition is scaffolded by technology (Scaife and Rogers 1996) or that it extends into the external world (e.g. Clark 2008). Affect too has enjoyed a renaissance and is no longer ignored or regarded as a vestigial embarrassment (Norman 2004). Its role in decision making, user experience, preference formation, (tele)-presence and our fondness for playing computer games has finally been

P. Turner (✉)
School of Computing, Edinburgh Napier University, Edinburgh, UK
e-mail: p.turner@napier.ac.uk

© Springer International Publishing Switzerland 2016
P. Turner, J.T. Harviainen (eds.), *Digital Make-Believe*,
Human–Computer Interaction Series, DOI 10.1007/978-3-319-29553-4_2

recognised (e.g. Damasio 1999; Lindgaard et al. 2006; Turner 2015b). Finally, the very notion of interaction as taking place between an intelligent agent and external technology is being challenged by the first tentative appearance of "cyborgs" which are the result of blending the organic and synthetic (Clark 2003). These successive anthropological, corporeal, social, external and affective turns have taken us a long way from Card et al. (1989) and their "model human processor" account. While we are now confronted by an HCI which is vibrant, truly multi-disciplinary and perhaps a little unmanageable, there remains the questions of how all of these different pieces fit together. We can no longer draw a neat, idealised and simplified "human" on one side and "technology" on the other separated by the word of "interaction". Indeed, this research has served to both expand and to fragment HCI.

This is further compounded by HCI itself having a number of different faces (cf. Long and Dowell 1989): firstly there is HCI as practice, including interaction design, user centred design, designing for accessibility and so forth; secondly, there is HCI as an academic discipline complete with theories, conceptual frameworks and specialist vocabulary and finally, there is HCI as the source, mediator and evaluator of a variety of user experiences.

Taken together, HCI is revealed as a disparate collection of concepts, tools and frameworks which makes it difficult to understand as a single, coherent piece. Indeed, it also seems unlikely that we can synthesize these different and occasionally incongruent elements into an over-arching super-theory or architecture, or by creating HCI's very own metaphysics. We need to look elsewhere and one avenue might be to adopt a narrative approach rather than conducting further scientific analyses.

Narrative here should not to be dismissed as just telling stories but as a description of one of the ways in which we think. For example, Bruner (1986) describes our two kinds of thinking which he calls *analytic* and *narrative*. He tells us that they represent the world to us in quite different ways. The former is well suited to dealing with the everyday world and is responsible for, among other things, scientific reasoning: the other makes sense of the world for us by telling us stories about it.

We have just seen the power of our analytic thinking applied to HCI – it has resulted in lots of detail but surprisingly little coherence, so what does the narrative aspect have to say about it? As our narrative thinking is about telling plausible stories, which story do we tell here? It is proposed that a narrative centred on *make-believe* may unify these different pieces.

It is not our intention to adopt Bruner's perspective wholesale but to recognise that it may be that our narrative thinking which is responsible for ability to make-believe (or, as it is suggested in the introduction to this volume, be a manifestation of motor cognition).

Make-believe is, for example, the means by which the characters and scenes of a scenario or persona are brought to life. Our analytic minds may have identified the necessary characters, their attributes and the settings for a successful scenario as part of a design episode, but it is our ability to make-believe which gives the scenario meaning, life and usefulness. Similarly, the Wizard of Oz technique

(Green and Wei-Haas 1985) which is used to evaluate the behaviour of low-fidelity prototypes goes a little further as it explicitly instructs us to pretend. The participants in a Wizard of Oz session make-believe that the prototype they are using is just like the "real thing" and they are instructed to "ignore the man behind the curtain" who is actually providing the computation, that is, simulating the opening and closing of "windows" and responding to the pressing of "buttons".

Numerous authors have told us (and still do) that we invoke a mental model to guide our use of interactive devices (e.g. Norman 1988). The mental model is used to reason about the steps we should take but we often "animate" these models, that is, we have the impression of rehearsing or practicing what we would expect to do and the steps we expect to take when using the technology. This is make-believe at work.

We also explicitly embraced pretence when we agreed that the graphical user interface is called the desktop. It is not a desktop, it does not particularly look like a desktop, it does not involve an analogy or metaphor of a desktop – instead we pretend it is. We behave towards it as if it were. This "behaving as if it were" is a defining characteristic of pretending.

Then, of course, if we regard interactive movies, video games, and virtual environments as existing along a loosely defined continuum of digital media, it becomes plausible that we are making-believe when we successfully engage with them. For example, it is difficult to conceive that we actually believe that playing a video game involves doing harm to others and that we must somehow suspend these beliefs while playing them. It is much more plausible that we are simply making-believe. Similarly, very few of us believe that the Force in the Star Wars™ movie series is real but we are all happy to make-believe that it can be used by the Jedi to restore peace to a troubled galaxy – eventually.

So, not only is it likely that our ability to make-believe bring to life our designs, visualisations, prototypes and scenarios but it also provides the means by which we engage with digital content (in movies, games and virtual environments). If make-believe does indeed have this pivotal, though silent and unrecognised, role in HCI, then it can also be seen as offering a *connecting narrative* which can bring together these very different aspects of HCI. After all it is what playing video games, the Wizard of Oz technique, the use of scenarios and personae, the use of "metaphor" in the design of graphical user interfaces, video games, virtual environments have in common. Having sketched the central argument of this chapter, we continue with a description of make-believe itself in this context.

2.2   Make-Believe

There is little shortage of terms describing our ability to create and embrace things which do not exist. We regularly day-dream, engage in reverie, imagine and fantasise to pass the time or to work out our frustrations. At night we are even more engaged elsewhere, babies spend most of their time in REM (or dreaming) sleep and even adults enter it approximately five times every night. These many different forms of "escape" may be related in that they share common brain structures, or are forms of neural or cognitive "garbage collection" or they may simply be the epiphenomena of our febrile minds or we might just find the world too much.

While this is still a matter of debate, we can be fairly sure that when children pretend, besides having fun, they are probably doing so for a purpose – to rehearse the necessary skills to manage social interaction (e.g. Jent et al. 2011); or to deal with their emotions (e.g. Seja and Russ 1999) or facilitate some aspects of their cognitive development (e.g. Lillard et al. 2012). Pretending has been researched and written about (primarily as pretend play) extensively but make-believe has not generally been treated as a psychological phenomenon demanding of this kind of attention as witnessed by the distinct absence of a research corpus. (Imagination, a term we have been careful to avoid, has also had a good measure of attention (e.g. Harris 2000; Byrne 2005).) We will argue that make-believe is at work within HCI and provides a rich domain of study for make-believe.

We argue that make-believe is not simply an expression of our cognition as it involves the exploration of possible worlds afforded by the use of a prop such as a hobby-horse, a "light sabre", or more seriously, a mathematical model or a what-if scenario. These artefacts do not merely shape the form the make-believe takes but both enable it and constrain it. A light sabre enables children (and far too many adults) to engage in Star Wars™ themed episodes of make-believe but explicitly not a Star Trek™ themed one. This is despite the fact that they are both examples of space-travelling fantasy involving exotic aliens and an array of energy-based weapons. The same is true of a make-believing with a mathematical model. Suitably armed a mathematician might be able to describe a new kind of space involving one-dimensional strings but to a very limited audience only.

Walton's (1990) make-believe theory it is not a psychological account, instead, it addresses the problem of representation in the arts. A key concept in his account is the concept of the *prop* (Walton 1993). Props can be found in instances of art such as paintings, sculpture, novels and so forth as well as in children's toys including dolls, teddy bears, and magic swords. These props provide the "seeds" from which an episode of make-believe can be spun. Despite these worlds not being the case, their make up and behaviour is governed by rules. Indeed, Walton also tells us that games, cinema, and a variety of other media are subject to their own "principles of generation" which are also "reality-oriented". This reality principle is, unsurprisingly, based on the similarity between make-believe and the real world. This principle ensures that make-believe worlds are comprehensive and ultimately believable (see Turner et al. 2015, for an extended discussion of this). However to facilitate the fantastic and make it believable, Walton also proposes the "mutual belief principle" which is based on a tacit agreement between the make-believer of these worlds and those who experience them. So, for example, travelling at faster than the speed of light is impossible in the real world, but we can agree to it for the sake of a story, a mathematical make-believe or to explore a possible world in physics. These principles, we argue, can be seen perhaps most directly in the spoken and unspoken contracts among participants in pretend play. Children regularly agree to object substitution, for example, water becomes coffee, and mud becomes chocolate, or a banana become a telephone. As we have already noted, this is not confined to the arts or children at play, as Toon (2010) has shown in explicitly adopting Walton's account to consider how theoretical models are used in scientific reasoning. He argues that these models are props in games of make-believe in a manner which "prescribe specific imaginings" that is, they afford and constrain particular kinds of reasoning analogous to the ways in which, say, Ninja Turtles (often rigidly) prescribe the pretend play of children. Further examples of make-believe in scientific reasoning include Einstein's famous thought experiment which involved him chasing a beam of light which ultimately contributed to the theory of special relativity and Kekulé's daydream about an ouroboros which offered him a clue as to the structure of benzene.

We would like to say the use of make-believe in HCI is quite distinct from playing with mud pies or the stuff of fairy-tales. But it is not. A fairy-tale is filled with scenes we have invented, and populated with characters who may or may not exist and who engage in a variety of ordinary and extraordinary things in a fairly ordered, rule-governed manner. We must stress that we are not drawing a fanciful parallel between telling fairy-stories (or equivalent) and the creation of, say, the next generation of smart phones instead we argue that making-believe is that form or mode of cognition common to both which enables us to create, reason about and experience things which are *not* the case. Thus, our interest here is not in trolls and wicked witches as such but in our ability to create and reason about things which do not *yet* (or might never) exist and to act as though they did. To this end, we recognise that make-believe has two components, the first is primarily behavioural and affective (i.e. pretending or acting as if or feeling as though) and the other is essentially what Clark (2008) would call extended cognition, that is, thinking with things – whether it is a Feynman diagram, a magic sword, or a work of art.

2.3   A Role for Make-Believe in HCI

As we noted earlier, in addition to the very many theoretical facets of current HCI, there are a number of different though fairly consistent and well-defined faces, namely:

1. HCI as **practice**. Here we include the range of tools and techniques which enable us to envisage and evaluate digital technology. The key tools are variations on scenarios, personae, and prototypes.
2. HCI as **theory**. We shall argue that the use of on-screen metaphor, such as the desktop, might be better thought of as "a fiction". We suggest that make-believe may have an important role in how we first engage with unfamiliar technology.
3. HCI as (user) **experience**. We will show that make-believe brings to life technology and the digital worlds it creates. The digital worlds found in games or as a product of virtual reality are transformed from moving pictures to engaging

vistas by virtue of our ability to make-believe. For example, we do not point the cross-hairs of our plasma rifles at animated patches of pixels but at aliens trying to kill our comrades in the space corps.

Our aim in this section is to examine examples of published work in both of these areas and offer alternate make-believe interpretations.

HCI as Practice

Design, like pretend play, is often characterised as alternating patterns of convergent and divergent thinking (e.g. Lawson 2005; Moggridge 2007). Coyne (2003), for example, observes that designers see the design process as a "series of successive rehearsals and revisions" and that design involves "a to-and-fro dialogical game". The former is solution focussed, while the latter is an example of "what-if" thinking. Kinsley (2012, p. 1557) tells us that all design relies upon make-believe in the process of reifying that which is not (yet), by drawing upon "anticipatory techniques [which] are a means of establishing the presence of what has not happened and may never happen..." and "stage the possible through some form of acting, gaming or pretending" (p. 1559, ibid.) From the early days of interactive systems design, designers have drawn upon a relatively unchanging collection of such envisionment tools in the exploration, communication and evaluation of systems, applications and user interfaces.

Scenarios and Personae

Scenarios were definitively documented as a design method in Carroll's *Scenario Based Design* (1995). They work by capturing potential use by way of stories. Scenarios have a beginning – user goals or intentions – a middle – interaction with the application features – and an end – realisation of the goal. In their richest form, their protagonists have roles (shift supervisor, shopper, parent ...) display a modicum of characterisation (apprehensive, in a hurry, short-sighted ...) and a backdrop of physical or organisational context may be evident (in an airport departure lounge, as part of a new work recording system). And, of course, much of this is typically make-believe.

For requirements engineers, scenarios are primarily a means of expressing and verifying user needs, while for designers they have a multiplicity of purposes from working through the practicalities of features and functionality in realistic use, to communication with colleague and client, and as the basis upon which to structure design evaluation with users. Each of these purposes demands different degrees of detail but all are grounded in knowledge, or at least assumptions, about the real world in which a design will be used.

In their evaluation guise – acknowledging that design and evaluation are iterative and intertwined – scenarios typically script episodes in which users "interact" with prototype representations of the application in question. However there are interesting variants here from the perspective of our argument. Howard et al. (2002) and Svanæs and Seland (2004) are among a number of sources which describe scenarios which are fully "acted out" by third-party actors or role-playing users, as resources for collaborative design. In the former example designers suggest innovations which are the means of "moving the design discourse between the poles of 'science fiction' (where all user problems are solved by a magical omnipotent device) and 'plausible fiction' (where the device imagined may not be ideal, but is both tractable and innovative)." (Howard et al. 2002). As both these contributions note, embodied scenario enactment was not a new development but dates back at least to the first participatory design initiatives (for example, among many others, Ehn and Kyng 1991). However, the rise of interactive technologies as consumer products and signifiers of personal identity in the last years of the twentieth century demanded a variation of the standard scenario to create a new representation technique which better reflected the nuances of user personalities and lifestyles, namely, personae. Popularised in Pruitt and Adlin (2006), although their genesis lies in the work, among others, of Cooper (1999), personae encapsulate individuals typical of one or more broad types who may use the technology in question. While the actors in scenarios may have absent or at best sketchy personalities, personae have names, ages, socio-economic profiles, likes, dislikes, values and aspirations, frequently complemented by an picture of the imaginary individual. This is not unlike a "profile" in a social media site although it is worth remembering that the person being described is typically make-believe. As in the case of scenarios, the most valuable personae rely on data about potential users in the real world. Their breadth and depth of detail serves not just to refine requirements on design, but, to allows designers "to put themselves in other people's shoes". To pretend to be that persona and to make-believe episodes of their "lives".

This is true, for example, every time we create personae "who", in the main, are not real people but may draw upon people we know or on information our focus groups have revealed, they are made-believe. Blyth and Wright (2006) have written of pastiche personae which draw upon fiction – including the Miss Marple stories, A Clockwork Orange and Nineteen Eighty-Four. They argue that these works of fiction add a believable "felt-life" aspect to their personae.

Prototypes

If scenarios and personae concern what is being played out, for what purpose, and by whom, prototypes demonstrate how this might achieved through interactive technology. In short, although many different typologies have been proposed, the primary dimensions concern the degree of interactivity afforded, the fidelity to the final intended implementation, the prototyping medium and the purpose of the prototype. This being said, while simple sketches and video prototypes primarily afford a means of expressing and communicating design concepts, most forms of prototype make-believe interaction to some degree. "Wizard of Oz" prototypes perhaps entail the strongest make-believe effects, relying upon "the man behind the curtain" to make systems "work". Of most interest for the current discussion are the variants of low-fidelity prototyping, whether mediated through paper or specialist prototyping software and the design team. A mock-up of the application interface screens and the more significant widgets is prepared, often literally on paper (Snyder 2003 offers a comprehensive account). Typically, users are briefed about the process to be followed and their role in it, the properties of the prototype and its limitations, and the scenario to be explored in the prototyping session, The session then unfolds, users attempting the specified as-if "tasks" (which may simply be exploratory) by moving, touching or simply pointing at interface objects while a member of the design team manipulates the prototype in response (if paper) or by clicking on interactive areas of the screen if software-mediated. Users are generally asked to comment concurrently or after the session on their perceptions of the interaction and "functionality" afforded, any difficulties encountered and fit with the real world equivalent of the situation being simulated. In sum, this is an active, collaborative, participative process being carried out "as if" the application would be used in everyday life, or "as though it were for real" as a well-regarded textbook has it (Rogers et al. 2011). The Wizard of Oz is an excellent example of explicit role-playing, which very closely resembles the structure and dynamics of a children's tea-party. Each participant holds a role which they act out. We see the substitution of objects in both: toy cups and water for coffee, paper prototypes for digital systems. Children pretend to drink coffee: we pretend to withdraw cash from an ATM. While children may be learning about social interaction, turn-taking and simply having fun, our more sober pretending can reveal problems with the sequencing of the transaction at the ATM. And, of course, we do not leave this use of Wizard of Oz at the purely behavioural as our next steps are to reason about what went well and what revealed problems in the design of the system. We typically apply ourselves to thinking with the prototype to determine whether we would trust/enjoy/find usable the design of such a system. And when we are done, we walk away, no tea has been split, no money withdrawn, and no software written.

It should be note that this "as if" quality is often unnoticed and usually unvoiced: the international standard ISO 9241-2010 for the human centred design of interactive systems advises that "When prototypes are being tested, the users should *carry out tasks using the prototype* rather than just be shown demonstrations or a preview of the design" (BSI (2010) clause 6.5.4, our italics.) They are not, of course, carrying out the tasks, but pretending to do so. They are acting out the purchase of tickets or watching a movie or searching for a flight to Rio. But no tickets are booked, no movie is watched and no flight schedule is searched.

HCI as Theory

As we have already discussed, HCI has an abundance of theories, fragments of theory and multiple theoretical perspectives. This section will briefly consider three different theoretical perspectives: the role of make-believe in the operation of mental models; make-believe rather than metaphor and the make-believe in initial engagement with digital technology. Again, we do not offer fresh empirical evidence but we do suggest alternative interpretations.

Mental Models

A *mental model*, as a description of how we use and think about interactive technology, was adopted in the 1980s within HCI with the publication of Norman's *Psychology of Everyday Things* (1988). The original idea, however, lies with Craik's *The nature of explanation* (1943) in which he describes them as a "small-scale model" of external reality in our head with which we are "able to try out various alternatives, conclude which is the best of them …" (p. 61). This concept was adopted by Johnson-Laird in his *Mental Models* (1983) in the service of deductive reasoning and by Gentner and Gentner (1983) to account for our use of interactive technology. The idea was readily adopted by other researchers and mental models became a popular means to account for how people reasoned about and used a wide range of interactive systems and devices. Specifically, a mental model is a (supposed) cognitive structure which enables people to make predictions about how things will work and guides their use of them.

From the perspective of HCI, it is assumed that we acquire a mental model of a given technology by exposure to it. This might take the form of formal instruction, observation, reading the manual, or by trial and error. So, having internalised the operation of the technology, what then? It is supposed that we then "run" it, that is, we are able to step through the operation of the model. There is no consensus as how this might actually be achieved though Thagard (2010) has proposed that mental models may be the result of patterns of activation in populations of neurons. Perhaps they do support our reasoning but phenomenologically, we often appear to animate the models in our "mind's eye". We might envision the steps we might take at the ATM or how we might save a file to "the Cloud" or change our printer from the local machine to the full colour network printer. Clearly there is some form of "everyday reasoning" or problem solving at work here but this is often accompanied by an unacknowledged episode of mental rehearsal, or as we prefer to phrase it, make-believe.

The Use of Metaphor

Less than 50 years ago, computers were unfamiliar, frightening and not something with which that the average man or woman had much contact. With the invention of the desktop metaphor in the 1970s, a means was established to provide a comprehensible interface to computers for the non-specialist. The desktop metaphor is now so well established that the current generation of users are probably more familiar with it than they are with the office desktops upon which it was based. Smith (1985), in an early retrospective, wrote of the first graphical user interface embodying the desktop metaphor on the Xerox Star system: *"Every user's initial view of Star is the Desktop, which resembles the top of an office desk, together with surrounding furniture and equipment. It represents a working environment, which current projects and accessible resources reside. On the screen are displayed pictures of familiar office objects, such as document folders, file drawers, in-baskets and out-baskets. These objects are displayed as small pictures or icons."* This use of the desktop "metaphor" is a very good idea but makes for it makes a great story not a metaphor.

A great deal has been written about the use of metaphor at the user interface to interactive technology, which is not confined to the desktop alone, much of which has been critical. Indeed it is difficult to see how the operation of the desktop is metaphorical as it does not correspond to any of the existing theories of how metaphor works. For example, Holyoak and Thagard (1989, 1995) tell us that a metaphor relies on an underlying analogy which maps a "source" to a "target". So, for example, the metaphor "my job is a prison", maps the source – a prison with the attributes of a cell, fellow inmates, pointless repetitive work, counting off the months to release, to the target – an office, workmates, pointless repetitive work, the prospect of retirement. There is a mapping but it is not perfect, for one thing my employers allow me to go home every evening, but what are the corresponding source and target of the desktop metaphor? A real world desktop and a graphical representation of another desktop? More recently, Lakoff and Johnson (1999) have proposed that metaphors are expressions of our bodily (sensorimotor) experiences. Specially, they tell is that "spatial-relations are at the heart of our conceptual system" (1999, p. 30) and that we learn about these relations through bodily interactions with the world. In turn, knowledge of these relations help us to make sense of the external world and are based on bodily projections such as "in front of us", "behind us", "to our right" – and so on. Our experiences of the world are not, of course, limited to spatial relationships but also afford direct experience of such concepts as FULL-EMPTY and BIG-SMALL. There is a simpler explanation. This "desktop metaphor" is not a metaphor and never has been. It works because we pretend, that is, we act as though it were a desktop. An odd desktop admittedly but it is where we put files and folders and the anomalous trashcan. Much the same is true of the other metaphors that are scattered about the landscape of a graphical user interface, e.g. scissors for cutting, a clipboard for pasting, a drawing pin for posting, a paperclip for attaching. We treat these all as though there were what they appear to be – there really is no need for a more complicated answer.

Engagement Precedes Interaction?

In recent years HCI has expanded its interest beyond usability to embrace all manner of desirable experiences one might have when using interactive technology, and engagement has emerged as an experience of recurring interest (e.g. Sutcliffe 2009). Though definitions of engagement vary, it is assumed that it is a consequence of sustained use of technology. This next anecdote suggests that this need not always be the case.

Fig. 2.1 An unknown green
device

We conclude this section with a story (a version of this story originally appears
in Turner 2010). A number of years ago my wife and I were on holiday in
Western Sweden and sometime during the second week we decided to have lunch in
Göteborg and took the train there. On the return leg of our trip we encountered the
following items of technology attached to partitions near the doors of the commuter
train we were travelling on (Figs. 2.1 and 2.2).

Neither device was accompanied by instructions but both had the air of being in
use, the blue device (on the right) having an active LCD display reading *Kortfråga*.
I felt compelled to investigate.

I took *Kort* to mean ticket (card) and having travelled on the Copenhagen
metro system I was familiar with their *Klipkort* system which physically removes a
portions of the ticket. I stood up and closely examined each device in turn looking
for an opening or slot into which to slide my ticket and have it stamped, clipped
or punched. There was none. I pressed the buttons. I waved my tickets in front of
each wondering if the magnetic strip might activate something. Nothing happened.
I tried to match the number system of the green artefact to the map of the journal

Fig. 2.2 An unknown blue device

posted above it – assuming that it operated a zoning system like most metro systems but again nothing. At this point I noticed that no one else had tried to use either device so I sat down. In due course the ticket inspector appeared and clipped our tickets. I took the opportunity to ask her about the devices and she told me that they were no longer used. Images of an Englishman waving his tickets at defunct technology, perhaps, but I had spent a little time engaging with both devices without successfully interacting with either. From this I conclude that it was quite possible that engagement precedes interaction. I had been engaged throughout this episode and this was predicated on making-believe potential use. I had constructed a number of scenarios of possible use, and anyone confronting a left-luggage machine at a railway station, ticket machines for an unfamiliar metro system, a self check-in system at an airport, or out of hours car park has had the same experience. Make-believe, the affordance and constraints offered by the technology are likely to guide our behaviour in these situations.

HCI as Experience

This aspect of HCI has come to the fore most recently, for example, McCarthy and Wright's *Technology as Experience* (2004) demonstrated that there was a good deal more to our encounters with technology than tasks, usability and mental models. In their book they introduced the HCI community to the work of Dewey and his "four threads of experience" which greatly expanded the consideration of the range of human experience which might arise in response to technology. HCI now actively designs for, and evaluates, the range of aesthetic and affective experiences which technology affords. We have witnessed "a turn to the phenomenological" identified first by Dourish (2001). The decades of objective usability testing are now being supplemented by a careful consideration of "felt experience", and questions as such "was it fun?" are now not only recognised as legitimate but are actively contributing to our understanding of how technology is experienced.

In parallel with this has been an extraordinary growth in digital entertainments such as games and, of course, the many different forms of virtual reality. While these technologies have quite distinct histories, it is impossible to deny that their boundaries are becoming blurred, allowing us locate all of them on a digital media continuum.

And, of course, we would argue that all of these different experiences typically involve acts of make-believe on our behalf.

Fun, aesthetics, the affective, and pleasure (for example): in short, those experiences associated with "user experience", we argue, rely on people making-believe. Being presented with items of technology and then asked, "which is more attractive?" or "which looks like the most fun to own?" requires people to make-believe themselves into situations where they feel able to make such judgments. A user's experience has been found to be closely identified with such issues as self-presentation and identity which also require the ability to make-believe oneself into another situation or role. "Is this phone really me?" is the kind of question which a potential purchaser will ask of themselves and to answer it will need to make-believe themself at the office, with their friends, out having fun. Hassenzahl (2004) calls this aspect of user experience "hedonic quality (identification)" and "self-presentation". He writes that, "identification addresses the human need to express one's self through objects" and that, "self-presentational function of products is entirely social; individuals want to be seen in specific ways by relevant others" (p. 222). Space does not permit the development of these arguments in full but this sense of *projection* is discussed in more detail by Susan Turner and her colleagues in the next chapter.

The other part of this argument (with respect to digital media) has also been developed elsewhere in some detail and the interested reader is directed to Turner (2015a). However, in brief, the role of make-believe in experience is as follows ... when we engage with games, movies, virtual environments (and other digital media) we decouple from everyday reality and embrace another. This embrace may result in immersion, or a sense of presence or we might even *flow*. Further, when we are engaged with a digital medium we are, by definition, making-believe. All of the hallmarks of make-believe are present. When we play a computer game we make-believe that we are killing aliens or driving a high performance motorcar. Similarly, being immersed in a virtual environment or an IMAX movie might lead us to believe that we are on the surface of Mars or deep underwater. In each instance, we act as though we were present or fighting or driving despite never having been actually transported beyond the bounds of the cinema, computer laboratory, or our bedroom: we are making-believe.

This is probably at its most striking when we consider the experience of presence, early definitions of which have included Slater et al.'s (1994) "the (suspension of dis-)belief" of being located in a world other than the physical one". The theme of the *suspension of disbelief* crops up periodically and is one which we challenge and would replace with *active making-believe*. To date there has been no suggestion of evidence that people actively disbelieve when they queue to see the latest Hollywood "blockbuster" and then suspend this disbelief during it, returning to their disbelief afterwards. Besides being suspicious of a double negative (suspension of disbelief), a simpler, more plausible explanation is that people "play along with" what they watch as active make-believe. As an argument there is no reason to believe that it does not apply to playing video-games or experiencing presence in a virtual environment too.

2.4   In Conclusion

This chapter began by observing that HCI as a discipline had become very fragmented, to the extent that it was becoming difficult to see it as a unified body of work. We suggested that what it needed was a story or narrative to help us to understand the many disparate parts of HCI. We have proposed that this story is based on make-believe. We have argued that make-believe is a form or mode of cognition which operates in conjunction with props which in turn, shape, direct and constrain the substance of the make-believe episode. These episodes follow what Walton calls the "principles of generation". They have their own logic, structure and rules. Breaking these rules, as we have argued elsewhere, leaves us open to straying from make-believe into something which is unbelievable. This is particularly important as pretending/making-believe involves decoupling ourselves from the veridical to other (close, adjacent but ultimately make-believe) realities.

Our argument is challenging but is it credible? Do HCI professionals really spend their time making-believe? If we compare this with what Russ (2004) tells us about pretending, namely, it "involves the exercise of alternating cycles of divergent and convergent thinking, that is, the abilities to generate a variety of different ideas, story themes, and so forth and to weave them together", then we can only conclude that they do.

References

Blyth MA, Wright PC (2006) Pastiche scenarios: fiction as a resource for user centred design. Interact Comput 18(5):1139–1164

Bødker S (1987) Through the interface: a human activity approach to user interface design. CRC Press, Boca Raton

Bruner J (1986) Actual minds, possible worlds. Cambridge University Press, Cambridge

BSI (2010) Ergonomics of human-system interaction, Part 210: human-centred design for interactive systems (BS EN ISO 9241-210:2010). BSI, London

Byrne MJ (2005) The rational imagination. MIT Press, Cambridge, MA

Card SK et al (1989) The psychology of human computer interaction. Erlbaum Associates, Hillsdale

Carroll JM (ed) (1995) Scenario-based design: envisioning work and technology in system development. Wiley, New York

Clark A (2003) Natural born cyborgs. Oxford University Press, Oxford

Clark A (2008) Supersizing the mind. Oxford University Press, Oxford

Cooper AL (1999) The inmates are running the asylum: why high-tech products drive us crazy and how to restore the sanity. Sams, Indianapolis

Coyne R (2003) Mindless repetition: learning from computer games. Des Stud 24(3):199–212

Craik K (1943) The nature of explanation. Cambridge University Press, Cambridge

Damasio A (1999) The feeling of what happens: body and emotion in the making of consciousness. Harcourt Brace and Co., New York

Dourish P (2001) Where the action is. MIT Press, Cambridge, MA

Ehn P, Kyng M (1991) Cardboard computers – mocking-it-up or hands-on the future. In: Greenbaum J, Kyng M (eds) Design at work: cooperative design of computer systems. Lawrence Erlbaum, New York

Engeström Y (1987) Learning by expanding: an activity-theoretical approach to developmental research. Orienta-Konsultit, Helsinki

Gentner D, Gentner DR (1983) Flowing water or teeming crowds: models of electricity. In: Gentner D, Stevens A l (eds) Mental models. Lawrence Erlbaum Associates, Hillsdale

Green P, Wei-Haas L (1985) The rapid development of user interfaces: experience with the wizard of Oz method. Proceedings of the Human Factors Society-29th Annual Meeting, Santa Monica, 470–474

Harris P (2000) The work of the imagination. Blackwell, London

Hassenzahl M (2004) The interplay of beauty, goodness and usability in interactive products. Hum Comput Interact 19:319–349

Holyoak KJ, Thagard P (1989) Analogical mapping by constraint satisfaction. Cogn Sci 13:295–335

Holyoak KJ, Thagard P (1995) Mental leaps. MIT Press, Cambridge, MA

Howard S, Carroll J, Murphy J, Peck J (2002) Using 'Endowed Props' in scenario-based design. In: Proceedings NordiCHI 2002. Aarhus, Denmark

Hutchins E (1995) Cognition in the wild. MIT Press, Cambridge, MA

Jent JF, Niec LN, Baker SE (2011) Play and interpersonal processes. In: Russ SW, Niec LN (eds) Play in clinical practice: evidence-based approaches. Guilford Press, New York

Johnson-Laird PN (1983) Mental models: towards a cognitive science of language, inference, and consciousness. Cambridge University Press, Cambridge

Kinsley S (2012) Futures in the making: practices to anticipate 'ubiquitous computing'. Environ Plan A 44:1554–1569

Lakoff G, Johnson M (1999) Philosophy in the flesh. Basic Books, New York

Lawson B (2005) How designers think: the design process demystified, 4th edn. Architectural Press, Oxford

Lillard AS, Lerner MD, Hopkins EJ, Dore RA, Smith ED, Palmquist CM (2012) The impact of pretend play on children's development: a review of the evidence. Psychol Bull 139(1):1–34

Lindgaard G, Fernandes G, Dudek C, Brown J (2006) Attention web designers: you have 50 milliseconds to make a good first impression! Behav Inform Technol 25(2):115–126

Long J, Dowell J (1989) Conceptions of the discipline of HCI: craft, applied science, and engineering. In: Sutcliffe A, Macaulay L (eds) People and computers V: Proceedings of the 5th conference of the British Computer Society. Cambridge University Press, Cambridge

Moggridge W (2007) Designing interactions. MIT Press, MA

Norman DA (1988) The psychology of everyday design. Basic Books, New York

Norman DA (2004) Emotional design. Basic Books, New York

Pruitt J, Adlin T (2006) The persona lifecycle. Morgan Kaufmann, San Francisco

Rogers Y, Sharp H, Preece J (2011) Interaction design, 3rd edn. Wiley, Chichester

Russ SW (2004) Play in child development and psychotherapy. Earlbaum, Mahwah

Scaife M, Rogers Y (1996) External cognition: how do graphical representations work? Int J Hum Comput Stud 45:185–213

Seja AL, Russ SW (1999) Children's fantasy play and emotional understanding. J Clin Child Psychol 28:269–277

Sheets-Johnstone M (2009) The Corporeal turn: an interdisciplinary reader. Imprint-Academic, Exeter

Slater M, Usoh M, Steed A (1994) Depth of presence in virtual environments. Presence 3:130–144

Smith DC (1985) Origins of the desktop metaphor: a brief history. Panel Presentation. The desktop metaphor as an approach to user interface design. In: Proceedings of ACM annual conference, 548

Snyder C (2003) Paper prototyping: the fast and easy way to design and refine user interfaces. Morgan Kaufmann, San Francisco

Suchman LA (1987) Plans and situated actions: the problem of human-machine communication. Cambridge University Press, Cambridge

Sutcliffe A (2009) Designing for user engagement: aesthetic and attractive user interfaces. Morgan Claypool, San Rafael

Svanaes D, Seland G (2004) Putting the users center stage: role playing and low-fi prototyping enable end users to design mobile systems. In: Proc. CHI 2004. ACM Press, New York, pp 479–186

Thagard P (2010) How brains make models. In: Magnan L, Carnielli W, Pizzi C (eds) Model-based reasoning in science and technology, vol 314, Studies in computational intelligence. Springer, Berlin/Heidelberg, pp 447–461

Toon A (2010) Models as make-believe. In: Frigg R, Hunter M (eds) Beyond mimesis and convention. Boston studies in the philosophy of science. Springer, Dordrecht, pp 71–96

Turner P (2010) The anatomy of engagement. Proc. ECCE 2010, 59–66

Turner P (2015a) Presence: is it just pretending? AI & Society, 2015, 1–10

Turner P (2015b) Affect, availability and presence. In: Lombard M, Biocca F, Freeman J, IJsselsteijn W, Schaevitz RJ (eds) Immersed in media. Springer, New York

Turner P, Hetherington R, Turner S, Kosek M (2015) The limits of pretending. Digital Creativity 26(3–4):304–17

Walton KL (1990) Mimesis as make-believe: on the foundations of the representational arts. Harvard University Press, Cambridge, MA

Walton KL (1993) Metaphor and prop oriented make-believe. Eur J Philos 1(1):39–57

Chapter 3
Make-Believing Virtual Realities

Susan Turner, Chih-Wei Huang, Luke Burrows, and Phil Turner

3.1 Introduction

A current concern in human-computer interaction lies in understanding how we experience virtual reality (VR). This chapter proposes that the VR experience relies on make-believe. The necessary decoupling from the real world to the make-believe world is costly in terms of the cognitive resources required but VR offloads some of the computation cost into the virtual environment (VE) itself. This is particularly true of high fidelity, immersive virtual environments. However, our ability to make-believe allows us to 'fill-in' the gaps in quite simple VR environments, with surprisingly effective results: we argue that this is because we have a propensity to see the world, including fictional and artificial worlds, as schematic.

We start by focusing our discussion by an introduction to that class of virtual environments that aim to provide an experience of real, or at least realistic, places. We then briefly review the concept of 'sense of presence' in this context. This leads to a consideration of how we decouple from real to technologically mediated worlds and – the main contribution of this chapter – how make-believe, and in particular its

S. Turner (✉)
Make-Believe Lab, Edinburgh Napier University, Edinburgh, UK
e-mail: susturner@gmail.com

C.-W. Huang
ZyXEL Communications Corp., Hsinchu, Taiwan
e-mail: vicky.huang@zyxel.com.tw

L. Burrows
Edinburgh Napier University, Edinburgh, UK
e-mail: luke-burrow@hotmail.com

P. Turner
School of Computing, Edinburgh Napier University, Edinburgh, UK
e-mail: p.turner@napier.ac.uk

schematic nature, plays a part in the experience of fictional worlds in general and virtual environments in particular.

Moving from theory to practice, the supporting role of schemata is illustrated by two case studies of the experience of simple, low fidelity desktop virtual environments that have nonetheless produced effective user experiences. The first of these relies on everyday schemata of travel abroad, the second on a schema adopting the artificial perspective of what Urry (2002) has termed the 'tourist gaze'. We conclude by extending our discussion of the role of schemata in make-believe to the contribution of episodic and autobiographical memory in what has been characterized as 'a capacity for self-projection' (Rabin et al. 2010).

3.2 Virtual Reality, Presence and Place

Many virtual environments are created to re-present real, or at least realistic, places, including, but not limited to: tourist destinations, museums, war zones, hospitals, ships, construction sites, and classrooms (among many other examples, Alsina-Jurnet and Gutièrrez-Maldonado 2010; Cohen et al. 2013; Goulding et al. 2012; Guerra et al. 2015; Rizzo et al. 2014; Sylaiou et al. 2010; Turner and Turner 2002), as contrasted to, say, fantastic landscapes or cities of the imagination. The purposes underlying the mediated experience of these virtual places broadly fall into the fields of education, training, tourism and psychotherapy.

Applications of Realistic Virtual Environments: Two More Specific Examples

By way of illustration of the variety of individual applications, we delve further into just the last two of this list. Guttentag (2010) identifies six types of touristic use: planning and management of tourist locations; marketing of destinations; education, including many applications which seek to recreate historical sites; enhancing the accessibility of locations; heritage preservation, and, of less interest to our theme, entertainment whilst visitors are actually in the destination. In a very different domain, the recent review in Spagnolli et al. (2014) of psychotherapeutic applications identifies the role of VR in the treatment of anxiety, addiction, eating disorders, various phobias, and stress. Among the most striking of these therapeutic environments are those for the treatment of post-traumatic stress disorder among military personnel returned from the battlefront. Rizzo and his colleagues (2014) for example, describe *Bravemind*, a system for prolonged exposure therapy. The system has customisable views of combat arenas in Iraq and Afghanistan and provides "Humvees, MRAP (mine- resistant ambush-protected) vehicles, or helicopters; vehicle-to-foot patrol transitioning; expanded weather and time-of-day controls;

customizable sound trigger profiles", complemented by directional 3D audio, vibra-tions and smells as appropriate. The authors also note that "higher-fidelity graphic art and animation have enhanced the stimulus content's realism and credibility". This may be a notably rich example of a virtual environment, but by far the larger proportion of other systems of the type identified in this short review employ high resolution visual effects of this nature, coupled with high fidelity audio, if not vibrations and, thankfully, smells. Coupled with this comprehensive content is a reliance on heavy weight technological platforms, at the least head-mounted dis-plays (HMDs) and in many instances cave automatic virtual environments (CAVEs) which surround their users and allow movement around a room-sized space.

It will be evident, therefore, that the scope of applications for virtual represen-tations of the real world is manifold and ranges from the trivial, commercial and meretricious to applications critical to human well-being. But whether explicitly or implicitly, the success of all such applications is predicated on evoking a sense of being in the environment in question, in other words a 'sense of presence'.

Being There: Presence

'Presence' has been a central issue in the VR research community from the emergent years of virtual environments and tele-operation technologies. Landmarks in the development of the concept may be found, among very many others, and in chronological order, in Heeter (1992), Steuer (1992), Slater and Wilbur (1997), Lombard and Ditton (1997), Witmer and Singer (1998), Biocca et al. (2003), Slater (2009), Riva et al. (2011), and Turner (2015). As Riva and his colleagues have observed recently, presence – often 'telepresence' in earlier work – was first conceived as the sense of being in a remote environment experienced by the operator of remotely controlled tools (Riva and Mantovani 2014). This conceptualisation of presence is indeed evident in the full title of the principal journal in the area, *Presence*: *Teleoperators and Virtual Environments*.

However, the original scope of the concept has long since been extended by presence researchers to apply to the experience of technologically mediated envi-ronments in the very broadest sense, from books through movies and television to full-spectrum virtual environments and to include *social presence*, the sense of being with others. The widely-used ITC-SOPI questionnaire instrument, for instance, was explicitly designed to span a wide span of media forms (Lessiter et al. 2001). In this chapter we follow Riva and Mantovani who distinguish this sense (which they term *media presence*) from the concept of presence as the general, foundational means of an individual's making sense of their place in the world (Riva et al. 2011) and extend the argument in Turner (2015) that presence necessarily entails make-believe.

Presence plays a dual role in empirical work with virtual environments and their implementation, treated both as a marker for the success of the user experience and, explicitly or implicitly, as a pre-requisite for the efficacy of any underlying therapeutic, educational, ludic, social or other purpose. As we have seen, many virtual applications mediate an experience of real, or realistic places, and here sense of presence becomes localised: one is not only present somewhere *else*, but present somewhere *in particular*. It is interesting to note, however, that while the concept is deeply entrenched in the broad field of the design, implementation, application, evaluation and theorisation of virtual environments, and has now attracted attention in the study of the performing arts (e.g. Poissant 2015) it has less currency in some apparently closely related fields, among them games research.

Contributory factors that support a sense of presence are generally held, after several decades of research endeavour, to comprise all or most of: realism, naturalness, a sense of being 'in' the physical space portrayed (a.k.a. spatial presence), of being 'with' other beings (social presence), engagement and immersion. These two last factors are of particular interest from the perspective of make-believe. Many researchers consider immersion and engagement to be positively associated with the degree of technologically-mediated sensory richness and interactivity facilitating isolation or *decoupling* from the real world. Slater and Wilbur (1997) add the factor of *plot*, defined as "the extent to which the VE in a particular context presents a story-line that is self-contained, has its own dynamic, and presents an alternate unfolding sequence of events...". However, just as evidence is mixed for the effects of ever-closer fidelity to the real sensory world, so it is for the completeness of the plot. The project manager for the full-spectrum, high-fidelity therapeutic *Bravemind* application discussed above, for example, emphasises that the virtual environment should be "real, but not too real. If the scenarios are too detailed, patients can't fill in the blanks with the parts of their experience they need assistance with." (Ungerleider 2014). In other words, there needs to be space for make-believe. We now move to a consideration of the relationship between make-believe and the experience virtual reality. In so doing, we observe that this moves the debate about the nature of presence from a focus on external factors – technology and story – to a focus on the experiencing individual's role in constructing other realities.

3.3 Decoupling, Make-believe and Schemata in Virtual Reality

To engage with virtual reality is to engage with, or be present in, a fiction: someone strolling through virtual Edinburgh, Hong Kong or New York is not necessarily located in that particular city. VR is thus one mode of instantiation of a fictional world, where engagement and immersion rely on the power of narrative supplemented by make-believe, just as in video games, movies or indeed, the simple black and white symbols on a printed page that comprise a book.

Decoupling from One World, Engaging with Another

A feature of the VR experience, but one which is rarely recognised, is that it involves de-coupling from the real world in order to engage with the fictional one. We simply cannot be present and engaged in the real world while being present and engaged in a virtual world simultaneously. Our attention or awareness, by definition, must be focussed in one or the other. Thus while we are engaged by media (of whatever kind) our experience of the real world is attenuated. Of course, decoupling from the real world is something we have all experienced. Occasionally we read a book which is so exciting and so compelling that we become immersed in it. While time passes without us noticing, we are not so decoupled from the everyday that we would miss a fire alarm or a cramped and complaining limb.

However, to decouple from the everyday and to maintain this separation requires significant cognitive (and potentially, affective) resources (Stanovich 1999; Stanovich et al. 2010). And here is the great power of VR as it can assume some of this burden. For example, in reading War and Peace we have to maintain and track a substantial cast of characters, locations, battles and so forth. This is cognitively demanding but a movie of War and Peace (an interactive VR version is yet to be created, as far as we are aware) would alleviate some of that effort by having principal characters reproduced on the screen, shifting the cognitive load from memory to perception and from recall to recognition. We recognise Napoleon, and we recognise a retreat when we see one. It is clear that such cognitive off-loading is supported by the realism and near full-spectrum sensory inputs afforded by high-fidelity immersive environments, but it is less immediately obvious how less technologically sophisticated environments succeed in holding us in thrall and isolated – decoupled – from the real world around us.

While there is little extant discussion of decoupling in the context of presence and VR, the phenomenon of being decoupled from the world has been long explored in relation to make-believe in the theorisation of fiction and narrative. Thus for Walton (1990) a fictional text is a "prop in a game of make-believe" while Ryan (2008) considers that interactive digital fictions are founded on an "act of make believe whose prototype can be found in children's role playing games". Make-believe not only transports the 'reader' to the fictional world, but serves to fill in the plot, the "gaps in the text" (Gerrig 1993), since even the most comprehensive of fictional narratives is inherently underspecified.

The Schematic Nature of Make-Believe

We hold make-believe to be strongly schematic in operation. Schemata are cognitive structures that hold representations of objects and the relations among them, whether simple or complex, individual or social, the contemporary concept of a schema originating in the pioneering work of Bartlett (1932) on memory and stories. Bartlett proposes that memory is a dynamic, situated, reconstructive process, memories being both stored in, and shaped by, culturally determined schema. Similarly, Piaget holds that a schema is "a cohesive, repeatable action sequence possessing component actions that are tightly interconnected and governed by a core meaning" (Piaget 1952, p. 7). In short, schema are held to organise our knowledge of the world and scaffold encounters with new situations and information. They are not, of course, static but evolve in the light of experience to assimilate and accommodate new knowledge – although the process is not universal nor always immediate.

While remaining a constant element in the development of the psychology of memory, as we discuss towards the end of this chapter, schema theory became more practically applied in the 1970s and 1980s by researchers working in the then emerging field of artificial intelligence, as a means of representing human information processing in a form which could be manipulated by machines. Here the most prominent work is that of Minsky (1975) on frames: fixed relational knowledge structures that have a number of slots which can be filled from a limited set of values. So a car frame has slots for wheels, paintwork, engine size and so forth, which might be filled by, for example, alloy, 1.4 l, pearlescent black; while the slots for a historic English city might include castle, cathedral, main square and market place. Importantly for our argument, slots that are un-instantiated in a current context are filled by default values. Finally, the dynamics of everyday life are captured through scripts, or schemata for action (Schank and Abelson 1977). Thus Schank and Abelson's most familiar example, the restaurant script, prescribes how to behave in a variety of restaurants by simply changing the contents of the "slots" from, say, Chinese to Italian. (Note that while schemata, scripts, frames and so forth have provided useful tools for describing and reasoning about the cognitive representation of knowledge, including in this chapter, how far they actually exist as cognitive structures remains contested.)

The basis for attributing a major role for schemata in make-believe, as we have discussed elsewhere at greater length (Turner et al. 2015) draws on the literature in child development (almost all psychological studies of make-believe and pretending concern childhood behaviours and cognition) the philosophy of the arts and narrative theory among other domains. Thus, Nichols and Stitch (2005, p. 34) argue that schematic "clusters or packets of representations whose contents constitute "scripts" or paradigms detailing the way in which certain situations typically unfold" govern episodes of childhood pretend play, while Walton (1990) and Gatzia and Sotnak (2014), among others, suggest that readers rely on background assumptions or propositions to populate the landscape of fictional narrative. Wolf (2014)) contributes a further elaboration, proposing that the act of make-believe that constitutes the fictional world is underpinned by schemata embodying both real-world knowledge and familiar fantastic genres. Alber (2013) makes a similar argument, but adds that real-world and fantastic genres are frequently blended, and that the unnatural in fiction may also be attributed by the reader in a schematic manner to dreams, fantasies or hallucinations. Rather interestingly for any consideration of VR environments which seek to influence perceptions or behaviour, Alber argues that such cognitive strategies in processing of fictional narrative in turn permit a fresh view of the real world.

Schemata, Presence and VR

Just as in other fictional worlds, we propose that schemata underpin the make-believe spaces and places of virtual reality and that this may explain the relative success of comparatively simple VR environments. (We distinguish this aspect of research into schemata and presence from the exploration of body schema – the unconscious, adaptive model of the performance and morphology of the body – in virtual environments and tele-operation. Stevenson Won et al. (2014) provide a recent review of this area.) Our argument here builds on a number of earlier proposals which may be summarised thus: schemata play a role in the enjoyment of hypertext and interactive narrative; the sense of presence may be inhibited by the lack of relevant schemata, and primed by content-relevant schemata; and during the experience an interplay exists between cognitive phenomena such as schemata and stimuli from the VR environment (Douglas and Hargadon 2000; Heeter 2003; Nunez and Blake 2003; Ladeira et al. 2005; Pinchbeck and Stevens 2005; Turner et al. 2005b; Jones 2007 respectively). A further group of studies explore lower level psychological processes, broadly concluding that the degree of real-world schema consistency influences memory for, and recognition of, objects in VEs (e.g. Mourkoussis et al. 2010; Mania et al. 2010). Finally Chertoff et al. (2008, 2010) suggest a role for schemata in enhancing "experiential design" for presence but do not develop this work further beyond a survey instrument designed to capture the effects of cognitive inputs from schemata and other structures.

Our argument expands the theoretical context of existing work by placing schemata in the broader context of make-believe on the part of users. As Nunez and Blake (2003) state that "presence does not simply occur as a consequence of sensory input only, but that it is a constructive process in which the VE user creates an experience using both sensory and psychological inputs." We suggest that this constructive, creative process is make-believe.

We conclude this introductory section with an instance of the very powerful priming effect of schemata in sustaining make-believe when interacting with a virtual environment. This particular VE employed (then) state-of-the-art techniques to produce 360° photo-realistic visual representations of places which were supplemented by an appropriate soundfield and augmented by computer-generated objects. The aim was to convey not only an impression of the physical space, but also a sense of the place itself (Turner and Turner 2006). In the later stages of the project, user trials evaluated how far this had been achieved. One such trial presented a re-creation of a distinctive stairway and landing in a historic university building, augmented by a computer-generated desk. Participants donned a head-mounted display and sat at a real desk placed to correspond with the position of the computer-generated desk in the re-creation, the environment maintaining veridicality as participants stood up or looked around. No other people, real or simulated, were present in the artificial environment. We also introduced a contextualizing schema. Before the VE experience, participants were asked to imagine – or make-believe – that they were a security guard and to report any incidents to control room staff (played by the project team). The sound of breaking glass was introduced part way through the 10 min VE session to enhance the scenario, but otherwise the audio environment was designed to be silent. However, it emerged after the trial sessions that several participants were able to hear unintended, extraneous sounds of conversation and people moving around in the (real) trial location. These were duly reported as suspicious events and one participant even mentioned a 'shadowy figure': the make-believe world had evoked the sight of an intruder where none existed in the depopulated virtual scene.

The VR application just described was a relatively rich environment. However, the operation of schema-based make-believe becomes even more compelling where the environments themselves are much more impoverished. We now turn to two more extensive case studies, firstly where a low fidelity VR experience of arriving in a new city is underpinned by everyday schemata of travel and city life; secondly where the concept of the schematic 'tourist gaze' is used to engage participants in a deliberately heightened VR cityscape. As we shall see, both these rather different types of constrained, mediated experience require participants to *make belief* and both engender a sense of being present in the places represented.

3.4   Application 1: A Taste of Edinburgh

The scenario below portrays the initial experience of an international student in a new country. More specifically, it encapsulates the challenges in coping with an unfamiliar geographical location, relating to its culture and praxis and interacting with its inhabitants.

Shu-hui is a 27 year old Taiwanese student undertaking a masters degree in Edinburgh. It is her first time in the UK. Before departure, she was unconcerned about adjusting to her new life, because she was an experienced traveller. She had, however learned that the weather is the most frequently discussed subject in everyday British conversation!

However, none of this prepared her for the penetrating cold and damp on her arrival, nor for her first challenge while buying something to eat. British coins are hard to distinguish for newcomers, and she felt embarrassed because it took too much time to find the right coins and she did not know how to respond politely to the cashier. (It is expected in Taiwan to show friendliness and politeness to others, especially to strangers and acquaintances.) Later, Shu-hui tried to locate her student accommodation. This was difficult since she found the addresses in Edinburgh differed from the format in Taiwan. Eventually, arriving at the main building and expecting a reception desk, she rang the bell, only to be told that the place was not a hotel and she was not allowed to move in yet. She wondered if she had misunderstood something but at least she learned where the building was. Finally, she then took the bus towards the university campus but got on it from the wrong direction, because she did not realise that in the UK vehicles drive on the left.

The interactive application *A Taste of Edinburgh* was designed and developed by the second author with the intention of better preparing students for the transition encapsulated in this scenario.

Design and Implementation

To support this, the application aimed to evoke a feeling of being in the city, and to afford a limited degree of simulated social interaction – a sense of both the spatial (or tele-) and social aspects of presence – for those 'arriving' for the first time. We were interested to see how far this could be achieved with an intentionally constrained environment, constructed and experienced through simple technologies.

The application was designed around the scenario presented above. Images, text, video and audio material were incorporated in a desktop VR application simulating arrival in Edinburgh. At the start of the experience, a textual narrative introduction described what the participants were expected to achieve during their mediated experience of Edinburgh. This comprised taking the bus from the airport to the city, visiting an art gallery, finding the flat where the participant would be living and buying food from a sandwich bar. It was phrased in a manner intended to arouse curiosity and interest and miminise uncertainty as to what the participants were required to do in 'Edinburgh' and how this would be achieved. More detailed textual instructions were provided at the start of each segment of the application.

Once the application proper had been started, images, video and audio clips conveyed an impression of the bus ride (Fig. 3.1) and arrival at the various destinations, while virtual characters afforded a limited degree of interaction with the participants. These were created, captured, edited and presented using simple web and digital media technologies. Audio output was presented through headphones and interaction mediated by conventional mouse and keyboard.

The images and videos were captured from the individual's viewpoint, including walking along streets, looking for an address, and the view from the front seat on the top deck of the bus. Spatialised sounds corresponding to the photorealistic scenes were presented during the entire set of sequences. The sounds were recorded at the locations used. In order to allow the virtual agents to 'speak' to the participants, the conversations between them were pre-scripted and audio clips captured from volunteers with Scottish accents. Thus, interaction with virtual agents was primarily achieved through images, pre-scripted text with limited opportunities for user input, and audio clips. In the sandwich bar, for example, it was possible to choose food and tender the right Scottish money to complete the transaction. Figure 3.2 shows one of these steps.

As will be evident from the above description and the screenshots we have included, the application as implemented did not appear conducive to a high degree of immersion. While both audio and video material were available in the application,

Fig. 3.1 A step in the sequence of buying a bus ticket

Fig. 3.2 Dialogue in the sandwich bar – adding a bacon roll to the order

as was a degree of interaction, media were presented at quite low fidelity and interaction minimal and pre-scripted. Moreover the 'flow' of experience in the application was punctuated by introductions at the start of each new sequence. To reiterate: the low degree of media richness and fidelity of interaction was intentional, in order to investigate the effect of such relatively simple virtual experiences.

Evaluation

A first prototype was trialled with 20 participants who were Asian students studying in the UK. The results served to refine the evaluation procedure, principally by counter-balancing order of post-experience questionnaires, as well as to fine-tune the prototype itself. A second prototype was the subject of the main evaluation which is reported here.

Participants were 26 Taiwanese and Chinese students who were considering, or had already undertaken, study abroad. Their ages varied from 20 to 42, with most being in their late twenties or early thirties. To avoid any uncontrolled effects from being in the real location depicted in the virtual environment, we used participants who were located outside the UK at the time of the evaluation. All gave their informed consent to the trial procedure and possible publication of their data.

Two questionnaires were administered post-experience, the ITC-Sense of Presence Inventory (ITC-SOPI), Lessiter et al. (2001) to capture data on spatial presence – the sense of being there – and engagement with the environment, complemented by the Networked Minds instrument (Biocca et al. 2001) for assessing the degree of social presence experienced in the 'company' of the virtual bus driver and shopkeeper. Both instruments are well-established in the presence research community.

The trial was conducted remotely over the internet, using audio communication between experimenter and individual participants, who ran the application on their own desktop computers. They were informed that the experience would take around 10 min to complete and asked to read the introductory text, then to carry out two simple tasks, buying a bus ticket and ordering food. They then completed the post-experience questionnaires. In order to preclude potential order effects we used a counterbalancing approach, asking half the participants to complete the ITC-SOPI first, followed by Networked Minds and the reverse order for the other group. Several items in both instruments were adapted in very minor ways from their original paper-based form to facilitate administration online.

Results and Discussion

We first report the results from the two questionnaire instruments, then discuss this data in the context of schema-based make-believe.

Spatial Presence and Engagement: ITC-SOPI

The SOPI instrument has four scales: spatial presence (the sense of being in the environment), engagement (with the environment), ecological validity/naturalness (of the environment) and negative effects (such as dizziness); results for the first two of these are reported here. Nineteen items defines the first factor 'Spatial Presence',

Table 3.1 Selected SOPI
results, a taste of Edinburgh

$N = 26$	Spatial presence	Engagement
Mean rating	3.32	3.52
Max	4.21	4.31
Min	2.37	2.46
Standard deviation	0.41	0.45

Table 3.2 Comparing SOPI ratings from a taste of Edinburgh to results from other applications

	Spatial presence	Engagement
A taste of Edinburgh	3.32	3.52
Tang et al. (2004) (VE discussion about phones mediated by avatars and head-mounted displays)	2.60	2.83
Bruce and Regenbrecht (2009) (Exposure therapy for claustrophobia; interactive VE and head-mounted display)	3.23	3.21
Villani et al. (2012) (simulated job interview in immersive CAVE-based VE)	2.93	Data not reported

such as "*I felt I was visiting the places in the displayed environment*" and "*I had a sense of being in the scenes displayed*". Thirteen items relating to psychological involvement and pleasure are classified as 'Engagement', including the questions, "*I would have liked the experience to continue*" and "*I responded emotionally*". All scales have 5 points, 5 being the most positive rating and 3 the 'neither agree nor disagree' option. The main SOPI results aggregated across participants may be found in Table 3.1 above.

The sense of 'being there' reflected in these apparently modestly positive scores is best appreciated in the context of results reported by other scholars. Reported data for *individual* SOPI scales is surprising rare in published material, but we have identified the following instances. It should be noted that these were obtained from trials of much heavier weight VR environments using head-mounted displays or a CAVE. As can be seen from Table 3.2, *A Taste of Edinburgh* is, relatively, very successful in this respect.

Social Presence: Networked Minds

The Networked Minds instrument developed by Biocca et al. (2001) enables researchers to measure the subjective degree co-presence, psychological involvement, and behavioural engagement, which in their model form the fundamental dimensions of social presence. Eight sub-dimensions underlie these dimensions: isolation/aloneness, mutual awareness, attentional allocation, empathy, mutual understanding, behavioural interdependence, mutual assistance, and dependent action. The 16 co-presence items include, for example, "*I hardly noticed another individual(s)*" and "*Others were often aware of me in the room*". Items such as "*The other individual(s) was influenced by my moods*", and "*My thoughts were clear to my partner*", contribute to the 12-item dimension of 'Psychological Involvement'.

Table 3.3 Selected networked minds results, a taste of Edinburgh

$N = 26$	Co-presence	Psychological involvement	Behavioural engagement
Mean rating	3.04	3.42	3.12
Max	3.56	4.17	4.17
Min	2.31	2.92	2.45
Standard deviation	0.37	0.38	0.45

The last dimension, 'Behavioural Engagement' also consists of 12 items, including *"My actions were dependent on the other's actions* and *"I worked with the other individual(s) to complete the task"*. As for the ITC-SOPI, all scales have 5 points, 5 being the most positive. The results for each dimension, aggregated across participants, are shown in Table 3.3 above.

Despite a thorough review it has proved impossible to identify comparison data from other VR applications but here again a positive sense of social presence, of being *with* the bus driver and the shopkeeper, as well as being *there* in Edinburgh is evident.

While *A Taste of Edinburgh* was crafted with a great deal of care, it remained a limited virtual environment which was non-immersive (in the technological sense of the term), minimally interactive and afforded only limited, pre-scripted 'communication' with its inhabitants. Yet, from the questionnaire results, participants experienced a reasonable degree of presence and social presence. For the former, this compares favourably with much more sophisticated environments. We suggest that these effects are facilitated by make-believe, bringing to bear existing schemata of travel, transport and commercial transactions to 'fill in the gaps' in the sparse landscape provided by the technology. This conclusion is supported by a vignette from the evaluation of the first prototype (not reported further here): when buying food in the shop, the dialogue box implied ordering a drink first. We noticed that some participants hesitated for a few seconds before continuing. It seemed they did not expect to order the drink first: schema driven expectations had been confounded. Schema theory would predict here that, in time, this and other schemata should assimilate such new patterns of everyday interaction, but further trials would be necessary to establish how far this had been achieved in this context, and also to establish how far the effects just discussed generalise beyond the particular case of this group of participants.

3.5 Application 2: Digital Visitor

Digital Visitor (Burrows et al. 2010; Turner et al. 2013) also sought to convey an experience of Edinburgh, but for a rather different purpose and with a very different style. Here, we were interested to explore whether adopting a particular schema, the 'tourist gaze', in the design of a limited VE would support participants in the make-believe that they were *there* in the city.

The Tourist Gaze

Urry (2002) argues that the "tourist gaze" is "directed to features of the landscape, which separate them off from everyday experience. Such aspects are viewed because they are taken to be in some sense out of the ordinary." The gaze is often static and managed, from a vantage point such as a balcony or promoted viewpoint, and insulated from the real world, as in the case of a tourist office's sign-posted walk. In other words (ours, not Urry's), the tropes of tourism form a genre of make-believe. The gaze is directed *inter alia* by anticipation, by the promotional narratives of the tourism industry, by the film, broadcast and internet media, by cultural stereotypes and expectations (Turner et al. 2005a). In short, though Urry himself does not use the term, it is itself a schema, informed by a set of other schemata. English visitors to provincial France, for example, will expect a small town to have its market place hosting a twice-weekly market, a clutch of specialist food shops which close at lunchtime, a dark and rather forbidding bar, a couple of reasonable restaurants and very likely a historic church. Aspects that do not fit the schema (the ubiquitous budget supermarket where most shopping is actually done ...) figure much less prominently in anticipation, in images captured by visitors or incorporated in promotional literature. Finally, the attractions made available to be gazed upon are frequently carefully manicured and their salient features, sometimes quite literally, as in the case of floodlit monuments, highlighted. This is the aspect of tourism which is characterised in Lengkeek's thoughtful, sociological discussion as the 'mode of amusement, where the "stories and metaphors *that suspend reality* are so well known and trusted that they do not create any tension with everyday reality." (Lengkeek 2001, our italics.) Thus, a tourist experience makes an ideal subject for mediation through the medium of VR: much of the irregularity and unpredictability of everyday reality is already designed out while the participant is primed to expect the *expected*.

Design and Implementation

Digital Visitor was a small-scale desktop application designed and developed by the third author to embody the 'tourist gaze' metaphor through the simple means of an Edinburgh conveyed by 'walking through' a selection of well-known photographed viewpoints. Images were supplemented by narrative descriptions similar to that found on the information panels that abound at real-world sites and appropriate sounds sourced from the position of image acquisition. Visitors were guided on a tour of five well-known locations in and around the city. They could explore each location by changing their point of view, much as a tourist admiring a landscape or landmark might, and to a limited extent, move 'through' the location. Two forms of visual effects were implemented. Firstly, the images comprised multiple layers creating a '2.5 D' effect and secondly, the appearance of the sky was exaggerated for each location by strikingly colourful colourful visual

Fig. 3.3 Calton Hill, Edinburgh (From *Digital Visitor*)

enhancements. The aim here was to reinforce the sense of a make-believe world and
to counter the effect encountered in photo-realistic virtual reality applications, that
the very fidelity of the images paradoxically draws attention to any flaws and thus
removes the observer from the scene. Figure 3.3 shows a typical image from the
application.

Evaluation

The evaluation of Digital Visitor was conducted with 25 participants, a mix of
undergraduate and postgraduate students and a range of professionals. Their ages
ranged from 19 to 45, comprising 14 males and 11 females: all were computer-
literate and familiar with the city. All gave their informed consent to the trial
procedure and possible publication of their data.

The intention was to emulate the representative use of a desktop application and
was conducted in a two settings: a typical home location and a busy university
computer lab. Each participant was briefed about the nature of the trial and the use
of the application, and then allowed to engage with the application independently,
at their own pace, observed by the third author. Time spent by the participants
ranged between 2 min 23 s and 7 min 44 s, the mean being a little over 5 min.
Post-use, participants completed a set of 11-point rating scales designed to elicit
structured responses to aspects of the experience of particular interest to its designer:

navigation, sound, text, interaction, locations, images, aesthetics and engagement,[1] of which the last is of most relevance here. Finally, a semi-structured interview was conducted, probing more general reactions to the application, and concluding with one additional scale item adapted from the Slater-Usoh-Steed presence instrument, as reported in Usoh et al. (2000). This last item asked the question "When you think back about the experience, do you think of *Digital Visitor* more as images that you saw, or more as somewhere that you visited? This required a response on a scale from 1 (images) to 5 (somewhere visited).

Results and Discussion

In this section we briefly review the qualitative data from the interviews, then consider the quantitative results from the 'images or place' and 'engagement' scale items. We then return to the role of schemata in the experience of this version of virtual Edinburgh.

Discussion around the *Digital Visitor* experience during the interviews was very much focussed in the main on the design of the application, rather than the experience itself. However, several participants volunteered remarks that suggested that they had, in some sense, visited the locations presented. A representative examples is quoted verbatim below.

> ...the background noise, it obviously made me feel like I was in sort of like, in the city... driving in the city, nice! ...and it felt like, you know, you were actually exploring the city, even though you were just looking at motion graphics, you're able to get a feel for the place. (Participant C, T-shirt printer)

> ...it felt like you were going on a journey through it, rather than it just being a sort of static... it felt like you were kind of moving through it, rather than it just being pictures. (Participant N, landscape architect)

> ...I just felt like I was coming to town from this place... the home screen. (Participant W, postgraduate psychology student)

This sense of a visit was reflected in the ratings obtained on the '*images seen – somewhere visited*' scale item. Here the mean rating was 3.6 on a 5 point scale, but with the modal rating of 4 being awarded by 17 of the 26 participants. Consideration of results from this item to those reported in evaluations of fully immersive VEs (Usoh et al. 2000; Juan et al. 2006) suggests that that *Digital Visitor* performed well by comparison. Finally engagement with the *Digital Visitor* experience was rated highly positively on the scale item concerned, achieving a mean rating of $+3.40$ on a scale from -5 to $+5$. No negative ratings were obtained, while the modal rating was 4.

---

[1]Please note that this is not the operationalization of engagement captured in the engagement scale in the ITC-SOPI instrument.

Overall, it appears that the design of this very technologically simple and non-immersive application, constructed around the schema of the tourist gaze, had been successful in evoking make-believe in a 'visit' to Edinburgh. This is supported to some extent by what was *not* said in the interview discussions. Participants all knew the city well, and there were several ideas volunteered for other tourist venues and vistas that might have been included. Yet none suggested including the sights of the mundane, workaday, and often less than picture-perfect city.

3.6 Overall Discussion: Lightweight VR and Make Believe

The above accounts demonstrate that simple, lightweight non-immersive VEs are capable of generating a solid sense of presence and social presence (in the case of *A Taste of Edinburgh*) and a sense of somewhere visited (*Digital Visitor*). How far the conclusions from these empirical explorations can be generalised is naturally limited: evaluation in both cases was conducted with relatively small numbers of participants, the results may be subject to the kind of demand characteristics which beset any evaluation where subjective responses are elicited and more systematic comparisons with higher-fidelity environments would be interesting and desirable. Nonetheless, there is a strong case that the experiences evoked are attributable to the ability of participants to make-believe, drawing upon existing schemata: in the first instance of travel, wayfinding and social interaction in an unfamiliar city; in the second of the experience of a touristic honeypot – the 'tourist gaze'. In turn, successful real-world applications need to be designed to support schema accommodation to new data. However, schemata may not be the whole story.

Does the Story End with Schemata?

As we have seen, schemata and closely associated constructs have been applied by AI researchers and are also intrinsic to the theorisation of story, narrative and fiction.[2] But what of the wider role for schemata in the psychology of memory?

A review of this vast, complex, specialist, field in psychology and neuroscience is beyond the scope of this chapter, so what follows highlights just a few selected studies of particular relevance. To set the scene, very many studies suggest that schemata not only hold generalised semantic knowledge, but also play a role both in episodic (or event) memory – for personally experienced, specific events – and

---

[2]And indeed there is also a large body of research, in AI-based storytelling.

therefore in autobiographical memory: the knowledge of the self, of the entire collection of remembered life events, and pertinent semantic knowledge, often considered to be a constructed narrative; our life story, in more popular parlance. (The exact definition, relationship and scope of these concepts and terms is both contested and varies considerably among memory researchers; for a recent review of the state-of-the art readers are referred to Rubin and Umanath 2015).

Further, and significantly for this chapter, intriguing neurological data points to links between autobiographical memory, theory of mind – the ability to infer other people's cognitive and affective states – and more generally to a capacity to mentally inhabit 'the other'. Rabin et al. (2010), for instance, describe the growing body of evidence that "the processes responsible for the retrieval of past personal episodes also serve non-mnemonic purposes". This is supported by data from fMRI scans showing close correspondence between the brain regions involved in imagining alternative locations or future events. Intriguingly, there is also some evidence that people with impaired autobiographical memory have difficulty in comprehending familiar narrative structures such as fairy tales.

Rabin and her colleagues suggest several differing, but related, underlying explanations for the phenomenon. Firstly, evidence from Buckner and colleagues (2007, 2008) may indicate a "capacity for self-projection" which supports a mental shift to "alternate times, places, and perspectives". Schacter and colleagues (2007, 2008), however, regard personal memories as *constructed* from past event details, rather than as fixed representations, and thus events yet to be experienced may be mentally constructed in a similar, flexible manner. Finally, there is also an argument for a spatial (re)construction of scenes within which schemata-informed details can be imagined (O'Keefe and Nadel 1978; Hassabis et al. 2007; Hassabis and Maguire 2007; Rubin and Umanath 2015). Returning to the VR context, the observation in Cummings and Bailenson's meta-review (2015) that "presence is achieved through a two-step formative process, in which the user first constructs a spatialized mental model of the mediated environment . . . and then comes to accept this mediated environment over grounded reality as his or her primary frame of self-reference . . . " has clear resonances with this work.

Whichever account holds sway, however, there are now clear, evidence-based indications that underlying our ability to decouple from reality and to project or transport ourselves to fictional worlds (including minimal, non-immersive virtual environments) lies in the perception and interpretation of those alternative worlds in terms of our own life histories and personal knowledge. The make-believe which supports the sense of presence in a VR experience may be no different from that which allows us to remember the past, dream about the future or take another's perspective: we construct stories (about VR content and in make-believe more generally) drawing on our story- and schema-based autobiographical memory. Perhaps the best source of content in designing a VR application which aims to convey realistic events and real places might be to have people tell us their memories.

References

Alber J (2013) Unnatural narratology: the systematic study of anti-mimeticism. Lit Compass 10(5):449–60

Alsina-Jurnet I, Gutièrrez-Maldonado J (2010) Influence of personality and individual abilities on the sense of presence experienced in anxiety triggering virtual environments. IJHCS 68:788–801

Bartlett FC (1932) Remembering: a study in experimental and social psychology. Cambridge University Press, Cambridge

Biocca F, Harms C, Gregg J (2001) The networked minds measure of social presence: pilot test of the factor structure and concurrent validity. Media Interface and Network Design (M.I.N.D.) Lab, E. Lansing

Biocca F, Harms C, Burgoon JK (2003) Toward a more robust theory and measure of social presence: review and suggested criteria. Presence: Teleoper Virtual Environ 12(5):456–480

Bruce M, Regenbrecht H (2009, March) A virtual reality claustrophobia therapy system-implementation and test. In: virtual reality conference, 2009 VR 2009, IEEE (pp 179–182) IEEE

Buckner RL, Carroll DC (2007) Self-projection and the brain. Trends Cogn Sci 11:49–57

Buckner RL, Andrews-Hanna JR, Schacter DL (2008) The brain's default network: anatomy, function and relevance to disease. Ann N Y Acad Sci 1124:1–38

Burrows L, Turner S, Turner P (2010) Re-creating Edinburgh: adopting the tourist gaze. In: Proceedings of the 28th Annual European Conference on Cognitive Ergonomics, ACM Press, New York, pp 183–186

Chertoff DB, Schatz SL, McDaniel R, Bowers C (2008) Improving presence theory through experiential design. Presence: Teleoper Virtual Environ 17(4):405–413

Chertoff D B, Goldiez B, LaViola JJ Jr (2010) Virtual experience test: a virtual environment evaluation questionnaire. In: Virtual Reality conference (VR), 2010, IEEE, pp 103–110

Cohen D, Sevdalis N, Taylor D, Kerr K, Heys M, Willett K, Batrick N, Darzi A (2013) Emergency preparedness in the 21st century: training and preparation modules in virtual environments. Resuscitation 84(1):78–84

Cummings JJ, Bailenson JN (2015) How immersive is enough? A meta-analysis of the effect of immersive technology on user presence. Media psychology (ahead-of-print), pp 1–38 www.tandfonline.com/doi/abs/10.1080/15213269.2015.1015740, VbDDBniA5UQ; Last accessed 23 July 2015

Douglas Y, Hargadon A (2000) The pleasure principle: immersion, engagement, flow. In: Proceedings of the eleventh ACM on Hypertext and hypermedia. ACM press, New York, pp 153–160

Gatzia DE, Sotnak E (2014) Fictional truth and make-believe. Philosophia 42(2):349–361

Gerrig RJ (1993) Experiencing narrative worlds: on the psychological activities of reading. Yale University Press, Yale

Goulding J, Nadim W, Petridis P, Alshawi M (2012) Construction industry offsite production: a virtual reality interactive training environment prototype. Adv Eng Inform 26(1):103–116

Guerra JP, Pinto MM, Beato C (2015) Virtual reality-shows a new vision for tourism and heritage. Eur Sci J 11(9):49–54, www.eujournal.org/index.php/esj/article/view/5375. Last accessed 21.08.15

Guttentag DA (2010) Virtual reality: applications and implications for tourism. Tour Manag 31(5):637–651

Hassabis D, Maguire EA (2007) Deconstructing episodic memory with construction. Trends Cogn Sci 11:299–306

Hassabis D, Kumaran D, Maguire EA (2007) Using imagination to understand the neural basis of episodic memory. J Neurosci 27:14365–14374

Heeter C (1992) Being there: the subjective experience of presence. Presence: Teleoper Virtual Environ 1:262–271

Heeter C (2003) Reflections on real presence by a virtual person. Presence: Teleoper Virtual Environ 12(4):335–345

Jones M T (2007) Presence as external versus internal experience: how form, user, style, and content factors produce presence from the inside. In: Proceedings of 10th international workshop on presence, pp 115–126, astro.temple.edu/~lombard/ISPR/Proceedings/2007/Jones.pdf. Last accessed 23 July 2015

Juan MC, Banos R, Botella C, Perez D, Alcaniz M, Monserrat C (2006) An augmented reality system for the treatment of acrophobia: the sense of presence using immersive photography. Presence Teleoper Virtual Environ 15(4):393–402

Ladeira I, Nunez D, Blake E (2005) The role of content preference on thematic priming in virtual presence. Proceedings of the 8th International Workshop on Presence, London, pp 227–230. astro.temple.edu/~lombard/ISPR/Proceedings/2005/presence2005.pdf. Last accessed 23.07.15

Lengkeek J (2001) Leisure experience and imagination rethinking Cohen's modes of tourist experience. Int Sociol 16(2):173–184

Lessiter J, Freeman J, Keogh E, Davidoff J (2001) A cross-media presence questionnaire: the ITC-sense of presence inventory. Presence: Teleoper Virtual Environ 10:282–297

Lombard M, Ditton T (1997) At the heart of it all: The concept of presence. J Com-put Mediated Commun 3(2). Accessed from onlinelibrary.wiley.com/doi/10.1111/j.1083-6101.1997.tb00072.x/full. Last accessed 23 July 2015

Mania K, Badariah S, Coxon M, Watten P (2010) Cognitive transfer of spatial awareness states from immersive virtual environments to reality. ACM Trans Appl Percept (TAP) 7(2):9

Minsky M (1975) A framework for representing knowledge. In: Winston P (ed) The psychology of computer vision. McGraw-Hill, New York

Mourkoussis N, Rivera FM, Troscianko T, Dixon T, Hawkes R, Mania K (2010) Quantifying fidelity for virtual environment simulations employing memory schema assumptions. ACM Trans Appl Percept (TAP) 8(1):2

Nichols S, Stich S (2005) Mindreading: a cognitive theory of pretense. Oxford University Press, Oxford

Nunez D, Blake E (2003) Conceptual priming as a determinant of presence in virtual environments. In: Proceedings of the 2nd international conference on computer graphics, virtual reality, visualisation and interaction in Africa. ACM Press, New York, pp 101–108

O'Keefe J, Nadel L (1978) The hippocampus as a cognitive map. Clarendon, Oxford

Piaget J (1952) The origins of intelligence in children. International Universities Press, New York

Pinchbeck D M, Stevens B (2005) Presence, narrative and schemata. Proceedings of the 8th International Workshop on Presence, London, pp 221–226. astro.temple.edu/~lombard/ISPR/Proceedings/2005/presence2005.pdf. Last accessed 23 July 2015

Poissant L (2015) Performance arts and the effects of presence. Leonardo 48(3):216–216

Rabin JS, Gilboa A, Stuss DT, Mar RA, Rosenbaum RS (2010) Common and unique neural correlates of autobiographical memory and theory of mind. J Cogn Neurosci 22(6):1095–1111

Riva G, Mantovani F (2014) 1 Extending the self through the tools and the others: a general framework for presence and social presence in mediated interactions. In: G Riva, J Waterworth, D Murray (eds) Interacting with presence: HCI and the sense of presence in computer-mediated environments, Walter de Gruyter GmbH & Co KG, pp 9–31

Riva G, Waterworth JA, Waterworth EL, Mantovani F (2011) From intention to action: the role of presence. New Ideas Psychol 29(1):24–37

Rizzo A, Hartholt A, Grimani M, Leeds A, Liewer M (2014) Virtual reality exposure therapy for combat-related posttraumatic stress disorder. Computer 47(7):31–37

Rubin DC, Umanath S (2015) Event memory: a theory of memory for laboratory, autobiographical, and fictional events. Psychol Rev 122(1):1–23

Ryan ML (2008) Fictional worlds in the digital age. In: Schreibman S, Siemens R (eds) A companion to digital literary studies. Blackwell, Oxford, pp 250–266

Schacter DL, Addis DR (2007) The cognitive neuroscience of constructive memory: remembering the past and imagining the future. Philos Trans R Soc Lond Ser B Biol Sci 362:773–786

Schacter DL, Addis DR, Buckner RL (2008) Episodic simulation of future events: concepts, data and applications. Ann N Y Acad Sci 1124:39–60

Schank R, Abelson R (1977) Scripts, plans, goals, and understanding. Erlbaum, Hillsdale

Slater M (2009) Place illusion and plausibility can lead to realistic behaviour in immersive virtual environments. Philos Trans Royal Soc B: Biol Sci 364:3549–3557

Slater M, Wilbur S (1997) A framework for immersive virtual environments (FIVE): speculations on the role of presence in virtual environments. Presence: Teleoper Virtual Environ 6:603–616

Spagnolli A, Bracken CC, Orso V (2014) The role played by the concept of presence in validating the efficacy of a cybertherapy treatment: a literature review. Virtual Reality 18(1):13–36

Stanovich KE (1999) Who is rational?: studies of individual differences in reasoning. Psychology Press, London

Stanovich KE, West RF, Toplak ME (2010) 17 Individual differences and rationality. In: Manktelow K et al (eds) The science of reason: a festschrift for Jonathan St BT Evans. Psychology Press, London, pp 355–396

Steuer J (1992) Defining virtual reality: dimensions determining telepresence. J Commun 42(4):73–93

Stevenson Won A, Haans A, Bailenson JN, IJsselsteijn WA (2014) A framework for interactivity and presence in novel bodies. In: Riva G, Waterworth J, Murray D (eds) Interacting with presence: HCI and the sense of presence in computer-mediated environments. De Gruyter Open, Berlin, pp 57–69

Sylaiou S, Mania K, Karoulis A, White A (2010) Exploring the relationship between presence and enjoyment in a virtual museum. Int J Hum-Comput Stud 68(5):243–253

Tang A, Biocca F, Lim L (2004) Comparing differences in presence during social interaction in augmented reality versus virtual reality environments: An exploratory study. Proceedings of the 7th International Workshop on Presence, Valencia, 2005, pp 204–208. astro.temple.edu/~lombard/ISPR/Proceedings/2004/Tang,%20Biocca,%20Lim.pdf. Last accessed 23 July 2015

Turner P (2015) Presence: is it just pretending? AI & Society, 1–10

Turner P, Turner S (2002) Embedding context of use in CVE design. Presence: Teleoper Virtual Environ 11(6):665–676

Turner P, Turner S (2006) Place, sense of place, and presence. Presence: Teleoper Virtual Environ 15(2):204–217

Turner P, Turner S, Carroll F (2005a) The tourist gaze: towards contextualised virtual environments. In: Spaces, spatiality and technology (pp 281–297). Springer, Dordrecht

Turner P, Turner S, Tzovaras D (2005b) Reliving VE day with schemata activation. In: Proceedings of the 8th International Workshop on Presence, London, pp 33–38. astro.temple.edu/~lombard/ISPR/Proceedings/2005/presence2005.pdf. Last accessed 23 July 2015

Turner P, Turner S, Burrows L (2013) Creating a sense of place with a deliberately constrained virtual environment. Int J Cogn Perform Support 1(1):54–68

Turner P, Hetherington R, Turner S, Kosek M (2015) The limits of pretending. Digit Creat 26(3–4):304–17

Ungerleider G (2014) Virtual reality for vets with PTSD recreates the smells, sounds, and feelings of an IED. www.fastcoexist.com/3031510/virutal-reality-for-vets-with-ptsd-recreates-the-smells-sounds-and-feelings-of-an-ied#1. Last accessed 23 July 2015

Urry J (2002) The tourist gaze. Sage, London

Usoh M, Catena E, Arman S, Slater M (2000) Using presence questionnaires in reality. Presence, Teleoper, Virtual Environ 9(5):497–503

Villani D, Repetto C, Cipresso P, Riva G (2012) May I experience more presence in doing the same thing in virtual reality than in reality? An answer from a simulated job interview. Interact Comput 24(4):265–272

Walton KL (1990) Mimesis as make-believe: on the foundations of the representational arts. Harvard University Press, Harvard

Witmer BG, Singer MJ (1998) Measuring presence in virtual environments: a presence questionnaire. Presence: Teleoper Virtual Environ 7:225–240

Wolf W (2014) Illusion (aesthetic). In: Hühn P (ed) The living handbook of narratology. Hamburg University, Hamburg

Chapter 4
Fiction for Design: Appropriating Hollywood Techniques for Design Fictions

Tom Flint

4.1 Introduction

This chapter offers approaches and ideas from outside the HCI arena and considers how they may be of use when producing fictions. What is offered is a set of tools for consideration when producing design fictions. The importance of fiction to the field of HCI is not a new consideration evidenced in the established practice of using scenarios; a practical tool for the production of interactive systems. Design Fictions are considered as a method for communicating speculative futures and a tool for engaging with those outside the laboratory. With a current demand for public engagement from universities (Vines et al. 2013) it is increasingly important that researchers become adept at communicating their visions and speculations. What is offered here are some effective tools for use in the production of fictions. This chapter concentrates on the effective production and structure of video for creating communications.

Considering how storytelling can be a tool for persuasion, this document takes a brief segue to consider the power of storytelling and make-believe in the creation of brands within the denim industry. The purpose of this aside is to demonstrates a tool from Freeman (2004) for developing characters. Branding and marketing argues for the treatment of companies as personalities and this is an important consideration if we are to present diegetic prototypes (Kirby 2009) in our fictions. The text then discusses the use of a company as an antagonist in the Alien movie franchise. What we learn from these sections is that diegetic prototypes are not produced outside of context and are products of a story world. The character of the producing company determines the shape and manifestation of the product.

T. Flint (✉)
School of Computing/Make-Believe Lab, Edinburgh Napier University, Edinburgh, UK
e-mail: t.flint@napier.ac.uk

© Springer International Publishing Switzerland 2016
P. Turner, J.T. Harviainen (eds.), *Digital Make-Believe*,
Human–Computer Interaction Series, DOI 10.1007/978-3-319-29553-4_4

49

The role of fiction has an important role in communication with the wider public. If we are trying to convince others of assertions, we must consider what it is to be convincing. Walton (1990) tells us that fictions serve as props in acts of make-believe. By creating believable fictions, it is more likely that our audience will indulge us by cooperating in acts of make-believe. This chapter presents some evidence for the role of structure in both memory and positive neurochemical response. This is followed by a presentation of Syd Field's paradigm and its effective use in Hollywood storytelling.

The final section in this chapter again looks beyond the laboratory at the phenomenon of crowd funding videos. Crowd funding videos are vital for their producers in that they are fictional accounts of products that have the aim of raising enough money to make these products a reality. They bridge fiction and non-fiction using storytelling as acts of realisation. A successful video is broken down in terms of the paradigm and demonstrates how structure enables the fiction it portrays.

This chapter does not aim to offer techniques that are to replace established methods. The tools discussed here have been shown to be effective in the act of storytelling. If it is our desire to tell stories that are aimed at the public and the wider world, we do well to consider them.

4.2   Fiction for Fiction

Stories are a way of mediating experience, watching a documentary on Everest can give a person a sense of the experience of being a Nepalese Sherpa. Similarly, watching The Terminator (Cameron 1984) mediates a sense of what it might be like to be hunted down by a ruthless cyborg. One of these stories is fantastical but we engage with it none the less, "because we would rather enjoy ourselves and accommodate the vagaries of a good story's speculations than dismiss it and step outside of the drama" (Bleecker 2010). Walton (1980) dismisses the idea of a "suspension of disbelief" or a "decrease of distance" instead arguing that audiences extend their presence into the fictional world. Extending presence, he argues is managed through pretending, an activity learnt in childhood.

For example, Benford and Giannachi (2011) demonstrate audiences who are keen to collaborate in the creation of fictions. This is similar to "This is Not a Game," a popular device in Alternate Reality Games (Örnebring 2007). Alternate Reality Games (ARGs) are games played across multiple media such as email, online videos, phone applications and live events; these games rely on mass participation and the creation of an alternate story world that plays across the real world. Those that participate in an ARG are expected to accept that they are participating in a game whilst simultaneously making-believe that they are not. Any interactions with characters or other players within the story world will not acknowledge the game as anything other than reality.

Audiences are willing to collaborate in fictions through the act of pretending. The popularity of ARGs and the success of Benford and Giannachi's work demonstrate that people will pretend in order to allow a narrative experience to continue. By locating their senses of presence into the fictional world, audience members have the tools to consider what the world might be like if a particular product exists. Audiences are sophisticated and are able to read media texts such as video at several levels. Taking a postmodern approach to understanding media (Barthes 1972; Berger 1972; Mulvey 1975) demands that we understand both imagery and relationship to other texts, something termed as the Under-Language (Moulthorp 2009). Although this method of reading texts is traditionally focused on cinema, fine art and literature, understanding this type of representation is essential when examining New Media such as Internet based videos (Lister et al. 2009).

A term for this type of representation is borrowed from rhetoric and is named a 'trope'. Tropes are described as "the order of things as a grid-like system of representative order" (Kellner 1981). Tropes are a method of "crafting meaning" to convey ideas that are "not literal but symbolic" (DiSalvo 2012). We can consider a relationship between tropes and archetypes allowing narratives to create emotional links with audiences (Huang-Ming et al. 2015). A contemporary cultural view of tropes borrows from literature, postmodernist theory and semiotics (Hall 2012; Howells 2003) and henceforth trope is the term used in this document for representational understanding.

4.3   Fiction in Design

Use of a computer system is never free from context, the challenge is to consider real world use and to this end, storytelling is an established tool within HCI. Personas and scenarios are tools that employ fiction. A persona is a description of a fictitious person, used to highlight specific motivations or needs when using a product or system. By considering how Julie, a professional lawyer of 50 with a busy home life might interact with a product it can be designed around the needs and motivations of real people. "The special aspect of a persona description is that you do not look at the entire person, but use the area of focus or domain you are working within as a lens to highlight the relevant attitudes and the specific context associated with the area of work" Nielsen (2014).

Scenarios are descriptive passages demonstrating established personas' attempts at navigating a system or product. By understanding the persona, it is possible to create a narrative vignette of the experience of a product. Ultimately, a scenario is a story of a persona interacting with a system. Personas can be argued as analogous to the creation of characters and scenarios as the creation of stories. According to Carroll (2000) the strength of scenarios is that they are simultaneously concrete and flexible. They are concrete in that they set out specific motivations and use cases and flexible in that they can be easily adapted and changed according to what is discovered in the design process. Scenarios encourage reflection and discussion in systems design allowing consideration of how different people might experience a system.

The same scenario can be used to explore different personas' approach to a similar interaction. The use of scenarios allows discourse with many stakeholders in the design process (Bodker 2000). Describing use in the form of a scenario or story allows non-experts to contribute to the design process, this is ultimately about future use with proposed systems. Scenarios have a beginning, middle and end, involve characters (personas) and are about these characters' progression through a series of events. Scenarios are driven by action and the motivations of characters to perform these actions.

Scenario based design focuses specifically on the user when interacting with systems, providing a useful and powerful tool for discussing the design of a system (Carroll 2000). Scenarios are text based descriptive narratives that are shared across organisations. How scenarios are used and how they are interpreted by different members of a team can cause tensions (Benyon and Macaulay 2002). What scenarios demonstrate is an established and relevant use of fiction for the design of a system.

4.4 Design Fiction

Design Fiction has been of interest in HCI for at least 10 years (Lindley and Coulton 2015). Design Fiction can be argued to hail from approaches of Research Through Design (Gaver 2012) and Speculative Design (Dunne and Raby 2013). Design Fiction lacks clear specific definitions or approaches (Lindley 2015), however it can be described as the use of story telling to encourage discussion of possible design. Typically Design Fictions look to an imaginary future and possible products that may be invented imminently.

There is no specific format for a Design Fiction though a common approach is to use video. The Near Future Laboratory is a design agency who employ design fiction in their work. They list a number of outputs for design fictions "case studies, events, workshops, fast-prototyped apps, innovative algorithms, curious objects, mock-ups, videos, fictional magazines, newspapers, product catalogs" (Near Future Laboratory date unknown). The intended audience is wide, meaning that Design Fictions tend to have high production values aiming to communicate a possible future reality. Design Fictions are presented as though they were documents of prototypes in action.

Design Fictions involve a diegetic prototype (Kirby 2009), these prototypes are often functionless mock ups but their manifestation enables the fiction producer to demonstrate what life would be like were this prototype in the world. These prototypes are props for acts of make-believe (Walton 1990). Unlike Scenarios, Design Fictions are not necessarily for the purpose of creating solutions, instead they "open up a space for discussion" (Dunne and Raby 2013 p. 51). Blythe (2014) promotes caution as Design Fictions can cause confusion, in danger of being interpreted as fact. Bleecker (2010) states that the strength of a design fiction is the placing of a prototype within mundane settings as though it were already a commonplace artefact within the world "The extraordinary becomes ordinary and, therefore, possible."

Design fictions have been used in high profile public communications, notably Is this your future? (Dunne and Raby 2004) "a collection of hypothetical products to explore the ethical, cultural and social impact of different energy futures" produced for the Science Museum London and exhibited in their energy gallery. Microsoft often release design fiction videos such as their Office Labs Vision 2019 (Microsoft 2009), these videos have no narration, allowing the unfolding story to communicate a vision of the future. The TBD Catalog from the Near Future Laboratory (2014) is a catalogue of "implications without making predictions" (TBD date unknown). This catalogue is reminiscent of the type of product catalogues that are sent with certain credit cards. Design Fictions can be argued to be artistically informed, concentrating on high quality output for a wide audience. Morrison et al. (2013) argue that design fictions "may too readily be influenced by notions and practices of designing to do with arriving at solutions to problems." It is important to delineate Design Fictions away from function and problem solving, this is the role of Scenarios.

Walton (1990) discusses the tensions between a text such as Darwin's Origin of Species, historical novels, outright fictions and requests to pass the salt amongst others. "If we are to believe the theory of evolution, it is because that theory is true, or because there is good evidence for it, not because it is expressed in The Origin of Species" (ibid p. 70). He tells us that a major difference between fiction and non-fiction is that the latter makes assertions, warning that there are also malleable delineations between the two. The pertinent fact in both is that something that is in one person's imagination is transferred to another's imagination. "To be fictional is to serve as a prop in games of make-believe" (ibid p. 102). Design fictions then are props in themselves as well as media that contain props in the form of diegetic prototypes.

Design fictions often inhabit a world between fiction and non-fiction and it can be argued that public communication of research thinking and speculation has a motive of persuasion. This can be simply as a form of marketing for the university or research group involved or as a method for encouraging funding investment. There is established use of story telling for persuasion in the field of marketing and the use of stories can be extremely powerful. This text will now examine how story telling was used to create and promote a new market of luxury denim transforming the view of denim from functional work wear to a high fashion item. This example is specifically used to demonstrate how the provenance of a product can be manufactured through character development tools and the use of tropes.

4.5   True Fiction

Denim is considered by some to be a specialist product and those that have this point of view seek particular types of denim in specific cuts and finishes with Japanese denim being considered the best quality. This market can trace its origin to a decision by Levi's to change the production methods of their signature 501 jeans. Levi's changed the type of loom on which the denim for their jeans was produced. The original shuttle loom process was notable for the fact that it produced a seam known as a selvedge. The selvedge marks the edge of the denim and runs up the outer inside of the leg of the trouser. Simultaneously Levi's changed the red badge on the back of the trouser, the E in Levi's was changed from an uppercase 'E' to a lower case 'e.'

In the early to mid 1980s a fashion ensued for buying second hand "big E" Levi's. Those who had a pair could easily signify this by turning up the bottom of their trouser legs to reveal the selvedge. The fashion became prevalent, particularly in Japan and due to their scarcity the price of second hand Levi's increased dramatically. Levi's have a particular brand story that is arguably one of the best-known in the world. This is the true story of a trader, Levi Strauss who ran a general trading shop in San Francisco during the gold mining era. Strauss came up with the idea of using rivets to strengthen his work trousers. The trousers were stocked on shelf number 501 and the denim jean, as we understand it today was conceived.

In 1998 Hidehiko Yamane began producing denim under the brand name Evis. These jeans were produced on shuttle looms meaning they had a selvedge. The jeans studiously recreated the cut of 1950s era Levi's 501 jeans and had similar details. The jeans were finished with a painted 'seagull' on the back pockets, the shape of these seagulls being very similar to the stitched shape on the back of a pair of Levi jeans known as the arcuate. There are unsubstantiated rumours that Yamane purchased Levi's old looms making him the only source of 'original' Levi's. These rumours were considered to be a fictional fabrication to aid his marketing (Sean 2012). Following legal action from Levi's, Yamane changed the brand name to Evisu and the company has since managed to create and dominate an international luxury denim market. Levi's have responded with their Levi's Vintage range, which produces replica items from the extensive Levi's archive.

Both Evisu and Levi's use the story of their founder to promote their product. Evisu and other Japanese denim manufacturers can be argued to have appropriated authenticity from Levi's (Keet 2011). Both companies' product catalogues are dominated by the story of their products, for example Levi's website (Levi's 2015) uses the following text for their 1933 replica jeans. "The Great Depression was causing tough times for Americans when these 501 jeans were released in the 1930s." The text continues, describing certain features of the jeans and their provenance.

This text now turns to Welsh company Hiut established in 2012. Hiut sell a premium denim range manufactured in Cardigan, South Wales. Factories in Cardigan used to manufacture denim jeans for Marks and Spencer, a popular UK high street retail store, until 2002 when production was moved to Morocco. Hiut employ storytelling to promote their trouser, the third link on their site, after 'Shop' and 'Fit Guide' is 'Our Story.' This is where they tell us:

Cardigan is a small town of 4,000 good people. 400 of them used to make jeans. They made 35,000 pairs a week. For three decades.

Then one day the factory closed. It left town. But all that skill and knowhow remained. Without any way of showing the world what they could do.

That's why we have started The Hiut Denim Company. To bring manufacturing back home. To use all that skill on our doorstep. And to breathe new life into our town.

(Hiut 2012).

Hiut have told a story of a large manufacturing facility closing and being revived through community practice. Using this particular story, they are able to charge a premium price for their product. The irony is that the original jeans manufactured for Marks and Spencer would have been produced and sold as a value product. Hiut employ a familiar trope of saving small town industry by community effort and this narrative is evocative. Without the luxury market created through storytelling by Evisu and other Japanese denim manufacturers, this story would be ineffective.

We argue above that the creation of personas is the act of creating characters and we now discuss brand personality as an established concept in marketing (Seimene and Kamarauskaite 2014). As an example Aaker (1997) defining brand personality as "the set of human characteristics associated with a brand" gives us personality traits associated with Coca Cola namely: cool, all-american and real as opposed to those of Pepsi: young, exciting and hip and Dr. Pepper: non-conforming, unique and fun.

Freeman (2004) has established a set of techniques he terms 'Emotioneering' for the establishment of effective characters. A specific tool Freeman has established is that of the character diamond. This is a set of traits allowing writers to consider how a specific character might act in the course of a fiction. The character diamond is termed a diamond because it is usually employed for human characters giving four dimensions. Freeman gives us the example of Star Wars character Han Solo's character diamond (Fig. 4.1). Freeman also describes a three pointed, triangular shape for non-player characters (NPCs), similar to Aaker's personality traits for soft drinks and a five pointed shape for more complicated characters. We could consider personality traits for the three denim companies discussed above (Fig. 4.2).

These brand personalities affect all aspects of a companies' interactions with the outside world. In this way, if we are to create a product from a fictional company, the product will communicate the brand personality in its structure. This reflects modern product design following principles of Total Design (Pugh 1991) where the design and manufacturing process are synthesised into an iterative process. In this way

Fig. 4.1 Character diamond for Han Solo

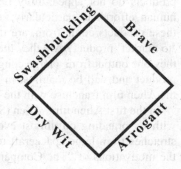

Fig. 4.2 Brand personalities of the denim companies discussed above

we can consider that a Samsung telephone will communicate the brand personality of Samsung through its shape, interface and marketing. Using Freeman's character diamonds enables us to consider what a family of products from the same company might be like.

4.6 Convincing Fiction

For Dunne and Raby (2013) it is important that speculative design is not something that could necessarily exist in reality, it is the discussions designs provoke that are more important. They also highlight a difference between speculative design and design fiction claiming that they are different disciplines with differing remits. Lindley and Coulton (2015) tell us "So a design fiction is (1) something that creates a story world, (2) has something being prototyped within that story world, (3) does so in order to create a discursive space." If, as argued above, we are asking our audience to cooperate through make believe in co-creating a story world we must take care that it is believable. Loveridge (2010) argues that Design Fictions occupy a space between the fantastic and the uncanny, for him it is imperative that we employ techniques from film, particularly science fiction in the creation of stories our audience will believe.

Design Fictions include prototype products and we must consider that these products do not appear fully realised from nowhere, they are the realisation of human effort and particularly entrepreneurial practice. We must consider where these products come from, are they the product of years of research realised in a 'to market' product? Are they the pursuit of a lone auteur and businessperson? Are they one output from a large conglomerate? These nuances will have bearing on the product and will be manifest in its construction. This is demonstrated throughout the Alien film franchise with the company Wayland Utani.

In the first Alien film, Alien (Scott 1979), this company has a dominant presence with its branding on almost every surface. Wayland Yutani's range of products stretches from large spacecraft to beer drunk by the crew. In this film series, it is the motivations of "The Company" that is the driving force of the narrative. This motivation is manifest by manipulating the crew to land on a planet in the hope that an alien specimen will be returned to Earth for study. Ash, a synthetic human and a product of Wayland Yutani, is the one character that is aware of the desire to capture an alien and that the human crew are considered expendable. This film establishes Wayland Utani as the major antagonist for the whole franchise. The alien though terrifying is simply acting to its nature; it is The Company that is the true monster.

In the first sequel, Aliens (Cameron 1986), Wayland Yutani have an outward public relations identity of attempting to help the human race settle extra terrestrially with a highly visible slogan of "Building Better Worlds." In this film, the company's interest in capturing a specimen is born out by the character Carter Burke, a corporate executive who conducts the protagonist Ripley's debrief and rehabilitation. Burke represents a familiar trope of an uncaring executive whose motivation is promotion and reward for fulfilling The Company's wishes. Through Burke, Wayland Utani is able to attempt to manipulate the capture of an alien. In Alien 3 (Fincher 1992), Ripley lands on a remote prison outpost and as soon as the warden reveals her identity to The Company, it becomes evident that she is of specific interest. In the final film of the original series, Alien Resurrection (Jeunet 1992), Ripley has been genetically resurrected by a secret arm of the military in order to breed aliens as a weapon. Throughout the franchise, it is the desire of external bodies to capture and study the alien that have been the underlying cause of the disasters that have befallen our heroine.

When Scott returned to the franchise in the prequel Prometheus (Scott 2012) he told the origin story of the discovery of the alien and the ancient ship that contained it. In this story we are introduced to Peter Wayland, founder and owner of the Wayland Corporation. During the film's narrative it becomes clear that Wayland's main motivation is to attempt to procure the secret to longevity. Although there is not a great deal of exposition of the character in the film, Scott turns to transmedia efforts (Von Stackleburg 2014) to expand on the character of Peter Wayland. On a corporate website for Wayland Industries (Fox date unknown), we are able to watch his revolutionary TED™ talk from the year 2023. We are also introduced to David, the first synthetic human developed by the corporation. In the feature film, David demonstrates a familiar disregard for the safety of crewmates when he deliberately infects a character with a substance discovered on the alien ship.

The tropes employed in the original franchise are of the overbearing corporation with little regard for people over profit. Combined with the trope of an uncaring, uncanny doppelganger (Freud 2003) or synthetic human, this makes for a powerful and believable element of the overall fabula. Scott uses this established trope to introduce the Peter Wayland character employing yet another trope of the driven megalomaniac inventor with a total disregard for anyone who may consider disrupting his machinations. Being made aware of this as an audience is credible because it makes sense of some of the situations in the first four films. In this way we can argue that any product that comes from the company should in some way be born of this narrative. In fact, David's fingerprints incorporate a large W, the Wayland Industries logo. When creating design fictions, we must be aware of the provenance of our products and implicitly design this narrative into their make up.

Our analysis reveals the careful construction of a story world in which various writers and directors have told entertaining stories. The Company itself acts as an antagonist throughout the series, operating malevolently in the background. If not for the motivations of this character, there would be no story to tell. There is a tension in the creation of narratives that are convincing and based on reality. Markusen and Knutz (2013) posit "if fiction is to be measured according to its resemblance to reality, then there will be no room for fictional worlds that do not resemble what we consider as real."

4.7 Vital Fiction

This chapter has so far discussed the use of storytelling in product design and demonstrated both its use in Hollywood and its power in creating brands. Our discussion now turns to the importance of structure. Individuals have greater recall of stories related to them that conform to specific structures (Mandler and Johnson 1977), implying stories and memory are linked. It is argued (Schank and Abelson 1977; Hassenzahl 2010) that phenomenological experience itself is made sense of and stored in memory as stories.

Paul Zak (2015) has found that oxytocin is secreted when a person is trusted and that this neurochemical promotes reciprocation. Oxytocin encourages a person to be more generous when donating money and it will make them more likely to give money to strangers. Zak's work has produced empirical evidence that engaging, structured narratives are effective in promoting the release of oxytocin, creating empathy and triggering charitable acts. This is important when we consider our next focus, crowdfunding videos on sites such as Kickstarter, Rockethub and IndieGoGo.

There can be no greater need for creating a convincing fiction than when seeking funding. A typical crowdfunding campaign proposes a product or service and asks members of the public to invest small amounts of money to support its development and production. A particularly successful crowd funded company is Flint & Tinder known for producing garments made in America. Starting with an idea to produce underwear they rapidly expanded into other products. Their durable 10-year hoodie was the first fashion product to receive over a million dollars in pledges (Kickstarter 2015). The language Flint and Tinder use in their promotional videos is based around domestic manufacturing and protection of US industry, echoing the story behind Hiut denim.

The majority of crowdfunding campaigns use video as the main promotion tool for their proposed product or service. Much of the motivation for investing in crowdfunding is feeling part of a community (Gerber and Hui 2013) so it is crucial that these fictions be convincing, promoting empathy and charity as well as creating feelings of community belonging. These campaigns are the act of telling the story of a fictional product in order to receive money to make it into being. It is possible to make videos engaging and involving using structure and many modern film writers use a tool termed "The Paradigm" (Fig. 4.3). Syd Field first introduced this structural

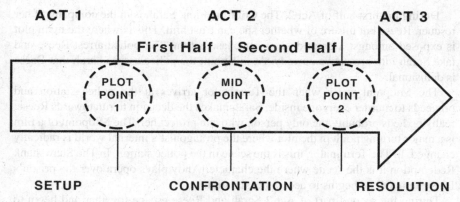

Fig. 4.3 A representation of Field's Paradigm drawn by the author

tool in 1979 (Yardley 2013) and it has become increasingly influential. Field (1984) describes the paradigm as a structure that acts as an open system allowing a writer freedom to create a compelling narrative. Drawing from Aristotle's Poetics, the paradigm breaks a narrative into a three-act structure commencing with a set up, moving to confrontation and finally resolution, these acts are navigated through "plot points."

The Paradigm has been used to deconstruct a number of films including The Shawshank Redemption (Darabont 1994). Plot points can be considered to be revealing points in the narrative where new facts are gained changing the protagonist's and thereby the audience's perspective of the story world. In Fig. 4.3 the arrow is used to represent the linear progression of narrative. Narratives are split strictly according to time, for example, if a film runs for 180 min, the first act will end 45 min into the narrative, with the second act finishing at 135 min.

We can deconstruct the film The Terminator (Cameron 1984) in terms of the Paradigm. In this film A Cyborg Assassin, a Terminator is sent back through time from a future where sentient machines are at war with humans. The Terminator's mission is to travel back to 1984 and murder a woman named Sarah Connor. In the future, Connor's unborn son John is the leader of the human army and will lead mankind to victory. If the Terminator succeeds in its mission, the whole of mankind is doomed. Sarah's only hope is a soldier from the future who has chased the Terminator back through time to protect her.

During Act 1, The Setup, we are introduced to the main characters. Both men arrive naked, steal clothes and begin looking for a woman named Sarah Connor. Sarah discovers that people with her name are being murdered and is scared to go home choosing to hide in a nightclub. Plot point 1 occurs in the nightclub where all three characters converge. This is where it is revealed to the audience that one man is there to kill Sarah and the other to protect her. It is also evident that the murderer is extremely resilient to gunshot wounds. Plot point 1 serves as a method of transforming our point of view from 'there are two suspicious men looking for a woman' to 'one is there to kill her, one to save her.'

During the first half of Act 2, The Confrontation, Sarah is in the company of her rescuer, Reese but unsure of whether she can trust him. This is where the main plot is exposed amongst a great deal of car chase action. The police arrest Reese and take Sarah into protective custody. At this point the police assure Sarah that Reese is delusional.

The Midpoint starts when the Terminator arrives at the police station and proceeds to murder everyone inside. Sarah makes the decision to run towards Reese, realising he is probably the only person who can protect her. The Midpoint of a film is a major turning point in the plot where the protagonist's internal world is radically changed. In The Terminator, this is the scene in the police station. In The Shawshank Redemption it is the scene where the character Andy plays opera over the prison's PA system and he begins to accept his situation.

During the second part of Act 2 Sarah and Reese escape together and begin to prepare to fight the cyborg. Plot point 2 and the beginning of Act 3, The Resolution, sees Reese declaring his love for Sarah and they have sex. This changes the mission into a personal act of protection for Reese. He is no longer simply protecting his leader's mother, he is caring for his partner. The film continues with a large amount of confrontation resolving with Sarah's successful destruction of the Terminator, Reese's death and the revelation that Reese is John's father.

Using the Paradigm enables filmmakers to pace their films successfully and The Terminator uses structure to great effect. We can consider how structure can help in the production of convincing crowdfunding videos and this is where this text now turns. There can be no greater need to convince with a design fiction than when trying to get people to part with money. To wit we examine a successful crowdfunding project whose video employs structure successfully. The crowdfunded product that will be focused on is Skylock™, a connected bicycle lock that communicates with smartphones. We examine this video (Skylock 2014) as an example of employing structure to impart a design concept.

To apply the paradigm to this video involves dividing it in time. The complete running time of the video is 2 min and 4 s. Strictly conforming to the Paradigm, we can expect that plot point 1 would be at 31 s, the midpoint at 1 min and 2 s and plot point 2 at 1 min 33 s. This is represented graphically in Fig. 4.4. All images are used with permission (Fig. 4.5).

Act 1 "The Setup"

Skylock employ the first act to introduce the video we are watching. The first 15 s of the video are concerned with various establishing shots and images of the product and the smartphone application. At exactly 15 s the shot focuses on the narrator, standing behind his bike, which is locked to a typical piece of street furniture outside a coffee shop. The initial 15 s are used to establish the fact that we are looking at a video about a bike lock, the subsequent 15 s are used by the narrator to confirm that this is a video about a bike lock, which he assures us is as strong as any lock on the market. Between 29 and 31 s, the narrator speaks the words "Skylock is keyless entry for your bike," this is the first plot point, it is asserted that we are not looking at an ordinary bike lock but keyless entry.

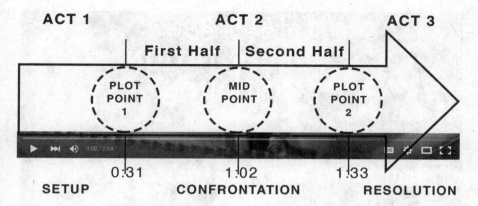

Fig. 4.4 A representation of the Paradigm with the Skylock video timeline super imposed

Fig. 4.5 Plotpoint 1 at 31 s

Act 2 "Confrontation"

The next 15 s establish the technology used and that the lock can be turned on and off with a telephone application. The narrator also points out that the lock has a solar panel "making sure its battery never runs out." We can argue that the video is employing a method of revealing functions over time, in this manner using a classic selling technique (Moncrief and Marshall 2005) known as 'overcoming objections.' Communication through video is mono directional so rather than wait for a consumer to voice their objections, the video uses pacing and slow reveal to create and then negate objections from the viewer. The first part of act 2 is employed here to make sure that the audience are clear that the lock is technically proficient.

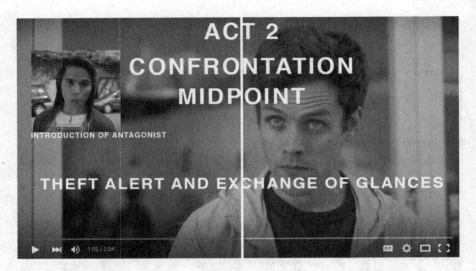

Fig. 4.6 Midpoint at 1 min 2 s

Midpoint

At 45 s the narrator is sat inside the coffee shop where he tells us "ordinarily I wouldn't leave my bike unattended for even an hour," he then goes onto explain that if he logs into the local Wi-Fi, the lock will alert him if anyone disturbs the bike. At 50 s, we see a hand shaking the bike, followed by an alert on the phone that prompts the narrator to leave the coffee shop. A young man has his hand on the bike and the narrator and the young man exchange glances. The midpoint is used here to present an antagonist, the youth, and the exchange of glances is used to present the theft alert capabilities of the lock (Fig. 4.6).

The narrator explains to camera that Skylock has an inbuilt accelerometer, finishing the midpoint. We are then told that the accelerometer can be adjusted for sensitivity and that the lock can be set to automatically open in response to proximity. The narrator then declares "let's talk safety (Fig. 4.7)."

Act3 "Resolution"

Plotpoint 2 is the narrator riding his bike into a post box. He uses this opportunity to explain the feature of the lock where it is able to contact emergency services in the event of an accident.

The video then cuts to an indoors shot where the narrator appears to be at home and a new female character is in the background. It is at this point that we are introduced to the bike sharing function of the application. The female character says goodbye to the narrator and we then see shots of her unlocking and taking his bike.

This video is divided into three acts and employs plotpoints to progress the narrative. Act 1 or the setup, explains the technology and that the video is discussing

Fig. 4.7 Plotpoint 2 at 1 min 33 s

a new type of bike lock, plot point 1 is where keyless entry is established. Act 2 or the confrontation is used to demonstrate the anti-theft attributes of the product. Plotpoint 2 is where our protagonist, the narrator crashes and is used to demonstrate the lock's ability to alert emergency services. The video is resolved with the protagonist safe at home, sharing his bike with his partner through the app.

This case study of Skylock is an example of structure helping to drive a narrative. By breaking down the essential information to impart, the video producers are able to employ structure to reveal important features of the product. The video is aided by its humour and deft use of cinematographic techniques such as composition.

Another example of a successful crowdfunding campaign is that of Tens sunglasses. Their campaign video (Tens 2014) elicited a great deal more funding than expected, allowing the company to expand and establish itself in the market place (Hurst 2014). In an interview discussing the making of their video, company director Tom Welsh stated "I was very aware of creating tension and pacing at particular points in our video. I made sure we edited it in a way that would reflect this."

4.8   Pulp Fiction

This chapter is about story telling and make-believe and offers some tools for public communication. It has established that stories are collaborative acts between communicator and audience. Treating audiences as sophisticated participants able to comprehend meaning on a number of levels allows us to tell engaging stories. The use of tropes is effective and relevant for a modern audience. The use of fiction in the area of HCI is not a new phenomenon and to this end the text has briefly focused on the use of scenarios. We have then discussed the relatively modern phenomenon of Design Fictions and introduced the concept of speculation rather than function.

The text digresses into the world of denim retail to make the point of brands as characters. If we treat brands as characters in our fictions, then we are able to create more convincing story worlds. This is evidenced with the example of Wayland Utani from Alien. By creating and establishing a believable company, Ridley Scott and others are able to use the story world as a constraint to embellish the story whilst maintaining continuity. The lesson here is that we should ensure that when we create diegetic prototypes that we consider where they come from.

Structure is introduced as a tool employed in Hollywood for establishing and maintaining tension through a narrative. Again we find ourselves having to move outside the laboratory to find effective examples of the use of structure. The acts of make-believe that are crowd funding videos ask us to pretend a product exists to such an extent that we are prepared to part with money to embody it.

The reader is asked to consider these tools when employing narrative in communication. Tropes allow a shorthand communication of familiar concepts to audiences. Character diamonds afford the creation of believable companies. Employing structure effectively makes video believable and memorable promoting action.

Acknowledgements The author would like to thank Velo Labs for allowing the use of their images. Thanks also go to Dr. Charles Kriel for the original deconstruction of The Terminator in terms of the Paradigm.

References

Aaker J (1997) Dimensions of brand personality. J Mark Res 34(3):347–356

Barthes R (1972) Mythologies. Vintage, London

Benford S, Giannachi G (2011) Performing mixed reality. MIT Press, Cambridge, MA

Benyon D, Macaulay C (2002) Scenarios and the HCI-SE design problem. Interact Comp 14(4):397–405

Berger J (1972) Ways of seeing. Penguin, London

Bleecker J (2010) Design fiction: from props to prototypes swiss design network conference 2010. Available from: http://www.swissdesignnetwork.org/daten_swissdesignnetwork/docs/Conference%20Book%20Swiss%20Design%20Network%20Conference%202010.pdf. Last accessed 8 Aug 2015

Blythe M (2014) Research through design fiction: narrative in real and imaginary abstracts CHI 2014. In: Proceedings of the SIGCHI conference on human factors in computing systems, Toronto

Bodker (2000) Scenarios in user-centred design – setting the stage for reflection and action. Interact Comput 13(1):61–75

Cameron J (1984) The Terminator. 20th Century Fox, Los Angeles, USA

Cameron J (1986) Aliens. 20th Century Fox, Los Angeles, USA

Carroll J (2000) Five reasons for scenario-based design. Interact Comput 13(1):43–60

Darabont F (1994) The Shawshank Redemption. Castle Rock, Los Angeles, USA

DiSalvo (2012) Spectacles and tropes: speculative design and contemporary food cultures. Fibrecul J Issues 20:109–122

Dunne A, Raby F (2004) Is this your future? Exhibition, science museum catalogue. Available from http://www.dunneandraby.co.uk/content/projects/68/0 Last accessed 24 July 2015

Dunne A, Raby F (2013) Speculative everything: design, fiction, and social dreaming. MIT Press, Cambridge, MA

Field S (1984) The screenwriter's workbook. Bantam Dell, New York

Fincher D (1992) Alien 3. 20th Century Fox, Los Angeles, USA

Fox (date unknown) Weyland industries. Available from http://www.weylandindustries.com. Last accessed 29 June 2015

Freeman D (2004) Creating emotion in games: the art and craft of emotioneering. New Riders, San Francisco

Freud S (2003) The uncanny. Penguin Books, London

Gaver W (2012) What should we expect from research through design? In: CHI 2012, Austin, Texas, USA

Gerber E, Hui J (2013) Crowdfunding: motivations and deterrents for participation. ACM Trans Comput-Hum Interact 20(6), Article 34:32

Hall (2012) This means this this means that a user's guide to semiotics, 2nd edn. Laurence King Publishing, London

Hassenzahl M (2010) Experience design, technology for all the right reasons. Morgan & Claypool, San Rafael

Hiut (2012) Our-town-is-going-to-make-jeans-again. Available from: http://hiutdenim.co.uk/blogs/story/5156362-our-town-is-going-to-make-jeans-again. Last accessed 26 June 2015

Howells R (2003) Visual culture. Polity. Cambridge

Huang-Ming C, Ivonin L, Diaz M, Catala A, Chen W, Rauterberg M (2015) Enacting archetypes in movies: grounding the unconscious mind in emotion-driven media. Digit Creat 26(2):154–173. doi:10.1080/14626268.2014.939985

Hurst S (2014) Indiegogo-success tens announces Singapore expansion. Available from http://www.crowdfundinsider.com/2014/10/52315-indiegogo-success-tens-announces-singapore-expansion/. Last accessed 15 Aug 2015

Jeunet J-P (1992) Alien Resurrection. 20th Century Fox, Los Angeles, USA

Keet P (2011) Making new vintage jeans in Japan: relocating authenticity. Text J Cloth Cult 9(1):44–61

Kellner H (1981) The inflatable trope as narrative theory: structure or allegory? Diacritics 11(1):14–28

Kickstarter (2015) The 10-year Hoodie: built for life, backed for a decade! Available from https://www.kickstarter.com/projects/jakehimself/the-10-year-hoodie-built-for-life-backed-for-a-decade. Last accessed 26 July 2015

Kirby D (2009) The future is now: diegetic prototypes and the role of popular films in generating real-world technological development. Soc Stud Sci XX(X):1–30

Levi's (2015) Levi's vintage clothing. Available from: http://levisvintageclothing.levi.com/GB/en_GB/#/1933-501-jean/showcase/fit. Last accessed 26 June 2015

Lindley J (2015) Researching design fiction with design fiction creativity and cognition 2015. In: Proceedings of creativity & cognition, Glasgow

Lindley J, Coulton P (2015) Back to the future: 10 years of design fiction. In: Proceedings of British HCI 2014, Lincoln

Lister M, Dovey J, Giddings S, Grant I, Kelly K (2009) New media a critical introduction, 2nd edn. Routledge, London

Loveridge R (2010) Fantastic form swiss design network conference 2010. Available from: http://www.swissdesignnetwork.org/daten_swissdesignnetwork/docs/Conference%20Book%20Swiss%20Design%20Network%20Conference%202010.pdf. Last accessed 8th Aug 2015

Mandler J, Johnson N (1977) Remembrance of things parsed: story and structure and recall. Cogn Psychol 1(9):111–151

Markusen T, Knutz E (2013) The poetics of design fiction DPPI 2013. Proceedings of designing pleasurable products and interfaces, 3–5 September 2013, Newcastle upon Tyne

Microsoft (2009) Microsoft office labs vision 2019 video. Available from https://www.youtube.com/watch?v=8Ff7SzP4gfg. Last accessed 7 Aug 2015

Moncrief W, Marshall G (2005) The evolution of the seven steps of selling. Ind Mark Manag 34(1):13–22

Morrison A, Tronstad R, Martinussen E (2013) Design notes on a lonely drone. Digit Creat 24(1):46–59

Moulthorp (2009) See the strings: watchmen and the under-language of media. In: Harrigan P, Wardrip-Fruin (eds) Third person authoring and exploring vast narratives. MIT Press, Cambridge, MA

Mulvey (1975) Visual pleasure and narrative cinema. Screen 16(3):6–18

Near Future Laboratory (2014) TBD catalog. Self published, USA

Near Future Laboratory (date unknown). http://nearfuturelaboratory.com. Last accessed 24 July 2015

Nielsen L (2014) Personas. In: Soegaard M, Dam RF (eds) The encyclopedia of human-computer interaction, 2nd edn. Aarhus: The Interaction Design Foundation. Available online at https://www.interaction-design.org/encyclopedia/personas.html

Örnebring H (2007) Alternate reality gaming and convergence culture. Int J Cult Stud 10(4):445–462

Pugh S (1991) Total design: integrated methods for successful product engineering. Addison Wesley, Boston, USA

Schank R, Abelson R (1977) Scripts plans goals and understanding. Psychology Press, London

Scott R (1979) Alien 20th Century Fox. Los Angeles, USA

Scott R (2012) Prometheus. 20th Century Fox. Los Angeles, USA

Sean (2012) Raw denim myths the truth about selvedge denim. http://www.rawrdenim.com/2012/08/raw-denim-myths-the-truth-about-selvedge-denim/. Last accessed 12 Oct 2015

Seimene E, Kamarauskaite E (2014) Effect of brand elements on brand personality perception. In: Proceedings of the 19th international scientific conference: economics and management, Riga, Latvia

Skylock (2014) Skylock – your bicycle. Connected. YouTube video. Available from: https://www.youtube.com/watch?v=6gyLPjDakAc. Last accessed 10 June 2015

TBD (Date Unknown) TBD catalog available from: http://tbdcatalog.com. Last accessed 4 Aug 2015

Tens (2014) Tens: #TheRealLifePhotoFilter. Available from https://www.youtube.com/watch?v=Q9N7hwJ29gQ. Last accessed 14 Aug 2015

Vines J, Thieme A, Comber R, Blythe M, Wright P, Olivier P (2013) HCI in the press: online public reactions to mass media portrayals of HCI research CHI 13. In: Proceedings of the SIGCHI conference on human factors in computing systems, Paris, France

Von Stackleburg P (2014) Tales of our tomorrows: transmedia storytelling and communicating about the future. J Futur Stud 18(3):57–76

Walton K (1980) Appreciating fiction: suspending disbelief or pretending belief? Dispositio V(13–14):1–18

Walton K (1990) Mimesis as make-believe. Harvard University Press, Cambridge, MA

Yardley W (2013) Syd field, who wrote the book on writing screenplays dies at 77. New York Times. Available from: http://www.nytimes.com/2013/11/19/arts/syd-field-author-of-the-definitive-work-on-writing-screenplays-is-dead-at-77.html?_r=0. Last accessed 10 June 2015

Zak P (2015) Why inspiring stories make us react: the neuroscience of narrative cerebrum. Dana Foundation, New York

Chapter 5
Designing for Service Experiences

Satu Luojus and J. Tuomas Harviainen

5.1 Introduction

In this chapter, we discuss the way service design processes are conducted through make-believe, and the contributions that service design and its modes of thinking can offer for HCI. Focusing on the experientiality of service, we through a review of design processes, business logics and sample techniques illustrate the presence of make-believe at all stages of fruitful design.

Modern technology is interactive and intelligent, and thus may appear complex or difficult to use from the user's point of view. Aspects of interaction between human and interactive technologies have traditionally been addressed by research and practice in areas such as Human-Computer Interaction (HCI) and Computer-Supported Cooperative Work (CSCW). The researchers and practitioners in HCI have recognized a need for understanding the relationship between people and technology in a more comprehensive manner. They have been trying to solve design problems by, for example, concentrating on designing for user experiences.

The rapid technologic evolution has raised new challenges for the various fields of design. Mager and Sung (2011) recognize two essential changes going on: (1) the role of design is shifting from being seen as styling through design as a process, towards design as a strategy, and (2) a continuous shift from the design of the tangible world to the world of interactions, moving frominteraction to experience

S. Luojus (✉)
Laurea University of Applied Sciences, Espoo, Finland
e-mail: Satu.Luojus@laurea.fi

J.T. Harviainen
Management and Organization, Hanken School of Economics, Helsinki, Finland
e-mail: tuomas.harviainen@hanken.fi

© Springer International Publishing Switzerland 2016   67
P. Turner, J.T. Harviainen (eds.), *Digital Make-Believe*,
Human–Computer Interaction Series, DOI 10.1007/978-3-319-29553-4_5

and then from experience to services. They go even further, for their design is "about strategies and structures, processes and interactions – altogether about services" (Mager and Sung 2011).

The digital revolution has raised new challenges for designing services as well. At the same time, while services have become the most important economic power in the world (e.g. Ostrom et al. 2010) the nature of services and the pace of change have shifted dramatically. Services have evolved into multichannel services where digital technology plays a significant role (Miettinen et al. 2014). According to Patricio et al. (2011) service fields agree that further research is needed to address these challenges in e.g. marketing, operations management, innovation management, interaction design, design, and service science. They emphasize that some areas need particular attention, such as the growing complexity of service systems, the emergence of multichannel services, and customer co-creation of service experiences (Patricio et al. 2011). Thus, traditional interaction design should be viewed in a more holistic way – through a service design lens.

Together these trends have resulted in the need for novel interdisciplinary approaches to respond to the increasing complexity of modern technology and modern business. New concepts, methods, and tools are needed to invent, identify and evaluate multidimensional services – and to make them intuitive and simple to use from the user's perspective. At the same time, designers have to understand the way in which people engage with new interfaces based on their existing mental models that come from previous engagements with products and services. Users intuitively make believe that the new actions they perform are similar enough with their existing patterns of behaviour, Comprehending this requires an understanding of the possible ways of interaction with interfaces and the role imagination plays in it. To acquire that, methods of make-believe are required, for both envisioning new services and for making sure that those services fit customers' needs and intuitive logics. Human experience (e.g. user experience, customer experience, service experience, tourist experience) research has received increasing importance in academic discussion in the design fields. Service design is a useful approach when trying to understand and design for human experiences.

The intent of this chapter is to outline how to engage interaction design and service design in fruitful dialogue, and how they connect to imagination and make-believe. It presents a short history of the different stages of current HCI research, from cognitive information processing psychology and studies of the user as rational data processor to user experience design and understanding technology as an experience, in many cases through the use of make-believe. Secondly, it briefly discusses the simultaneously paradigm shift and how the new business logics have dramatically changed the understanding of business thinking and value creation in the field of service marketing and managing. Finally, it presents service design approaches and processes. As an outcome, it introduces three innovative and creative service design methods that can be useful in the field of HCI.

5.2 Shifting Focus from Products to Experiences

A Short History of Current HCI

The roots of HCI extend at least to WWII, but in its current form, it started at the turn of the 1970s and 1980s when the use of computers became more common and the general public became aware of problems in understanding the interaction between humans and computers. When personal computers became more common, this field of research suddenly gained both social and financial significance, and HCI research quickly expanded both in companies and in universities. The model of human cognition was adopted as the information-processing paradigm of computer science in the early 1980s (Kaptelinin and Nardi 2006). Challenges for the dominance of the cognitive paradigm and observations about the limitations of the traditional information-processing paradigm began to appear as early as in the mid-1980s (e.g. Winograd and Flores 1986; Suchman 1987). The limitations of cognitivist thinking and the need for a broader focus in HCI research and development were acknowledged by the mainstream HCI community (e.g. Grudin 1990; Bannon 1991; Kuutti 1995) by the early 1990s.

When information technology or communication technology devices became more common and expanded into consumer products in the 1990s, new challenges for interaction design emerged. "Post-cognitivist" approaches were created in HCI research to understand the problems of living with technology. The term post-cognitivist refers to an approach based on the idea that it is difficult or impossible to address these issues by utilising cognitivist information-processing psychology, and thus researchers have strived to introduce new elements into the original theoretical basis of HCI. Theories have been developed in order to study (1) the human element when using computers from viewpoints other than cognition and (2) the human-computer use case in a broader sense than the immediate interaction (Kuutti 2009).

After the turn of the millennium, HCI researchers started to search a solution for design problems by focusing on designing user experience (cf. ACM series of Designing User Experience (DUX) conferences). This approach focuses on the role and activities of users not only as rational but also emotional beings and consumers seeking pleasure and status (cf. Pine and Gilmore 1998). User experience (UX) in itself is a new important concept that aims at describing the comprehensive relationship between a user and a product, as well as the service provided by the product (Jääskö et al. 2003). During the last dozen years UX has become a focus of attention in HCI research. The HCI community has recently recognized a need for a complementary conceptual-theoretical discussion about UX. Not only theoretical study of the phenomenon is needed but also analytical tools to more comprehensively analyse and understand UX (Luojus 2010).

The design of digital services increasingly utilizes these concepts. User experience design requires an understanding of customer needs, and service design excels in acquiring such data. Make-believe allows researchers and designers to then extrapolate from that data, creating an understanding of many customers' needs through insight into the needs of a few of them. This understanding is combined with a customer-oriented business approach, in order to create contexts where the HCI design's results are seen as means and tools for providing services and solutions to customers, not as products. Because this drastic shift in perspective is based on a different view of the market, we next examine the logics that underlie at the base of such an approach.

Shifting Focus from Products to Customers in Service Marketing and Managing

During the past decade, the academic discussion in service marketing and management has shifted from a manufacturing way of thinking, i.e. goods-dominant logic (GDL), towards service-dominant logic (SDL), service logic, and further, towards customer-dominant logic (CDL). Business logic refers to a strategic mindset of a company and its business activities that guide conscious decisions made in that company (Heinonen et al. 2010; Ojasalo and Ojasalo 2015). Focus of contemporary academic discussion on business logics is on the identification and creation of customer value (e.g. Vargo and Lusch 2008; Heinonen et al. 2010; Grönroos and Ravald 2011; Ojasalo and Ojasalo 2015).

According to goods-dominant logic every company has a position in a value chain, adding value to inputs and then passing them to the customers, who are the actors in the end of the value chain. In goods-dominant logic value creation takes place inside a company through its own activities (Ojasalo and Ojasalo 2015). Customers are seen as an external part and through segments, which the companies tried to capture and act on (Prahalad and Ramaswamy 2004; Lüftenegger 2014). Goods-dominant logic suggests that value is added in the units of output, and the outputs present the essential units of exchange (Vargo and Lusch 2008; Ojasalo and Ojasalo 2015).

New business logics, service-dominant logic (Vargo and Lusch 2004, 2008), service logic (Grönroos 2006, 2008), and customer-dominant logic (Heinonen et al. 2010; Voima et al. 2010) highlight customers' active role in value creation. The fundamental principle of the service-dominant logic is that the value emerges when the offering is used and experienced by the customer (Vargo and Lusch 2004, 2008). SDL emphasizes the co-creation of value, value-in-use and value-in-context, which are proposed as an alternative approach to the traditional notion of value-in-exchange (Ojasalo and Ojasalo 2015). The company offers value propositions and value is always co-created together between the service provider and the customer (Vargo et al. 2008). Lüftenegger (2014) proposes that SDL is focused on value co-creation as a collaborative process and the integration between the producer, the consumer, and other supply and value network partners (Lüftenegger 2014). While the ideas may come from marketing, for HCI this is an important shift in design perspectives: as we move to understanding the systems and interfaces we create as tools for delivering service, instead of as products, we are better able to imagine how the users will relate to that which we have produced. That insight, in turn, will enable better design, with a focus on delivering solutions for customer needs and wants.

Grönroos (2006, 2008) has further developed the idea of SDL and provides an alternative approach, service logic. Service logic proposes that customers are value creators during value-generating processes and in value-supporting interactions, while companies are the facilitators and co-creators that engage themselves in the customers' value creation processes. Thus, the customers not only define the value, but also control the value creation in their own processes (Heinonen et al. 2010; Voima et al. 2010; Grönroos and Ravald 2011). This means that companies search for possibilities to understand and support the customers' value creation processes (e.g. Grönroos and Ravald 2011; Grönroos and Voima 2013) and create resources and means to facilitate customers to create value for themselves (Grönroos 2006).

In the beginning of 2010s the service-dominant logic and service logic were argued to be still production and interaction focused (e.g. Heinonen et al. 2010; Strandvik et al. 2012). Although the customer was seen as a partner in co-creation, service was viewed from the perspective of a service provider. The customer-dominant logic (CDL) (e.g. Heinonen et al. 2010; Grönroos and Voima 2013) takes the SDL thinking further emphasizing a deeper understanding and knowledge of the customer's daily life and the service experience as a long-term, in a context related process. It is essential for companies to understand how the value emerges in the customer's mental and emotional experiences; to understand the customer experiences before and after the actual service interaction, and to know how the customer experiences the value in her/his own context, i.e., what is the customer doing in order to accomplish their goals (Ojasalo and Ojasalo 2015). CDL emphasizes that the value is emerged, when the service becomes embedded in the customer's own context, processes, activities and experiences. Service design therefore takes into account not only the customer, but optimally as many key actors and stakeholders in the service's ecosystem as possible. We next discuss how this is typically accomplished.

5.3 Service Design Approach

Design is an integrative discipline. Buchanan (1996) writes about 'wicked problems' of 'design thinking' common to all designers despite of professions and academic disciplines. He argues that different areas of design point towards certain kinds of objectivity in human experience, and the work of designers in each of these areas has to create a framework for human experience in contemporary culture (Buchanan 1996).

Stickdorn and Schneider (2011) discuss the five core principles of service design thinking: (1) user-centered; (2) co-creative (3) sequencing; and (4) evidencing, and (5) holistic.

(1) User-centered design approach is based on the principles that can be found in "Human-centered design for interactive systems" (ISO 9241-210) and that can

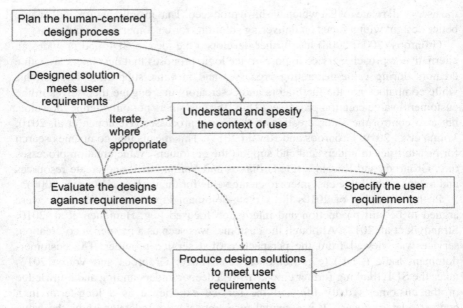

Fig. 5.1 Human-centered design for interactive systems (ISO)

be summarized in the following manner (Fig. 5.1): (A) the design is based upon an explicit understanding of users, tasks and environments; (B) users are involved throughout the design and development process; (C) the design is driven and refined by user-centered evaluation; (D) the process is iterative by nature; (E) the design addresses the whole user experience and (F) the design team has multidisciplinary skills and perspectives (ISO 9241-210).

(2) Co-creative. Mattelmäki and Sleeswijk Visser (2011) clarify the relationship of co-design and co-creation in the context of design research as follows: "Co-design is a process and the planning, adjusting tools and facilitation is built on a mind-set based on collaboration. Co-creation can take place within the co-design processes but focuses much more on the collective creativity of involved users and stakeholders." The notion of co-creation has adopted also in business literature. As noted before, there has been an apparent shift away from goods-dominant logic (GDL) that sees value embedded in products and services (value-in-exchange) to customer-dominant logic (CDL) where value is embedded in personalized experiences (value-in-use) (Prahalad and Ramaswamy 2004). In the value co-creation, the service company and its customer are together creating value for the customer, as well as for the service company (e.g. Gupta and Lehman 2005; Ramaswamy and Gouillart 2010). In the modern business thinking a company's co-creation approach is viewed from three angles: (A) Strategic thinking and the business model, (B) Customer interactions and relationships, and (C) Service design processes (Ojasalo 2010).

(3) Sequencing. Services are created through the interaction between the service provider and the customer in a dynamic process taking place over a certain period of

time. Each service process follows a three stage continuum from pre-service period to the actual service period and finally to the subsequent post service period. The service processes can be divided into single touch-points, when interaction between the service provider and the customer takes place. Thinking these touch points can happen through different interfaces, such as human to human and human to technology. According to service design these service moments should be visualized and well organized as a sequence of interrelated actions, enabling a pleasant rhythm and progress of the customer's mood by communicating the story inherently to the service through each touch point. This is a key area where make-believe comes in: using tools of imagination, extrapolations of deep customer insight data, desktop walkthroughs, and other similar means, service designers model the interaction and seek to optimize it (Stickdorn and Schneider 2011).

(4) Evidencing. Due to the intangible nature of service, physical evidence or artefacts, such as souvenirs, brochures, or signs, can enhance the customer experience by triggering positive associations and memories about the service moments. Physical or tangible service evidence can therefore prolong the service experiences from the actual service period far into the post-service period, potentially increasing customer loyalty and engagement. They allow users to return to the service experiences, reliving them through make-believe anchored by the physical reminders. It is crucial however that the service evidence is designed as an integral and natural part to the service and the sequence of touch-points (Stickdorn and Schneider 2011).

(5) Holistic. When designing services, the wider context of the environment, in which the service process takes place, should be considered. The service designers should understand and be consciously aware of what the customers may subconsciously perceive through their senses from the entire service environment. These subconscious perceptions can have a profound impact on the service experience. In addition, when designing a detailed touch-point, it is necessary to understand the whole customer journey and to know where this particular touch point lies in relation to the entire customer experience. Furthermore, the holistic approach needs to be incorporated to the entire organization of the service provider. The organizational culture, values, norms along with its structure and processes are important elements for the success of service design. Thus, there cannot be any inconsistencies between the corporate identity and objectives with the corporate image perceived by the customer (Stickdorn and Schneider 2011).

The service design approach is both a set of methods for service designers as well as an emerging academic field of design research (Ojasalo and Ojasalo 2015; Miettinen and Valtonen 2012; Miettinen et al. 2014) with a focus on complex and interactive experiences and processes. The multidisciplinary service design approach has been widely disseminated and rapidly adapted among designers, because the service design methods have proven to be very powerful in bringing customers and the service experience into the focus of service development process (Ojasalo et al. 2015; Ojasalo and Ojasalo 2015). Many of the tools rely on make-believe for their effect. For example, personas are imaginary target customers created by extrapolating from existing customer data and then used as a basis for designing for the segments which they represent. Academic research on service design is increasing (Ojasalo and Ojasalo 2015) and the basic concepts and paradigm are still developing (Miettinen et al. 2014).

Due to their inherent nature of being intangible, and being simultaneously produced and consumed (Vargo and Lusch 2004), services cannot be stored in an inventory like traditional products. Service is created through the interaction between the service provider and the customer (Zeithaml et al. 2013). According to Mager and Sung (2011) service design aims at *"designing services that are useful, usable and desirable from the user perspective, and efficient, effective and different from the provider perspective. It is strategic approach that helps providers to develop clear strategic positioning for their service offerings. Services are systems that involve many different influential factors, so service design takes holistic approach in order to get an understanding of the system and the different actors within the system."* (Mager and Sung 2011).

5.4 Service Design Process Models

There are several service design processes model or frameworks available usually consisting of three or even up to seven stages, but fundamentally all service design processes share the same logic and mindset (Stickdorn and Schneider 2011; Tschimmel 2012). Each service design process model is complementary to existing design methodologies and provides a service design thinking perspective that can be integrated into different design and development processes in a way that is appropriate to the particular context. In other words, various tools and methods can be used in each stage, depending on the desired outcome.

Stickdorn and Schneider (2011) emphasize that the service design processes are usually presented as having a clear and chronological structure, but in reality the service design processes are nonlinear and iterative by nature (see ISO 9241-210). The iterative approach is fundamental for service design processes, enabling the designers to learn from the mistakes and to take the process in the right direction based on these learnings. The idea is to notice the mistakes as early as possible in the design process and before actually implementing the new concept. The cost of iteration is marginal compared to changing the service concept that has already been launched full scale (Liedtka and Ogilvie 2011; Stickdorn and Schneider 2011). In the following section, a selection of perhaps the most well-known and used service design processes are introduced.

(I) The Double Diamond Model (or 4D Model) by the British Design Council has been divided into four distinct phases, *Discover*, *Define*, *Develop* and *Deliver*. (1) In the Discovery phase the designer identifies the problem, opportunities and need to be addressed through design, define the solution space and build a rich knowledge resource with inspiration and insights. (2) The Define stage acts as a filter in which the outputs of the previous phase are reviewed are analysed and the findings are synthesized into a reduced number of opportunities. Furthermore, the designer defines a clear brief for sign off by all stakeholders. The main activities in (3) the Definition phase are to develop the initial brief into a product or service for implementation, design service components in detail and as part of the holistic experience, and finally to iteratively test concepts with end users. In the last phase, (4) the Deliver stage, the final solution concepts are taken through final testing, signed-off, produced and launched (British Design Council).

(II) The 3 I model (*Inspiration, Ideation, and Implementation*) was developed by IDEO in 2001 in the context of social innovation. (1) The Inspiration stages includes the following stages: the identification of the service design problem motivating the search for solutions; the elaboration of the design brief providing the service design team a framework; and the observation of the customers for gathering deep insights about the behaviour and needs of the users in their own environment. (2) In the Ideation stage is the process of generating, developing and testing ideas. In this phase, the interdisciplinary service design team aims to synthesize the observations and learnings they have gathered in the Inspiration phase into insights reflecting opportunities and ideas for new solutions, i.e. the ideas for solving the initial problem or opportunity are brainstormed and visual representations of the new service concepts are made. The selected concepts are tested, iterated and improved through prototyping. (3) The Implementation phase takes the project from concepts to the market, i.e. once the final product or service has been created based on the feedback gathered from the users. The three overlapping spaces of innovation described above provide the necessary boundaries, without which the design simply cannot happen. Brown (2009) takes this thinking further by stating that the acceptance of these boundaries is the foundation of design thinking. He states that these constraints can be visualized as three overlapping criteria for successful concepts: feasibility (what is functionally possible), viability (is it possible to create a sustainable business model), desirability (what makes sense for people, do they want to use the solution and does it satisfy their needs) (Brown 2009).

(III) Moritz (2005) presents a service design (SD) process as a set of tasks that have been grouped into six categories: *SD Understanding, SD Thinking, SD Generating, SD Filtering, SD Explaining* and *SD Realizing*. The categories enable an easy application of the list of tasks and also tools to be utilized in a service design project. All categories have their objectives and each task acts as an intermediary step helping to reach these objectives. (1) SD Understanding is about researching the customers' both conscious and unconscious or latent needs. It is about finding out about the context, the constraints and resources as well as exploring different possibilities. In this stage, insights identifying areas the company should aim for are generated. This phase takes the project beyond things that the participants are already familiar with through exploring the customer's wants, needs, motivations and contexts as well as investigating the business and technical requirements and constraints, i.e. what do the customers' desire, what is feasible and viable. (2) SD Thinking identifies the purpose and objectives for the project, provides strategic direction for the service design project by setting the parameters for the other categories, making sure that all other categories work in line with the strategy. (3) SD Generating includes the development of relevant, intelligent and innovative ideas, the creation of role-, design- and concept alternatives as well as crafting details and consistency. In practice, this stage is about doing, creating and coming up with ideas and strong solution concepts, through the use of make-believe as a tool for imagining the potential end results. In addition, the service experience is developed, including all the details, spaces and elements required for providing superior experiences matching the customer needs. (4) In the SD Filtering stage, the most relevant and promising ideas are selected and evaluated against specific criteria, requirements and measures (e.g. subjective, heuristic, economic, technical and legal). The performance and quality and the service components of these selected solutions are tested and measured. Here, too, make-believe plays a significant role, as testing methods rely on tools that function through representation rather than model the eventual result perfectly. For example, websites are often feasibility tested by using simplified wireframes, servicescapes with methods such as LEGO® walkthroughs, and physical items rapidly prototyped with things like cardboard mock-ups. These anchors enable the testers to envision what using the service would roughly feel like (5) Comprehensive understanding of the main findings and insights, ideas and processes is vital for ensuring a successful of SD Explaining phase. This phase is a necessary step for creating shared understanding within the multidisciplinary team and stakeholders by visualizing the ideas and concepts; as well as testing the service experiences by prototyping. The same make-believe tools that help filtering play an even more important role on this stage, as the anchors make possible not just imagining, but also a shared imagining that results in common insight and understanding. (6) SD Realizing is about making it happen; developing and implementing prototypes, solutions and processes, writing business plans, instructions and guidelines as well as conducting training and briefings for ensuring consistent touch-points, i.e. everything that is needed to plan, specify and rollout a service. SD Realizing too can be done either by testing an experience prototype or the actual service, ensuring the best possible service performance. However, as service systems are complex and the environment likely to change, it will always be necessary to continue improving the service. Thus, this phase should be considered a new beginning instead of the end of the service design process (Moritz 2005).

(IV)   The service design process defined by Liedtka and Ogilvie (2011) is based on four basic questions, representing the four stages of the process: *What is*? *What if*? *What wows*? and *What works*? (1) The What is? phase explores the prevailing reality, aiming to define the job the customer is trying to get done and what are their current problems or dislikes. This means the framing of the design challenge based on the as-is situation. (2) The What if? phase is about synthesizing the information and emerging patterns gathered in the What is stage, developing hypothesis about the possibilities and the desirable futures as well as generating ideas and developing concepts based on these identified possibilities and future visions. Obviously, this stage is largely the realm of fruitful make-believe, yet it is important to note that it is still guided by the fact-base created during What is?. In the What wows? phase, the most promising concepts, meeting the customer needs and providing attractive profit potential, are prioritized and tested in the market via rapid prototyping in order to collect real-time data about the concept performance. The final stage, i.e. What works?, is about determining what works by inviting customers into an active and hands-on co-creation conversation and taking the service concepts into the market via careful launch planning and trials, ensuring that the concept will persuade the customers and get the awareness required for success (Liedtka and Ogilvie 2011).

(V) Stickdorn and Schneider (2011) present a service design process that has been divided into four stages: *exploration, creation, reflection* and *implementation*. In (1) the exploration phase, the service designer's task is to identify the problem to start working on. The objective and focus in the exploration phase is to define the problem and gain a clear understanding of the situation from existing and new customers' points of views. During (2) the creation phase, the objective is to create possible solutions based on the problems identified and insights generated in the previous phase, through make-believe. (3) The reflection stage means testing the ideas, and as discussed earlier, relies on tools that function as make-believing anchors. Thus, prototyping and gathering feedback from customers should take place. Stickdorn and Schneider (2011) remind that testing intangible services, the prototyping may be more complex. They suggest the utilization of e.g. comic strips, storyboards, videos or image sequences, and role-plays to guide the imagination. (4) The implementation should be based on the consistent service concept developed and tested in the previous stages of the service design process. There needs to be clear communication including the emotional aspects of the service, i.e. the desired customer experience the service provider aims to offer for its customers via the new or improved service. Employee engagement is one of the key success factors for the implementation. Including the employees in the interdisciplinary team throughout the service design process for developing and testing the service concept usually creates the required engagement (Stickdorn and Schneider 2011).

Due to the nature of service design thinking, it is impossible to provide a simple and easy to follow process model that would ensure the success of every service design project (Brown 2009). However, as noted before in this section, all these service design processes share the same service design thinking approach. The authors may have emphasis on different phases of the process. Characteristics of the service design processes are that them (1) aim at understanding human experience; (2) invite and involve users and other stakeholders to the design process to inspire design and to evaluate design solutions; (3) consist interlinking and overlapping phases in the iterative design process; and (4) rely on a combination of gathered data and guided, result-seeking make-believe. Some of the models, such as The Double Diamond

Model (or 4D Model) by the British Design Council, The 3 I model by IDEO and The service design process model by Stickdorn and Schneider describe roughly the design process as a continuum of few overlapping phases, not as a sequence of distinct and strictly defined steps happening in an orderly manner (cf. Brown 2009). Moritz's (2005) service design process model is more detailed, because the phases have two functions: to create a simple and generic framework helping to understand service design and to establish what various mindsets are needed in service design. He wants to emphasize that each phase can require a different set of skills, mindset, attitude, focus and environment (Moritz 2005). The service design process defined by Liedtka and Ogilvie (2011) and by Stickdorn and Schneider (2011) emphasizes that the successful implementation of a new service concept usually requires elements from change management and has to be planned properly, as well as reviewed after the actual implementation has taken place (Liedtka and Ogilvie 2011; Stickdorn and Schneider 2011). The 3 I model (Inspiration, Ideation, and Implementation), on its behalf, is developed for the context of social innovation. In the next segment, we further discuss some of the key tools of service design and their connections to make-believe.

5.5   Service Design Methods

Service design has adopted methods and working traditions from several fields (Miettinen et al. 2014). Service design methods come from several knowledge fields, such as arts, engineering, marketing, anthropology, and psychology. Sleeswijk Visser et al. (2005) divide methods into three categories according to the focus of the method: say/think, do/use and know/feel/dream. "Say/think" relates to interviews and to explicit knowledge, whereas "do/use" relates to observing the situation of usage. "Know/feel/dream" refers to physical or visual aids to allow people to visualize and describe their expectations and dreams, or tacit knowledge (Fig. 5.2) (Sleeswijk Visser et al. 2005). The focus of service design has shifted towards more creative approaches which seek to understand people's subjective values, attitudes and desires.

Users' creative input is an important source of design ideas. Thus, designers' creativity is not targeted only towards creating new design solutions, but increasingly towards creating opportunities for creative collaboration among users and developing tools that enhance their creativity (Brandt 2006; Vaajakallio 2012). There is a quantity of design methods recently established that represent credible ways of collecting user data through creative means. Creative and innovative methods are usually identified by their participatory nature, creative engagement and outcome, and their relatively specific application to design research (Hanington 2003). These methods are meant to support both the designers and the users in their creativity and interpretations during the design process. The service design approach favours creative research methods because research data gathered by these methods

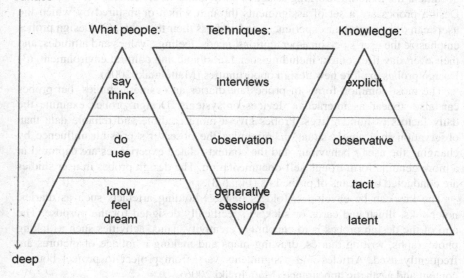

Fig. 5.2 Division of user research methods by Sleeswijk Visser et al. (2005)

provide stimuli that allow ideas and insights to be created and enable opportunities to share them (Mattelmäki 2006).

In the following paragraphs three innovative, make-believe related service design methods are introduced: design probes, design games and Lego serious play. All of the methods are specifically designed for the users in specific design context to enhance their creativity and encourage them to express themselves. Since design probes is based on self-documentation, specifically designed material packages are given to the users to document their private lives, contexts and experiences. Design games and Lego serious play are based on playful approach. Polaine (2010) argues that play is such a fundamental building block of culture, society, technology and cognition that it is a central vehicle through which to understand the interactive experience. Play is versatile enough to cross boundaries and fundamental enough to be understood intuitively. Taking play as a central feature in design enables us to understand interactivity in more comprehensive manner (Polaine 2010).

Design Probes

Probes are an approach for understanding human experience and exploring design opportunities (e.g. Gaver et al. 1999; Gaver 2001). Probes are based on self-documentation. Mattelmäki (2006) identifies the three features describing the probes: (1) Users have an active role in gathering research data. The users gather and document the material, working as active participants in the service design process. Design probes are a set of assignments through which or inspired by which the users can document their experiences and express their thoughts. (2) Design probes emphasize the user's personal perceptions, needs, feelings, values and attitudes, and their everyday life context including social, aesthetic and cultural environment. (3) Design probes explore new design opportunities (Mattelmäki 2006).

The most common forms of probes are diaries and camera studies, but probes can also appear as interactive devices or systems. Design probes examine the daily factors of human lives. Probes give a more credible and reliable data than observation in a single situation, minimize the observer's possible influence by changing the user's behaviour, and the context-related experiences are captured in a more genuine form trough self-documentation. The design probes in user studies are conducted by means of probe kits (Fig. 5.3).

The kits can be envelopes, folders or bags holding artefacts such as diaries, notebooks, illustrated cards or stickers specifically designed for the purpose. The aim of the design probes is to encourage creativity. Thus, activities such as taking photographs, writing diaries, drawing maps and making a collage of pictures are frequently used. Articles and assignments vary from project to project both in content and aesthetic appearance (Mattelmäki 2006).

Mattelmäki identifies five different phases in the use of design probes. The first phase *"tuning in"* consists of the definition of the uses, purpose, and subject of the

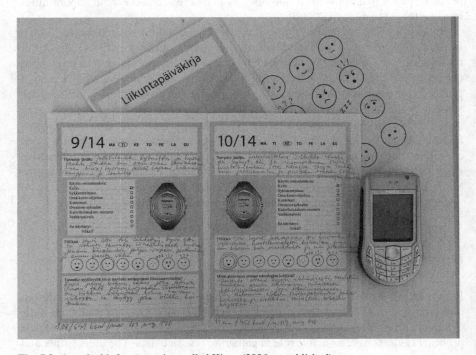

Fig. 5.3 A probe kit from a project called Kinos (2006, unpublished)

probes. The second phase is *"reaching out to the target group"* helps defining the principles of selecting the user group. The third phase *"designing the probes"* is actual probing with instructions for practical work. The fourth phase *"a follow-up on the probe material in an interview"* is the methods to be applied with probes, interviews in particular. The last phase *"interpretation and results"* is to draw interpretations and results out of the material (Mattelmäki 2006).

Design probes represent the data-gathering aspect of service design. While not themselves connected to make-believe, they exemplarily create precisely the kind of information which can then be used by the designers for imagining possible solutions to existing problems and new services that fill needs of which the probe providers themselves may not even be aware. Probes function as a condensation of human experiences, for the purpose of others then expanding again, through make-believe and empathy, from that summarization.

Design Games

There is no generally accepted definition for the concept of design game. Instead, there are several different descriptions of the characteristics of design games. Most descriptions agree that design games are about staging participation, that there is seldom competition over who wins the game and that there are rules and tangible game pieces that guide the design moves (Brandt 2006; Vaajakallio 2012). Design games are not games in a traditional sense, because the application area of early concept search and co-design, define them. Vaajakallio (2012) argues that there are some characteristics of play, games and performance that could describe design games as well: they are bounded with regard to time and space, they proceed according to explicit rules, are typically intensive and they utilize the magic circle of play, fostering make-believe (Vaajakallio 2012).

Design games can be approached from different perspectives and seen for example (1) as a tool for addressing the three needs of co-design: organising dialogue, supporting empathic understanding and gaining several contributions in order to identify, frame and solve design problems. (2) For the players, design games appear as a mind-set that creates an experience of being in a special game world, which is a physical and ideal playground with a special ordering of time, roles and rules that are not bound by the laws of ordinary life and where fruitful make-believe is therefore much easier – and more easily shared between stakeholders. (3) From a game designer's point of view, design games are a structure with tangible game materials, explicit rules or fixed elements, and performance roles that can be manipulated depending on contextual needs (Vaajakallio 2012).

Vaajakallio (2012) identified two basic components of design games, context and play-qualities, which define them. Instead of being a well-defined method, a design game is an expression that emphasizes the exploratory, imaginative, dialogical and empathic aspects of co-design. The objectives of applying design games are rooted in the design context. Design games are tools for co-design that purposefully highlight play-qualities such as playful mind-set and structure, which are supported by tangible game materials (e.g. game board, playing cards, and pieces) and rules (Vaajakallio 2012). The objectives of the design games are to inspire design and to help facilitate a participatory design process. By being context-specific, yet playful, they allow participants to engage in make-believe within the topic, while the rules of the game provide both direction and facilitation (Vaajakallio and Mattelmäki 2014). Framing collaborative design activities in a game format improves idea generation and communication between stakeholders. By shifting focus to the game, power relations and other factors that might complicate idea generation, are downplayed (Brandt 2006). According to Vaajakallio (2012) *"the means for reaching these objectives are drawn up in addition to the design (e.g. tangible mock-ups and user representations) from the world of games (e.g. role-playing, turntaking, make-believe) to deliberately trigger participants' imagination as a source of design ideas"* (Vaajakallio 2012) (Figs. 5.4 and 5.5).

LEGO Serious Play

LEGO® SERIOUS PLAY® (LSP) is a make-believe based team collaboration method developed by LEGO and IMD, a business school based in Lausanne, Switzerland. The basic principle of LSP is that LEGO bricks are simple to use and provide ready-made, powerful and multi-purpose symbolic pieces, known to most people and across different cultures (Cantoni et al. 2009). LEGO bricks (1) are simple to use and do not require particular motor abilities in order to be able to build models, (2) provide ready-made powerful symbolic pieces, such as little men and women representing e.g. many professions and cultures, as well as animals, plants, vehicles, furniture, and tools, (3) are known to most people as a toy and as a joyful part of their own childhood, and (4) are present in many different cultures. LSP offers a refined means for a team to share ideas, assumptions and understandings, as well as to engage team members in rich dialogue, by anchoring the imagination with tangible, playful representations. LSP's statement is that everyone can contribute to the discussion and help creatively generate solutions (Cantoni et al. 2009). In addition, the creative, reflective process of making something stimuluses and can open new perspectives. (LEGO® SERIOUS PLAY®).

LSP is based on four theoretical approaches (1) constructivism (e.g. Piaget), (2) constructionism (e.g. Papert), (3) play and (4) imagination (Moeller and Tollestrup 2013). In practice, LSP follows a structured process, where the participants use the bricks to create models that express their thoughts, reflections and ideas. The three elementary phases of the process: (1) *the challenge*, (2) *building*, and (3) *sharing*. (1) Considering the objectives of the workshop in advance, the facilitator formulates building challenges in a way that enhance dialogue and reflection. Each building challenge is posed to the participant one at a time. The building time is made clear and the facilitator asks participants to build a model with the bricks that expresses their thoughts and simultaneously response to the building challenge.

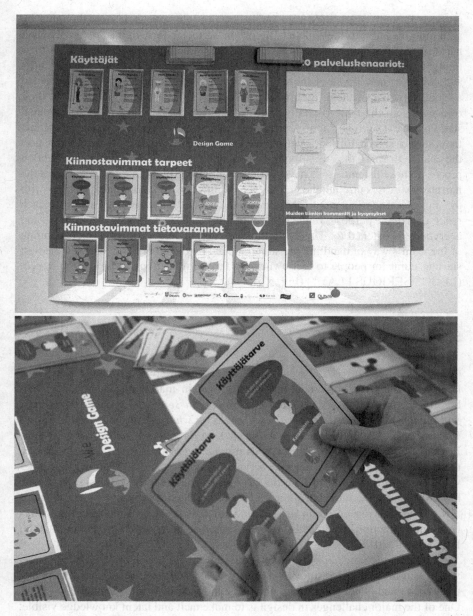

Figs. 5.4 and 5.5 A design game from a project entitled WeLive (2015) (Photo: Janne Lahti)

The challenge for the facilitator is to formulate the building task so that it best serves the purpose of the workshop while following the basic principles of the method. (2) The participants construct their response to the building challenge with LEGO bricks. During construction, the individual participant under goes a reflective process through which they gain more deep insight into their own thoughts by assigning meaning to their models by means of metaphors, figures of speech, and narratives. Using their hands to build concrete, three-dimensional models of their thoughts and reflections, gives the participants easier access to their experiences and catalyses new trains of thought. (3) When all participants have a constructed a model in front of them, each of the participants has an opportunity to set their own issues on the table (literally and metaphorically), and they all have an equal standing. Next, one at a time, each participant shares the meaning and story that they have assigned to their own model. It is necessary that each participant gets the chance to share the story about their model, because the sharing is a reflection process. Those listening also have an opportunity to explore in more detail what the narrator expresses through the model. The facilitator asks facilitating questions with the aim of get participants to share more about their thoughts and ideas with each other. One of the purposes of the LSP process is that each person's voice is heard and everybody is listened to. This is on the one hand to create a shared understanding of the team's way of handling the situation, and on the other hand to create the best starting point for people to feel ownership for the reflections and ideas expressed. (LEGO® SERIOUS PLAY®) (Fig. 5.6).

5.6 Discussion

Ojasalo and Ojasalo (2015) argue that service design approach would bring new kinds of means for implementing service logic in marketing and management, because the principles of service design support *"the service logic since the process and outcomes of service design are not based on what an offering can do, but on what customers want to achieve and what they do with the service* (e.g. Wetter-Edman 2011)". Service design methods provide a practical set of tools to explore their customers' world, to develop service experience and to facilitate customer value creation (Ojasalo and Ojasalo 2015). It seems that service design approach has awakened some interest within the HCI research community as well. First steps towards identifying common ground and towards creating supportive structures between interaction design and service design have been taken (e.g. Holmlid 2007; Polaine et al. 2012).

The innovative methods are intended to understand people's feelings, pleasure, values and dreams, often through data-based make-believe. Sometimes the objectives are thoughts never really thought, or expressed in words (Mattelmäki 2006). One of the major challenges in design is to make tacit and latent knowledge visible. These types of studies require methods for examining phenomena that cannot be grasped by means of direct observation and understanding. Tacit knowledge turns visible through appropriate research methods and tools (Luojus 2010). There are two ways how innovative methods can enhance in making tacit knowledge visible: (1) the innovative and creative methods are based on the process of making something, utilising the 'hand-mind connection' (e.g. design probes, design games and LSP).

Fig. 5.6 A LEGO® SERIOUS PLAY® from a project entitled COM'ON (2012) (Photo: Jukka Malkamäki)

The process of building and collaborating often produces insights which simply would not have appeared in regular discussions (e.g. Gauntlett 2007, 2011). (2) The innovative and projective methods (e.g. design probes and LSP) help the users to express themselves through make-believe, metaphors and associations, sometimes revealing very delicate and irrational motives. Creative and projective methods offer these ways. Projections reveal things that people do not wish to see, or are incapable of seeing. The principle of psychoanalytic interpretation is that the factors affecting the emotional reactions evoked by images are subconscious, not conscious. Projective methods are used for collecting qualitative data about the users and their values, dreams and needs for understanding and inspiration, and for further development of design (Mattelmäki 2006).

Human experience research has received increasing importance in academic discussion in the various fields of design. Human experience as an object of design provides a way to perceive more comprehensive understanding of the various elements of the design challenge. An experience is always personal and therefore designers always work through make-believe, when they try and create experiences for others. The components of each single experience are dependent not only on the subject and object of the experience but also on the comprehensive interaction between these two. This requires UX research that approaches the phenomenon in a more comprehensive manner and analytical tools to analyse and understand UX. Multidisciplinary service design approach seems to be a useful framework when trying to understand and design for human experience in more comprehensive manner. By using and understanding data-based make-believe, designers are able to better tailor the experiential value that they propose to users through the services that they design.

References

Bannon LJ (1991) From human factors to human actors. The role of psychology and human-computer interaction studies in system design. In: Greenbaum J, Kyng M (eds) Design at work: cooperative design of computer systems. Lawrence Erlbaum, Hillsdale, pp 25–44

Brandt E (2006) Designing exploratory design games: a framework for participation in participatory design? In: Proceedings of the 9th conference of participatory design (PDC 2006), ACM Press, New York, pp 57–66

British Design Council. http://www.designcouncil.org.uk

Brown T (2009) Change by design: how design thinking transforms organizations and inspires innovation. HarperCollins, New York

Buchanan R (1996) Wicked problems in design thinking. In: Margolin V, Buchanan R (eds) The idea of design. A design issues reader. The MIT Press, Cambridge

Cantoni L, Marchiori E, Faré M Botturi L, Bolchini D (2009) A systematic methodology to use LEGO bricks in web communication design. In: Proceedings of the SIGDOC'09, ACM Press, New York

Gauntlett D (2007) Creative explorations: new approaches to identities and audiences. Routledge, London

Gauntlett D (2011) Making is connecting: the social meaning of creativity, from DIY and knitting to YouTube and Web 2.0. Polity Press, Cambridge

Gaver W (2001) The presence project. RCA.CRD Research Publications, London

Gaver W, Dunne T, Pacenti E (1999) Cultural probes. Interactions 6(1):21–29

Grönroos C (2006) Adopting a service logic for marketing. Mark Theory 6(3):317–333

Grönroos C (2008) Service logic revisited: who creates value? And who co-creates? Eur Bus Rev 20(4):298–314

Grönroos C, Ravald A (2011) Service as business logic: implications for value creation and marketing. J Serv Manag 22(1):5–22

Grönroos C, Voima P (2013) Critical service logic: making sense of value creations and co-creation. J Acad Mark Sci 41:133–150

Grudin J (1990) The computer reaches out: the historical continuity of interface design. In: Proceedings of the SIGCHI conference on Human factors in computing systems: empowering people. ACM Press, New York, pp 261–268

Gupta S, Lehman DR (2005) Managing customers as investments. Wharton School Publishing, Philadelphia

Hanington B (2003) Methods in the making: a perspective on the state of human research in design. Des Issues 19(4):9–18

Heinonen K, Strandvik T, Mickelsson K-J, Edvardsson B, Sundström E, Andersson P (2010) A customer dominant logic of service. J Serv Manag 21(4):531–548

Holmlid S (2007) Interaction design and service design: expanding a comparison of design disciplines. Nordes 2007 (No. 2). University of Arts, Crafts and Design, Stockholm, Sweden

ISO 9241-210 (2011) Human-centered design processes for interactive systems. International Organization for Standardization, Geneve

Jääskö V, Mattelmäki T, Ylirisku S (2003) The scene of experience. In: Haddon L, Mante-Meijer E, Sapio B, Kommonen KH, Fortunati L, Kant A (eds) God, bad, and the irrelevant. University of Art and Design Helsinki, Helsinki, pp 341–346

Kaptelinin V, Nardi BA (2006) Acting with technology: activity theory and interaction design. MIT Press, Cambridge

Kuutti K (1995) Activity theory as a potential framework for human-computer interaction research. In: Nardi B (ed) Context and consciousness: activity theory and human computer interaction. MIT Press, Cambridge, pp 17–44

Kuutti K (2009) HCI and design – uncomfortable bedfellows? In: Binder T, Löwgren J, Malmborg L (eds) (Re)searching the digital Bauhaus. Springer, London

LEGO® SERIOUS PLAY®. http://www.lego.com/fi-fi/seriousplay/

Liedtka J, Ogilvie C (2011) Designing for growth: a design thinking tool kit for managers. Columbia University Press, New York

Lüftenegger ER (2014) Service-dominant business design. Doctoral dissertation. Proefschiftsmaken, Eindhoven University of Technology, The Netherlands

Luojus S (2010) From a momentary experience to a lasting one. The concept of and research on expanded user experience of mobile devices. Doctoral dissertation. University of Oulu, Oulu

Mager B, Sung TJ (2011) Special issue editorial: designing for services. Int J Des 5(2):1–3

Mattelmäki T (2006) Design probes. Doctoral dissertation. University of Art and Design, Helsinki

Mattelmäki T, Sleeswijk Visser F (2011) Lost in co-X: interpretations of co-design and co-creation. In: Proceedings of the 4th world conference on design research (IASDR 2011), Delft, The Netherlands

Miettinen S, Valtonen A (eds) (2012) Service design with theory: discussion on value, societal change and methods. Lapland University Press, Rovaniemi

Miettinen S, Valtonen A, Markuksela V (2014) Service design methods in event design. In: Richards G, Marques L, Mein K (eds) Event design. Routledge, New York

Moeller L, Tollestrup C (2013) Creating shared understanding in product development teams. How to 'Build the Beginning'. Springer, London

Moritz S (2005) Service design – practical access to an evolving field. Koln International School of Design, University of Applied Sciences Cologne, London, pp 187–239

Ojasalo K (2010) The shift from co-production in services to value co-creation. Bus Rev 16: 171–177

Ojasalo K, Koskelo M, Nousiainen AK (2015) Foresight and service design boosting dynamic capabilities in service innovation. In: Selen W, Roos G, Green R, Agarwal R (eds) The handbook of service innovation. Springer, London

Ojasalo K, Ojasalo J (2015) Adapting business model thinking to service logic: an empirical study on developing a service design tool. In: Gummerus J, von Koskull C (eds) The Nordic school – alternative perspectives on marketing and service management. Hanken School of Economics, Helsinki

Ostrom AL, Bitner MJ, Brown SW, Burkhard KA, Goul M, Smith-Daniels V, Demirkan H, Rabinowich E (2010) Moving forward and making a difference: research priorities for the science of service. J Serv Res 13(1):1–33

Patricio L, Fisk RP, Cunha JF, Constantine L (2011) Multilevel service design: from customer value constellation to service experience blueprinting. J Serv Res 14(2):180–200

Pine BJ, Gilmore JH (1998) The experience economy. Welcome to the experience economy. Harv Bus Rev 76:97–105

Polaine A (2010) Developing a language of interactivity through the theory of play. PhD thesis, Faculty of Arts & Social Sciences, University of Technology, Sydney

Polaine A, Løvlie L, Reason B (2012) Service design from insight to implementation. Rosenfeld Media, New York

Prahalad CK, Ramaswamy V (2004) The future of competition – co-creating unique value with customers. Harvard Business Press, Boston

Ramaswamy V, Gouillart F (2010) Building the co-creative entreprise. Harv Bus Rev, October

Sleeswijk Visser F, Stappers PJ, Van Der Lugt R, Sanders EB-N (2005) Contextmapping: experiences from practice. CoDes J 1(No. 2):119–149

Stickdorn M, Schneider J (eds) (2011) This is service design thinking: basics – tools – cases. BIS Publishers, Amsterdam

Strandvik T, Holmlund M, Edvardsson B (2012) Customer needing: a challenge for the seller offering. J Bus Ind Mark 27(2):132–141

Suchman L (1987) Plans and situated actions: the problem of human-machine communication. Cambridge University Press, Cambridge

Tschimmel K (2012) Design thinking as an effective toolkit for innovation. In: Proceedings of the XXIII ISPIM conference: action for innovation: innovating from experience, Barcelona, Spain

Vaajakallio K (2012) Design games as a tool, a mindset and a structure. Doctoral dissertation, Aalto University

Vaajakallio K, Mattelmäki T (2014) Design games in codesign: as a tool, a mindset and a structure. CoDesign 10(1):63–77

Vargo SL, Lusch RF (2004) Evolving to a new dominant logic of marketing. J Mark 68:1–17

Vargo SL, Lusch RF (2008) Service-dominant logic: continuing the evolution. J Acad Mark Sci 36:1–10

Vargo SL, Maglio PP, Akaka MA (2008) On value and value co-creation: a service systems and service logic perspective. Eur Manag J 26(3):145–152

Voima P, Heinonen K, Strandvik T (2010) Exploring customer value formation: a customer dominant logic perspective. Working papers. Hanken School of Economics, Helsinki

Wetter-Edman K (2011) Service design – a conceptualization of an emerging practice. Licentiate thesis, University of Gothenburg, Gothenburg, Sweden

Winograd T, Flores F (1986) Understanding computers and cognition: a new foundation for design. Addison-Wesley Publishing Company Inc, Menlo Park

Zeithaml VA, Bitner MJ, Gremler DD (2013) Services marketing – integrating customer focus across the firm. McGraw-Hill, New York

Chapter 6
Gameworld Interfaces as Make-Believe

Kristine Jørgensen

Make-believe is an important part of our engagement with many aspects of our lives and is often seen as central to our engagement with representational media. When playing video games, players must make sense of a range of information, and gameworlds include a selection of signs that either point to the game system, or to the fictional aspects of the game. The combination of health meters, experience bars, and symbols floating around in the world, with a recognizable environment featuring anthropomorphic inhabitants with intentions and motivations may appear paradoxical, but players tend to accept this contradiction without any confusion. With reference to Kendall Walton's (1990) theory of make-believe where virtually anything has the potential of being props in the imaginative process, the aim of this chapter is to expand the understanding of make-believe by exploring how it is employed when players interact with gameworlds.

Springing out of game studies, the chapter builds on the idea that gameworlds are not simply game rules in fictional worlds as Jesper Juul claims in *Half-Real* (2005), but world environments designed for gameplay (Klevjer 2007; Jørgensen 2013). This environment is a complex world construct that draws on conventions from fictional media as well as interactive systems, often in combination, and where players must employ different kinds of imaginative processes simultaneously. Finding support in cognitive theory and play theory, the chapter challenges the notion that the engagement with games can be reduced to pretence and "acting as if", and shows that other imaginative processes are also part of the playful processes that take place when players engage with gameworlds. The chapter stresses imagination over make-believe as a better concept for illuminating the imaginative processes,

K. Jørgensen (✉)
Department of Information Science and Media Studies, University of Bergen, Bergen, Norway
e-mail: kristine.jorgensen@uib.no

© Springer International Publishing Switzerland 2016
P. Turner, J.T. Harviainen (eds.), *Digital Make-Believe*,
Human–Computer Interaction Series, DOI 10.1007/978-3-319-29553-4_6

and presents thus an expansion of Walton's sense of make-believe that takes a game-specific approach to the imaginative process used when interacting with gameworlds.

The chapter starts with two sections introducing the theory of gameworld as interface, and the concepts of imagination and make-believe. Once established, these concepts are brought together through Walton's idea of props in an argument stressing that gameworlds spawn different kinds of imaginative processes. In the following sections this argument is developed and reinforced through a discussion of how players experience gameworlds. The empirical data that supports the argument was collected during a 2008–2010 research project focusing on how players engage with information in a gameplay context in four different game genres. Players were observed while playing, and subjected to a research interview immediately after the play session. In addition, one focus group was conducted in which a group of five players discussed game information on the basis of a number of screenshots from selected games. Although the data has been discussed in closer detail in Jørgensen (2011, 2013), the contribution of this chapter is to give greater attention to the role of make-believe and imagination in connection with gameworlds.

6.1   The Gameworld Interface

Before we can go into the concept of make-believe and its role in the engagement with gameworld interfaces, it is important to delimit and discuss what a gameworld is. Gameworlds are world representations designed for the playing of games, structured as arenas for participation and contest (Klevjer 2007, 58). Although modern video games include powerful physics engines, gameworlds are primarily governed by game mechanics; that is, standardized game interactions and operations restrained by game rules (Rollings and Adams 2003, 9; Sicart 2008). Gameworlds are also world systems, representing a habitable and self-contained world-like environment (Bartle 2004: 1; Ryan 2001: 91). Communicating the game system by way of a world metaphor, gameworlds are interfaces to the game system. In human-computer interaction, an interface is traditionally understood as the part of the computer system that allows communication between the user and the system (Lauesen 2005, 4). As an environment that connects the player with the game system, the gameworld invites a particular kind of gameplay interaction, and provides relevant information to support this (Jørgensen 2013, 3–4).

As both interfaces and world environments, gameworlds are complex representational systems: First, the gameworld is a metaphor that makes an abstract game system more concrete; or in other words, the gameworld *reifies* the game system (Beaudouin-Lafon 2000, 449). Second, the gameworld is also, like other representational media such as literature and film, a representation of a fictional reality. As world representations, gameworlds contextualize and make the game system understandable. This contextualization is based in recognizable tropes from fiction and narratives, making the gameworld not only a stage for contest but also a fictional world of imaginary characters and powerful narratives. This duality in terms of representation is made evident and strengthened through the fact that gameworlds combine two kinds of semiotic systems. Gameworlds use some signs that point to the fictional reality of the game, presenting a world environment with more or less recognizable topography, landscape, objects and inhabitants (Ryan 2008, 251); and other signs that point directly to the game system hidden beyond to hood, using features that we do not recognize from the interaction with the natural ecology such as blinking arrows above character heads, health and ammo bars, minimaps, and inventories. We may call game information *ecological* when it is represented as integrated into the gameworld environment in a way that resembles how information exists in our actual physical environment; and *emphatic* when it adds new information about, comments on, or augments ecological features (Jørgensen 2013, 79–80). Examples of ecological information span from walking paths that indicate the safest road through the environment in *The Elder Scrolls 5: Skyrim* (Bethesda Game Studios 2011), to the integration of the HUD into the avatar's helmet in a first-person shooter such as *Crysis* (Crytek 2007). In *The Witcher 3: The Wild Hunt* (CD Project Red 2015), we witness emphatic information when using "witcher's senses" to get a heightened perception of the surroundings, illustrated through a filter that marks clues in the environment as bright red. Ecological and emphatic information are both natural to the gameworld interface because they support the player's direct interaction with the game and have a direct relationship with actions and events that takes place inside the game. Often seen as part of the graphical user interface of the game, such features are integral parts of the gameworld to the degree that it makes little sense to separate them from it. For this reason the gameworld is not only an interface, but the interface is also part of the gameworld (Jørgensen 2013, 57–58, 143–144). In the following I will use gameworld and gameworld interface interchangeably, but they both refer to the gameworld environment that players engage with when playing games, and the idea that gameworlds are informational spaces and for this reason interfaces to the game system at the same time as they are fictional worlds.

6.2 Imagination and Make-Believe

Combining conventions from different media and interactive systems, gameworld interfaces appeal to different forms of engagement and cognitive processes. The two different information systems described above – ecological and emphatic information – invite the players to activate different imaginative processes. This subchapter will discuss make-believe with reference to imagination, and argue why imagination may be a better term when discerning between the different kinds of imaginative processes that are active when engaging gameworlds.

Make-believe presupposes an active cognitive process of creating belief, or to make something believable. As such it is often used as synonymous to pretence, fantasy and imagination. Crudely speaking, we can describe make-believe as a mental process in which one actively enters a mindset where one gives in to a non-factual situation and pretends to believe that it is real in the context of the particular situation. Make-believe can be understood as a cognitive process related to imagination, but it may also be understood as an aspect of play. As play, make-believe is often associated with children's play (Piaget 1962; Walton 1990, 4).

As a cognitive process, make-believe is more commonly discussed as *imagination* in the fields of psychology and the philosophy of mind. Imagination is a cognitive process that includes the formation of a mental representation of something (Gendler 2013). Imagination covers a range of related processes, spanning from "the ability to think of something not presently perceived" to "the ability to create works of art that express something deep about the meaning of life" (Stevenson 2003, 238). Imagination appears to have a more general application than make-believe in that it includes sophisticated processes of reasoning such as hypothesis-making and the considering of possible and counterfactual situations, as well as dreaming, fantasy and fictional engagement (Byrne 2005; Gendler 2013; Mithen 2007; Turner and Harviainen 2016).

Make-believe is an essential part of Caillois' understanding of play. In connection with the activity of play, make-believe opens up for a "special awareness of a second reality" (Caillois 1958, 10). For Caillois, play can be governed by rules or make-believe. This means that some games can be more heavily rule-bound, while other games are based in make-believe. Make-believe and rules are closely related in play; rules themselves may create fiction, and make-believe may substitute rules as a guiding principle in the activity of play.

Most importantly for this chapter is the idea that make-believe has a central role in connection with play activities, and that it works in conjunction with rules. Since gameworld interfaces combine conventions from game and fiction, they are governed by rules as well as make-believe. In connection with gameworld interfaces we may for this reason see rules and make-believe as two parts of a continuum, where one might be more heavily activated than the other at any given time during play. With reference to reversal theory, psychologist Michael Apter identifies two mindsets connected to play: the *telic* and *paratelic* state. The telic is a goal-oriented mindset in which the play activity is engaged in for a purpose. This mindset is activated when a play activity is heavily rule-bound. The paratelic, on the other hand, is at work when the activity is important in itself (Apter 1992, 56, 202n; Stenros 2015, 66, 167). We can recognize this mindset in play activities that are more heavily oriented towards make-believe. Central to the reversal theory is the idea that those engaging in such activities may experience an oscillation between the two mindsets (Apter 1992, 29–31).

Combining Caillois and Apters' theories with a broader understanding of imagination from cognitive theory, we may distinguish between two kinds of imaginative processes that are central for players engaging with gameworld interfaces. Make-believe or *fictional imagination* is connected to the paratelic state and allows players to interpret what happens in the gameworld as part of a fictional reality separate from the physical world and where particular laws apply. *Ludic imagination* is telic in nature and connected to the kind of hypothetical reasoning that allows us to imagine alternative possible outcomes or moves that can be undertaken in the problem solving process of gameplay. This mindset corresponds with what Bernard Suits calls the *lusory attitude* (Suits 2006, 188–190); the rule-oriented mindset focused on the game activity, stressing interaction with the game system and accepting the rules of the game even when they are not in coherence with the fictional world of the game. Simply described, players who are most interested in the narrative experience and the consistency of a fictional world stress their fictional imagination, while players who are mostly engaged in the game mechanisms and the manipulation of the system focus on ludic imagination.

The two mindsets are active when players engage with gameworld interfaces, and while some players may stress one rather than the other, they may experience an oscillation or rapid change between the two during the course of play. Also, they may experience that apparent contradictory information, such as emphatic symbols in an otherwise ecologically oriented gameworld representation, are not experienced as a paradox, but as a convention to gameworld interfaces. This will be explored more thoroughly below.

6.3 Props and Models in Gameworld Interfaces

How does the imaginative process work in the context of gameworld interfaces? According to Kendall Walton, *props* are important cues in the imaginative process. Props are "generators of fictional truths, things which, by virtue of their existence, make propositions fictional" (Walton 1990, 37), and anything that is being used in the imaginative process for the purpose of establishing and maintaining a fictional reality can be considered props. When something serves as a prop, it becomes a fictional representation in a game of make-believe. As world representations, gameworlds have the potential for employing, and for themselves being, props. Although Walton explicitly connects props to the activity of make-believe, props may support any kinds of imaginative process. Understood as a cue that guides our attention or supports our interpretative processes, they are helpful not only for fictional imagination, but also in processes of hypothetical reasoning and meaning-making associated with ludic imagination.

We find support in cognitive science for the idea that representations or objects may assist us, not only in the make-believe process, but also in other cognitive processes. Research in cognitive science has shown that we often use external models or artefacts are helpful for human cognition process of sense-making (Kirsh 2010; Scaife and Rogers 1996). The idea that representations and models may help us understand complex processes is fundamental both to the use of illustrations for explanatory or pedagogical purposes, and for the idea of training simulations and simulation-based learning. Scaife and Rogers argue that a particular way of representing an underlying structure will affect comprehension and problem solving. Models that visualize or put into motion how things work may reduce the cognitive effort required to understand what is being represented or solve a problem, and such models can also cue a particular interpretation of an abstract structure (1996, 188–189).

Using Walton's terminology, the model or representation becomes in these cases a prop that allows the player to envision how the system works and can be interacted with, and thus it works to support the imaginative process. As the gameworld itself models the underlying, abstract game system in terms of a more comprehensible world environment, the gameworld is a prop that cues the player's understanding of how the game system works. By exploring the gameworld and testing its interactive limits, the player uses the gameworld to envision possible scenarios and solve problems. Players stressing a ludic over a fictional mindset will approach the gameworld as a model that helps them understand how to interact with and master the game, and their imaginative process will stress problem solving rather than immersing themselves into a fictional reality.

When the player enters a gameworld that addresses them in a way that resembles the physical world, for instance through a recognizable topography and inhabitants that address them with tasks they can solve, he or she is given cues that strongly invite them to imagine this world as if it were real. Corresponding with the idea of a coherent fictional world, ecological information may seem particularly enticing as props, and as world representations, gameworlds have the potential for employing, and for themselves being, props. However, props can also be of a less world-like or more abstract nature. According to Jesper Juul, players are invited to imagine a fictional world in games through the combination of graphics, sound, haptics, rules and player actions (2005, 133–134). As augmentations of ecological features in the gameworld, emphatic information, such as blinking arrows above character heads, health and ammo bars, minimaps, and inventories, is also powerful because they highlight particular aspects of the gameworld, direct attention towards particular features, and may thus prescribe specific imaginings (Toon 2010) in the player. Although they may be unfamiliar to our physical environment, such informative features are natural to the gameworld interface because they support the player's direct interaction with the game and have a direct relationship with actions and events that takes place inside the game.

6.4   Players' Imaginative Engagement with Gameworlds

In this sub-chapter I will use interview data to show how actual players describe their imaginative involvement with in-game information when interacting with gameworlds. I will discuss how players interpret game information with point of departure in the imaginative process in which they are engaging.

Gameworlds and Fictional Imagination

Players who employ fictional imagination seek to frame the game experience as a fictional experience.

Common for these players is the idea that the gameworld is primarily a fictional world, and that the fictional world is the source system that all game information available in the gameworld refers to. For this reason they will interpret information from this perspective regardless of whether the information is presented as ecological or emphatic. How players with a fictional mindset choose to tackle game information varies between players as well as between genres.

While most players tend to accept the mixture of emphatic and ecological information as a convention to the video game medium as long as it provides meaningful information in a given gameplay context (Jørgensen 2012, 2013), some players find that the mixture between fiction and game system to be potentially disturbing for fictional imagination. When discussing the first-person shooter *Crysis* (Crytek 2007), a player states that "if a score appeared above the heads of the monsters when you shot them [. . .], immersion would disappear instantly" (Peter, focus group, Nov 2008). When playing *Crysis*, Peter finds emphatic information to be a sign of fictional incoherence (Juul 2005, 123) that hinders him from imagining a consistent fictional world, and which thus activates *imaginative resistance* (Gendler 2013). Of course, as a first-person shooter that focuses on ecological information while downplaying emphatic to the degree that it explains the HUD as being part of the avatar's helmet, *Crysis* is aiming for the audio-visual style of *immediacy*, where "the goal is to make the viewer forget the presence of the medium (. . .) and believe that he is in the presence of the objects of representation" (Bolter and Grusin 1999, 272–273).

The ideal of immediacy aims for photorealism and is based in the idea that the sense of involvement is enhanced when the game appears unmediated, and for some players this stylistic coherence is an important prop in the process of fictional imagination. For many players, abstract information or game system information inside the gameworld environment is imagined as referring to an event or object relating to the fictional reality in the game. For example, when employing fictional imagination, an exclamation mark above a character head in a role-playing game such as *Diablo 2* (Blizzard North 2000) is not system information, but representative of a fictional event. In Scott's words, the avatar "would perhaps see it as a person trying to make contact with her, not as an exclamation mark above the head" (Scott, interview, Dec 2008). For Scott, the emphatic information becomes a prop that inspires fictional imagination, and with reference to Toon (2010) we may also argue that its caricature style prescribes a particular interpretation: It draws attention to itself and stresses the importance of the character in question.

Gameworlds and Ludic Imagination

Players who stress ludic imagination may frame information completely different from those who focus on fictional imagination. Ludic imagination is activated when players frame information as representative of the game system, regardless of mode of presentation. For instance, when a player accepts that Mario has three lives by referring to the game rules (Juul 2005, 130) they are engaging in ludic imagination. For these players, the game system is the source system, and the fictional world is a metaphor that contextualizes and makes the abstract game rules more concrete and easier to understand. Thus, emphatic information is for them a direct representation of the game system, while ecological information is seen as a metaphor for the abstract game rules.

Games that leans on emphatic information and does not attempt to mask it as fictional follow the style of *hypermediacy*, which aims to "remind the viewer of the medium" and draw attention towards itself and the communicative process (Bolter and Grusin 1999, 272). Games using this approach focus on the formal aspects of the game and the fact that it is a system to be played. With reference to *Diablo 2*, one player argues that such games "never ask you to relate to [the game] as a realistic world. They only ask you to play it as a game" (Peter, focus group, Nov 2008). When encountering emphatic information such as overhead exclamation marks or floating, highlighted symbols in the gameworld, these players do not imagine a fictional explanation for these, but explain them as representative of certain game mechanics. According to one player, symbols such as health meters are "an abstraction, not of emotions, but of, well, avatar status" (Oliver, focus group, Nov 2008). Oliver's interpretation shows that he is attentive to the instrumental function of this information with respect to game state, and that emphatic information becomes props in his process of ludic imagination. While it is possible to argue that this explanation is caused by fictional incoherence, for these players it seems that considering the gameworld through ludic imagination is the most rational interpretation. However, this interpretation is not limited to situations of fictional incoherence. Another player discusses the light that surrounds the avatar in caves in *Diablo 2*: "Well, I don't think they light a torch and then they draw the sword. That light is part of the game mechanics, to give you better overview." (Tom, interview, Dec 2008). This shows that information that are more in tune with the fictional universe of the game can be used as a prop that fuels ludic imagination.

Gameworlds and the Importance of Mixed Imagination

Although gameworld interfaces invite players to stress either fictional or ludic imagination when they interact with gameworld interfaces, most players tend to accept a combination of emphatic and ecological information in gameworlds as long as it provides relevant information in the gameplay context (Jørgensen 2011). This is demonstrated by the remark made by one of the respondents when playing *Crysis*:

"Regardless of how cinematic a game is (. . .), since you're making the decisions yourself, give orders and move things, you need something that provides some kind of feedback on what is going on" (Eric, interview, Nov 2008). Even the most immediate gameworld using largely ecological signs needs a system that provides clear and relevant information in the right context to make the game playable.

Many of the respondents appear to accept the combination of emphatic and ecological information not as a necessary evil, but as a stylistic convention of modern video games. According to one respondent, "It's like cartoons, right? [. . .] We accept the speech bubbles because that's the way cartoons work" (Oliver, focus group, Nov 2008). Likewise in games, emphatic information "is something we have become accustomed to, partly because we need some aids in order to register what is happening" (Carl, interview, Nov 2008). The relativist position shows that players have no problems combining the two kinds of imagination when playing games. Although players may favour one of the imaginative processes when interacting with gameworld interfaces, they may experience an oscillation or rapid change between the two during the course of play. Players may also engage in both processes simultaneously and appreciate that games are at one and the same time fictional experiences as well as ludic. They may experience that apparent contradictory information, such as emphatic symbols in an otherwise ecologically oriented gameworld representation, are not experienced as a paradox, but as a convention to gameworld interfaces. However, it is important to stress that conventions from the game medium and also from specific game genres may take the role as props in the imaginative process as well. Whether a particular combination of props inspires fictional or ludic imagination, or a combination of the two, appears to be an individual endeavour.

6.5 Conclusions

Combining cognitive theory and play theory, this chapter has discussed the role of make-believe in the interaction with gameworlds. By arguing that props can spawn different kinds of imagination, the chapter presents an expansion of Walton's theory of make-believe that includes the engagement with gameworlds. Because gameworld interfaces are complex representative systems where the gameworld environment may be understood as a fictional reality, or as a metaphor for the underlying game system, players may engage with them as fiction or as game. The fact that gameworld interfaces draw on conventions from both fictional media as well as interactive systems, often in combination, players must employ different kinds of imaginative processes at the same time. Further, it is important to stress that although the use of ecological information is in correspondence with a coherent representation of a fictional world, and the use of emphatic information has an abstraction level that is in conflict with a coherent fictional world, we cannot conclude that ecological information sparks fictional imagination and emphatic information sparks ludic imagination. As we have seen both informational types can function as props in both processes.

But are the imaginative processes in question make-believe? The answer to this is yes and no.

Players leaning towards the fictional mindset may interpret the gameworld interface mainly as a fictional world. They may either choose to interpret all features in the game as representative of something fictional, or they may choose to ignore it. In this fictionalization lies a high degree of make-belief, understood not as pretence, but as acting or thinking as if they believed that the fictional world and its events were real. This also allows them to imagine the gameworld as a bigger fictional universe than is actually presented in the gameworld. The fictional element is an important part of modern video games, and also a major motivator for many players. However, make-believe is not the only kind of imaginative process that takes place when players engage with gameworld interfaces. Players leaning towards a ludic approach towards games stress the gameplay experience of interacting with the game mechanisms, the challenges and working towards the goal of the game. The imagination that they employ is related to rational thinking and allows us to consider alternative possibilities and scenarios. They choose to see the gameworld as instrumental in the problem solving process of gameplay, and are thus using the gameworld as an artefact that helps them reason. And this process is not what we normally understand as make-believe, since players are not acting or thinking as if they believe that their pursuit towards the game goal matters. Instead their actions do matter, and their imaginative process is for this reason more closely associated with problem solving and rational thinking. The player may not have killed a dragon, which would be an act of make-believe; but they may in fact have defeated the main boss and received an in-game reward for that. While this is the categorical answer, the details about the relationship between these activities and how the combination of imaginative processes affects our interpretation of what fiction is in the context of games, and what games are in the context of fiction, may be clearer with more research on the matter.

This chapter shows the strengths of using cognitive theory in combination with play theory in exploring how players engage with imaginative processes when making sense of games. Also, the chapter has demonstrated how individual interpretations and preferences influence the imaginative process. Not least, the chapter stresses that the idea of gameworlds as a particular kind of world construct with its own rules and characteristics is a fruitful base for a game-specific understanding of the imaginative process.

References

Apter MJ (1992) The dangerous edge. The psychology of excitement. The Free Press, New York
Bartle R (2004) Designing virtual worlds. New Riders, Indianapolis
Beaudouin-Lafon M (2000) Instrumental interaction: an interaction model for designing post-WIMP user interfaces. In: CHI'00: Proceedings of the SIGCHI conference on human factors in computing systems. ACM, New York, pp 446–453
Bethesda Game Studios (2011) The elder scrolls 5: skryim. Bethesda Softworks [Xbox 360]

Blizzard North (2000) Diablo 2. Blizzard entertainment [PC]

Bolter JD, Grusin R (1999) Remediation: understanding new media. MIT Press, Cambridge

Byrne RMJ (2005) The rational imagination: how people create alternatives to reality. MIT Press, Cambridge, MA

Caillois R (1958) Man, play and games. University of Illinois Press, Champaign

CD Project RED (2015) The witcher 3: the wild hunt. Namco Bandai Entertainment [Xbox One]

Crytek (2007) Crysis. EA games [PC]

Gendler T (2013) Imagination. In: Zalta EN, Nodelman U, Allen C, Perry J (eds) Stanford encyclopedia of philosophy. Stanford University Press, Stanford

Jørgensen K (2011) The user interface continuum: a study of player preference. In: Gamasutra, April 12. Available via Gamasutra.com. http://www.gamasutra.com/view/feature/134715/the_user_interface_continuum_a_php. Accessed 1 Mar 2016

Jørgensen K (2012) Between the game system and the fictional world. A study of computer game interfaces. Game Cult 7(2):142–163

Jørgensen K (2013) Gameworld interfaces. MIT Press, Cambridge

Juul J (2005) Half-real. Videogames between real rules and fictional worlds. MIT Press, Cambridge, MA

Kirsh D (2010) Thinking with external representation. AI Soc 25:441–454

Klevjer R (2007) What is the Avatar? Fiction and embodiment in avatar-based, single-player games. PhD dissertation, University of Bergen

Lauesen S (2005) User interface design. A software engineering perspective. Addison-Wesley, Harlow

Mithen S (2007) Seven steps in the evolution of human imagination. In: Roth I (ed) Imaginative minds. Oxford University Press for The British Academy, Oxford, pp 3–29

Piaget J (1962) Play, dreams and imitation in childhood. Norton, New York

Rollings A, Adams E (2003) Andrew rollings and Ernest Adams on game design. New Riders, Indianapolis

Ryan M-L (2001) Narrative as virtual reality: immersion and interactivity in literature and electronic media. Johns Hopkins University Press, Baltimore

Ryan M-L (2008) Fictional worlds in a digital age. In: Schreibman S, Siemens R (eds) A companion to digital literary studies. Blackwell, Cambridge, pp 250–266

Scaife M, Rogers Y (1996) External cognition: how do graphical representations work? Int J Hum-Comp Stud 45:185–213

Sicart M (2008) Defining game mechanics. Game Stud 8:2

Stenros J (2015) Play, playfulness and games. A constructionist ludology approach. PhD dissertation, University of Tampere

Stevenson L (2003) Twelve conceptions of imagination. Br J Aesthet 43(3):238–259

Suits B (2006) The grasshopper: games, life and utopia. Broadview Press, Peterborough

Toon A (2010) Models as make-believe. In: Frigg R, Hunter M (eds) Beyond mimesis and convention, Boston studies in the philosophy of science. Springer, Dordrecht, pp 71–96

Turner P, Harviainen JT (2016) Introduction. In: Turner P, Harviainen JT (eds) Digital make-believe. Springer, Cham

Walton K (1990) Mimesis as make-believe. On the foundations of the representational arts. Harvard University Press, Cambridge, MA

Chapter 7
Make-Believe in Gameful and Playful Design

Sebastian Deterding

7.1 Introduction

On an unassuming summer day in 2012, The Hague became witness to a monster. The "Man-Eater", as the press would later call it, was first spotted around noon by a passenger on tram number 6, between Stuyvesantplein and Centraal Station. Roughly the size of a bulldog, with fins and telescope eyes, it floated through the air like a deep water dweller above the ocean ground, biting off the head of any pedestrian it passed, swallowing them whole in one swift, clean gulp, *shlupp*: just like that.

The Man-Eater is, of course, a creature of make-believe, summoned into The Hague as a thesis project by designer Daniel Disselkoen (2015). It was little more than two stickers: One thumb-sized, in the shape of a deep sea fish, attached on eye level to the inside of a tram window, and a second, larger sticker with a set of rules pasted on the back of the seat in front. The rules instructed the passenger to look through the window with one eye closed, such that the sticker would appear as a big fish floating in the panorama beyond. Moving her head up or down, the passenger could make the fish appear to float up or down in turn. The goal: between two tram stops, eat as many pedestrians as possible by visually capturing their heads in the Man-Eater's mouth (Fig. 7.1).

Disselkoen's Man-Eater is a great little example of a recent wave in interaction design (IxD) and human-computer interaction (HCI) that has been variously called gamification, gameful design, or playful design. Although each term captures slightly different phenomena, the underlying idea is the same: Play is the paragon of enjoyable, intrinsically motivated activity, associated with a wide range of

S. Deterding (✉)
Digital Creativity Hub, University of York, York, UK
e-mail: Sebastian@codingconduct.cc

© Springer International Publishing Switzerland 2016
P. Turner, J.T. Harviainen (eds.), *Digital Make-Believe*,
Human–Computer Interaction Series, DOI 10.1007/978-3-319-29553-4_7

Fig. 7.1 Daniel Disselkoen's man-eater

positive effects on experience, motivation, social interaction, learning, and well-being. Games and toys are artefacts purpose-built to afford play and its positive effects. Hence, game and toy design might hold design elements and guidelines for affording enjoyment, motivation, and the like that can be applied to other activities and systems (Deterding 2015a).

In our example, Man-Eater added rules and a goal to a daily tram commute to turn it into an eye-street coordination challenge – a *game* (Juul 2005). And not just that: It combined the game with a little fiction of head-chomping urban fish, anchored in words ("Man-Eater") and a fish-shaped sticker. It produced *make-believe*, a fundamental form and aspect of human play and its appeal (Burghardt 2005; Lillard 2014; Pellegrini 2009). Man-Eater materializes for us adults to see what children naturally discover on the backseat of a car ride: that something quotidian like a rain drop running down a car window can be made engaging by wrapping its fate in a bit of pretence. And we do not have to go back into childhood to see the engaging power of pretence: any look into a movie theatre or library will find ample adult faces entranced in a piece of make-believe.

Now in some sense, games and make-believe are separable: To turn the tram ride into a game, it would have sufficed to state the rules and paint an abstract targeting reticule on the window. Likewise, the two stickers could have merely prompted passengers to imagine the Man-Eater, without any rules. And yet make-believe and games also share something fundamental. Both are instances of "counting-x-as-y", of layering alternative meanings and functions on top of existing ones. In make-believe, a stick can suddenly count as a "magic wand"; by virtue of the shared agreement between players, its holder can command others to "drop dead". Games formalize this loose shared agreement into explicit rules and numbers: this stretch of the lawn now counts as "out", and crossing it with this leather ball in your hand counts as one "strike", and whoever scores the most "strikes" in so-and-so many minutes is the "winner."

We can already see that play, games, and make-believe are entangled in many interesting ways, both in and beyond gameful and playful design. This chapter hopes to disentangle them at least somewhat, with two provisos. First, it focuses on make-believe as part of the user experience. Many interaction design practices involve make-believe in a playful or gameful manner, such as "gamestorming" (Gray et al. 2010) or service theatre. These are covered elsewhere in this volume (see Turner, this volume; Luojus and Harviainen this volume). Second, given the largely non-existing existing research on make-believe in gameful and playful design, the present chapter is quite theoretical, chiefly drawing on neighbouring fields to suggest future research trajectories. To this end, it first introduces the concepts of games and play, gameful and playful design, and make-believe. A survey of existing design literature and empirical research finds that make-believe has been largely neglected in gamification and gameful design, and is conceptually and empirically best situated in playful design (Sect. 7.2). The majority of the chapter breaks out five major design aspects of make-believe: theming; storification; scripting, ruling, and framing; role-playing; and their integration in unified experiences. Each aspect is presented with potentially positive psychological and behavioural effects and explanatory theories; main design elements and strategies used to evoke these effects; empirical studies, if existing; and illustrative examples (Sect. 7.3). The chapter closes in summarizing the potential positive effects as well as drawbacks of make-believe; how and why playful make-believe designs differ from current gamification in form (often artistic one-offs) and technology (often audio); and what limitations future research should try to overcome (Sect. 7.4).

7.2 Concepts

Gameful and Playful Design

Designs like the Man-Eater are but the most recent outgrowth of a long history of applying games and play to 'serious' purposes, reaching back at least to Plato's Republic (Krentz 1998) and Chinese military leaders using Go to train in the art of war during the sixth century BCE (Halter 2006). Important waymarks are the emergence of the simulation and gaming movement starting in the 1960s, the rise of edutainment software in the 1990s, and of digital serious games in the 2000s (see Deterding 2015b for a fuller history). In HCI, Malone (1982), Carroll (1982), and Carroll and Thomas (1988) early on suggested to derive heuristics and models for "fun of use" from games, followed in the 2000s by researchers interested in the "funology" (Blythe et al. 2004) of "pleasurable products" (Jordan 2002). Designing for playfulness became a particular focus of this work (Korhonen et al. 2009; Fernaeus et al. 2012). But it was arguably start-ups, think tanks, and digital agencies that in the 2010s brought large-scale attention and investment to applied games and play. Under the catchword "gamification," they promised massive gains in customer and employee engagement through the use of game design (Deterding 2015b). Today, serious games, playful design, and gamification are growing and intertwined industries and research fields.

Naturally, several terms and definitions have been suggested to capture these phenomena. As for "games" and "play", despite or because of decades of research across disciplines, scholars mostly agree on what they disagree about (see Sutton-Smith 1997; Henricks 2015, for play, and Stenros forthcoming, for games). "Play" is generally seen to refer to a kind of *activity* and/or psychological-behavioural *mode of engagement* with the world, whereas "games" typically refer to *objects* or *systems* designed for that activity (see Stenros forthcoming for exceptions). For *animal and childhood play*, ethology and developmental psychology provide convergent empirical descriptions of play features (Burghardt 2005; Pellegrini 2009): play is intrinsically motivated, autotelic; it transforms and recombines other, functional behaviours – exaggerating, varying, repeating, representing them, rendering them incomplete so they lack their 'serious' consequence and thus, their obvious immediate instrumental or survival value; finally, play tends to occur when no other immediate inner or outer pressures are felt. In game studies, Salen and Zimmerman (2004) and Juul (2005) have provided influential recent syntheses of *game* definitions. Juul's oft-cited "classic game model" defines a game as "a rule-based system with a variable and quantifiable outcome, where different outcomes are assigned different values, the player exerts effort in order to influence the outcome, the player feels emotionally attached to the outcome, and the consequences of the activity are negotiable" (Juul 2005, p. 36).

Moving on to applied games and play, definitions are likewise still contested, particularly with regard to *gamification* (see Seaborn and Fels 2015 for a review). There is consensus that gamification refers to a design process, activity, or strategy, not its end result. Beyond that, some definitions have framed gamification through particular means (game design elements like points, badges, leaderboards, cf. Deterding et al. 2011), others through particular ends (gameful experiences like competence, competition, etc., Huotari and Hamari 2012). Some include serious games (Zichermann and Cunningham 2011), others exclude them (Deterding et al. 2011; Huotari and Hamari 2012). Some delimit gamification to non-game contexts, on the grounds that 'adding game elements to a game' is tautological (Deterding et al. 2011); others don't, holding that a game can be made 'gamier' (Huotari and Hamari 2012); yet others view priming users to re-frame a non-game as a game to be a sub-form of gamification (Lieberoth 2015). This chapter adopts the matrix suggested by Deterding and colleagues (2011) and Deterding (2015a), for two reasons. First, it is well-established and widely adopted (cf. Seaborn and Fels 2015). Second, it explicitly maps the full space of applied games and play, which is particularly relevant for make-believe (Fig. 7.2).

Their matrix uses two (plus one) dimensions with two poles each. The first is taken from Caillois (2001), who noted that all human play exists on a spectrum between unruly, free, exploratory play or *paidia* (found prototypically in children's pretend and rough-and-tumble play), and the orderly, rule-based striving for

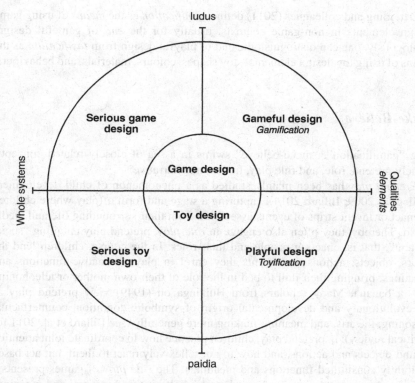

Fig. 7.2 A conceptual map of applied games and play practices

challenging goals or *ludus*, as found in classic gaming and competitive sports.[1]
Second, Deterding and colleagues distinguish between *wholes* and *qualities* as the
object of design. Combining these dimensions, they arrive at the following four
quadrants:

- Serious game design or creating "ludic wholes": designing and/or deploying full-
  fledged games for 'serious' purposes;
- Serious toy design or creating "paidic wholes": designing and/or deploying full-
  fledged toys for 'serious' purposes;
- Gameful design or affording "ludic qualities": designing to afford the experiential
  and behavioral qualities characteristic for gaming;
- Playful design or affording "paidic qualities": designing to afford the experiential
  and behavioral qualities characteristic for playing.

---

[1] *Ludus* and *paidia* do not map onto games vs. play understood as objects vs. activities/modes.
Rather, they characterize particular *styles* of play activity/engagement, which are afforded more
or less well by particular *genres* of games (see Barr 2007, also for empirical evidence regarding
Caillois' conceptual distinction). They *do* roughly map on the psychological distinction of pretend
and role vs. rule play (Pellegrini 2009). This is reflected in the following by talking of *playing* (=
paidic play) and *gaming* (= ludic play).

Deterding and colleagues (2011) define *gamification* as the *means* of using game design elements in non-game contexts, usually for the *end* of gameful design. Analogously, one can distinguish the end of playful design from *toyification* as the means of using toy design elements – toy shapes, colours, materials, and behaviours.

Make-Believe

Like "gamification", "make-believe" swims in a sea of closely related concepts, namely pretend, role, and rule play, fiction, and narrative.

Pretend play has been mainly studied as a phenomenon of child development (Pellegrini 2009; Lillard 2014), capturing a stage and form of play where children re-enact or invent strips of events assembled from their surrounding life and media world. Thereby, they often also engage in *role-play*, pretend play entailing "social content", that is, enacting people and their roles. In the course, children lend the actors, objects, actions and events they enrol in play alternative functions and meanings: bringing their doll to bed in the role of their own mother or telephoning with a banana. Many scholars from Huizinga on (1949) view pretend play as the evolutionary and developmental origin of symbolic cognition, counterfactual reasoning, the arts, and meaning-making more generally (see Lillard et al. 2011 for a critical review): in pretend play, children practice how to coordinate joint attention around objects and actions, and how to not reflexively react to them, but act based on jointly constituted functions and meanings. The *rule play* of games presents a later development of pretend play, where said alternative functions and meanings are formalized in the shape more or less explicit, not spontaneously renegotiable rules (Pellegrini 2009; Lillard 2014).

As such, pretend, role, and rule play *double* the foundational process in which members of a society jointly constitute the functions and meanings of their social world: this piece of paper counts as "20 Euros", these two people now count as "man and wife", stepping onto this street before that light has switched to green counts as "jaywalking" (Berger and Luckmann 1967; Warfield Rawls 2009; Searle 1995). Our everyday world is filled with entities that may have been made little more durable with the help of material objects (traffic lights and wedding rings and specially printed paper), but would ultimately not exist without us continually acting *as if* (or more precisely, *such that*) they exist. What sets pretend and rule play apart from canonical social functions and meanings is that the former are voluntary, temporary, and "as if": enacted to hold no lasting reality beyond the play episode.

Which brings us to *fiction*, mainly the subject of literary theory and philosophy. Prototypically encountered in literature and other fictional media, fiction is commonly seen as a genre of discourse (Searle 1975) characterized by its "as if" truth or reality status (Zipfel 2001). Authors have variously distinguished *fictionality* (Cohn 1990) – the syntactical, formal properties that allow us to tell apart a fiction film from a documentary; *fictiveness*, the semiotic, logical, or ontological status of propositions expressed in a work of fiction; and fiction as a pragmatic *institutional practice*: the running agreement between fiction producers and receivers to co-intentionally treat them "as if" (Lamarque and Olsen 1994). Works of fiction involve a *fictional world* – e.g., J.R.R. Tolkien's *Lord of the Rings* renders the fictional world of Middle Earth, just like pretend play may generate a pretence world of pirates (Zipfel 2001; Ryan 2014).

Although fiction has often been equated with *narrative*, they are analytically separable (Ryan 2008). Put plainly, narrative is about telling a story. It relates to a certain semantic type of statement (a temporal sequence of events); a formal quality of communications (being organized and presented in a way we would recognize as 'typical' for stories: re-tellable, eventful, sequential, etc.); and a certain pragmatic communicative situation, consisting of a narrator relating the narrative to a narratee (Abbott 2014). To be sure, all narratives convey a story world (Ryan 2014), and this story world is very often fictional (see Middle-Earth). Vice versa, the overwhelming majority of works of fiction is narrative. But as narrative journalism and maps of fictional countries demonstrate, there is non-fiction narrative and non-narrative fiction.

To summarize, pretend play, role-play, rule play, and fiction strongly overlap in the constitution of alternative, "as if" functions and meanings. They often involve narrative: pretend and role play re-enact or invent narrative sequences of events, rule play generates sequences of events that are often retold as a story afterwards, and fictional media usually take a narrative form. And this overlap has led multiple scholars to reason that all four phenomena share an evolutionary and developmental origin in play.

Prominently – turning to *make-believe* – Kendall Walton suggested in *Mimesis as Make-Believe* (1990) that literature, movies, theatre plays, and paintings "are best seen as continuous with children's games of make-believe." (p. 11) Make-believe emerges from the interaction of "props" – toys, pictures, written or spoken words that prompt, anchor, focus and coordinate individual and shared imagination (ibid., pp. 19–21) – , and "principles of generation": "rules about what is to be imagined in what circumstances", based on a given prop in a given game of make-believe (ibid., p. 40). These principles are part of a larger shared "convention, understanding, agreement in the game of make-believe" (ibid., p. 38) to treat those generated imaginations "as if". In contemporary humanities, make-believe is chiefly understood with Walton as this *constitution of fictional, "as if" functions and meanings found both in play and representational art* (Bareis 2014). Because of its wide adoption, including the conceptualization of make-believe in games (Bateman 2011), we here subscribe to the Waltonian definition of make-believe.

The main point of remaining scientific contention is *how* the constitution of make-believe works. The traditional family of views holds that make-believe involves some mental (meta-)representations: things symbolically "stand in for" other, non-existing things, prompting mental images or propositions of those non-things, be it through simple association or some rule-based calculus (Rucinska 2014; this volume). An alternative, emerging family of socio-material, ecological, or enactive accounts views make-believe as a practical accomplishment emerging from the embodied dispositions of actors and affordances of involved objects (ibid.).

Here, functions and meanings are not cued or rule-generated mental representations with propositional content, but learning-shaped organizations of one's perception and action systems how to perceive and engage with certain objects in certain contexts that bottom out in the responses of the material environment and the running agreement of the co-present social group.

Positioning Make-Believe

Following Caillois, make-believe (or "mimicry", as he calls it [2001, p. 19]) is squarely a matter of *paidia*: games are "ruled *or* make-believe" (ibid., p. 9, emphasis in original), and make-believe lacks "the continuous submission to imperative and precise rules" (ibid., p. 22) that characterizes ludic gaming. Developmental psychology, as we have seen, likewise distinguishes pretend and role-play from rule play. In our matrix of applied games and play, this would put make-believe in the paidic half.

Game research since Caillois has unfortunately been more concerned with the relation of games to narrative than make-believe, particularly in the so-called "ludology/narratology" debate, which often conflated narrative and fiction (Frasca 2003). To establish games as a subject matter in its own right, early game studies engaged in what Bateman (2015) labelled "fiction denial": It drew a sharp conceptual distinction between "rules" and "fiction," holding that only rules are essential to games, conceding that digital games often comprise (analytically distinct) rules *and* narrative/fiction in one piece of "half-real" or "ludo-narrative" software (Juul 2005; Aarseth 2012).

From a Waltonian make-believe standpoint, this view is incorrect in that *both* rules and fiction are forms of make-believe (Deterding 2009; Bateman 2011, 2015). It is correct in that games and player communities can differently facilitate and emphasize *ludic*, rules-and-goals-focused gaming, or *paidic*, pretense-and-roles-focused playing (Barr 2007; Linderoth 2012). For instance, the genre of role-playing games particularly formalizes and facilitates pretend and role-play (Deterding and Zagal forthcoming).

A look into gamification and gameful design lends further support to Caillois' view, suggesting if not a fiction denial, then a fiction neglect: In most gamification design literature, make-believe is simply absent (e.g. Zichermann and Cunningham 2011; Kim 2011; Paharia 2013; Deterding 2015a). If it appears at all, then as a single bullet point or paragraph listing *avatars* or *story*. For instance, Werbach and Hunter (2012, pp. 78, 80) name "narrative (a consistent, on-going storyline)" and "avatars (visual representations of a player's character)" as game dynamics and mechanics, to then never return to them. Reeves and Read (2009, pp. 64–66, 68–71) enumerate "self-representation with avatars" and "narrative context" as two of the "ten ingredients of great games". In contrast, both books spend whole chapters on ludic design elements like points, badges, and leaderboards. And neither avatars nor narratives are necessarily make-believe.

Gamification research shows a similar picture. A systematic review by Hamari et al. (2014) identified 24 empirical papers on gamification, only 6 of which involved "story/theme" (versus 10 with leaderboards, and nine each with points and badges). In another review, Seaborn and Fels (2015) found 31 studies, of which only 3 featured avatars, 1 featured roles, and 1 a story (compared to 18 with points, 17 with badges/achievements, and 11 with leaderboards). Seaborn and Fels furthermore identified seven theories currently in use in gamification research – none of which explicitly speak to the effects of make-believe.

While both practice and research are in their infancy, this comparatively curt, superficial, and conflating treatment is indicative of the inferior role of make-believe – and paidic play more generally – in gamification and gameful design. Among current rhetorics and connected forms of applied games and play, only one explicitly focuses make-believe: the rhetoric of performance (Deterding 2015b). Notably, its proponents typically *distance* themselves from gamification or gameful design, preferring play forms and terms like alternate reality games, play in public, or live-action role-play (ibid., pp. 42–43). Proponents of this rhetoric commonly approach games and play as the collective performance of temporary reframings of everyday life. They value the paidic opening such performance produces for exploring and creating new, alternative behaviours, meanings, and experiences. As such, they connect to older rhetorics of play as identity – a strong shared experience that bonds a community – and play as imaginary: a realm of creative imagination (Sutton-Smith 1997). Given how their work foregrounds open exploration and backgrounds goals and rules, it is most easily classified as playful design.

7.3 Forms and Effects

Gameful and playful design, we noted, attempt to afford gaming- and playing-characteristic experiences and behaviours with non-game/play activities and systems, typically for an ulterior goal like enjoyment, motivation, or learning. To this end, they often employ design elements from games and toys. This raises the question what desirable effects make-believe has on user experience and behaviour, and what the 'active ingredients' of games and toys are that bring these effects about. Put more formally, what are the *affordances* of games and toys regarding make-believe: the functional compounds of design features and user dispositions that give rise to particular desirable experiences and behaviours (Deterding 2011)?

As noted, although foundational to pretend, role-, and rule play, make-believe has been chiefly employed as part of playful design interventions (and serious role-playing games, see below, Sect. 7.3.4). Even here, practitioners and researchers have been more focused on the design and effects of systems and make-believe as a whole than teasing out individual affordances. As suggestions for future research, we here highlight four design aspects: theming; storification; scripting, ruling, and framing; and role-playing.

Theming

In games and other design spheres, *theme* commonly refers to a particular semiotic domain (Gee 2003) or frame (Fillmore and Baker 2009) that a design evokes or "is about": a recognizable chunk of real or fictive life world like "pirates", "high fantasy", "Wall Street banking", "Japan", "hospital", or the like. *Theming* describes how a given design is "dressed up" in a domain (in contrast to *simulation*, where the system is intended to model a domain).

Maybe the most prominent design domain of theming is not games, but themed spaces (Grove and Fisk 1992; Gottdiener 2001; Ritzer 2009; Lukas 2013). As part of the larger shift towards an experience economy (Pine and Gilmore 2011), corporations are increasingly trying to transform interactions with customers into memorable and entertaining experiences – either as their chief product, or as a marketing tool to differentiate themselves from competitors and put customers into a positive, consumption-fostering mood. Examples are theme parks like Disneyland, theme restaurants like the Jekyll & Hyde Club in New York City, theme shops like the Time Travel Mart in L.A., and theme events like a party set in a 1940s WWII bunker by the Parisian event group WATO. There are even examples in the workplace, like start-ups trying to create a more playful office environment by designing meeting rooms as a James Bond villain's secret underground lair (Mäyrä et al. 2013).

The main tools for theming are art direction and language (Lukas 2013): Spaces, objects, actors, events and actions are audio-visually (and sometimes also in smell and interaction) designed and verbally labelled to evoke elements from the target domain: In a hypothetical hospital-themed restaurant, waiters might wear white overcoats and stethoscopes and call themselves "nurses", the drink menu may be labelled "medicine", the walls may be painted in hospital white and light green, etc.

Several desirable effects can be identified for theming: First, the novelty of a themed system or space can evoke curiosity in users, driving exploration to discover what else the designers might have themed how, as well as pleasurable surprise at unexpected theming (Silvia 2006). Paradoxically, theming is also seen to relax users through familiarity: themed spaces usually only evoke the most universally well-known semiotic domains and use the most stereotyped, clichéd signifiers (the doctor's stethoscope) to both make the theming easily legible and create a safe, calming space (Gottdiener 2001). In the case of franchises or fictional worlds with significant lore and fan communities, recognizing allusions and 'insider jokes' that are non-obvious for casual consumers may also generate positive experiences of cultural competence and belonging (Jenkins 2006).

A further positive effect often highlighted is facilitating understanding and learning through (metaphorical) external representations (Imaz and Benyon 2007). Providing novice users with concrete representations from a well-familiar source domain for a novel or abstract target domain allows them to use existing knowledge to infer and learn about the target. A well-known example in interface design is the desktop metaphor (ibid.).

In HCI, Malone (1982) first observed that wrapping interaction in a "fantasy" is one characteristic that makes video games more interesting and motivating. Carroll and Thomas (1982) similarly suggested that boring computer jobs like monitoring factory parameters on a screen could be made more motivating by representing them as e.g., landing an airplane in rough weather. Particularly with regard to learning, Malone (1982) distinguished "intrinsic" fantasies, where the theme maps onto and supports the skill to be learned, from "extrinsic" ones, where the theme is an arbitrary, exchangeable add-on. This distinction has since been articulated and tested as *intrinsic integration* (Habgood and Ainsworth 2011): Evidence supports that a learning game where the skill to be learned is both the central game challenge and fitting the fictional domain representing the challenge is more conducive to engagement and learning than a not-fitting one (e.g., calculating angles is intrinsically integrated with a game where the challenge and fiction is to load, aim, and shoot a catapult to destroy an enemy's castle, whereas translating words to fire the catapult would not be). The explanation is that intrinsically integrated fictions provide metaphorical mappings (see above), and that clashing fiction and game mechanics disrupt enjoyable immersion in the task – a phenomenon also called "ludonarrative dissonance" (Hocking 2007).

In playful and gameful design, few if any research has focused on theming. Birk and colleagues (2015) studied the effect of theming on four standard psychological tasks. For instance, a go/no-go task where users are to respond on one stimuli (circles) but not another (squares) was redressed as shooting zombies, not civilians. Birk and colleagues found that theming actually *decreased* performance and user experience, presumably because it added complexity and cognitive load and set up expectations of enjoyable gameplay that were not met by the underlying basic experimental tasks. Mollick and Rothbard (2014) found that having choice in the theming of a workplace game (in their case, between a fantasy and farming theme) positively affected user consent to the game, which moderated its affective and performance effects.

In design practice, one can highlight two examples. One is the ubiquitous commercial practice of theming websites and smartphone applications. For instance, during special events like Halloween or Christmas, interface elements are being redrawn with snow or pumpkins on them. At the high end of this practice are websites and applications around a fictional entertainment product, such as promotional websites for movies and film. Here, akin to attempts in game user interface design to create immersive interfaces (Fagerholt and Lorentzon 2009), interface elements are often designed to appear as if they are (a) taken out of the fictional world (e.g., a button in a website about the Stone Age looks like a rough-hewn stone) and/or (b) actually exist within the fictional world. For instance, in the (now-retired) first version of the website Pottermore.com, focused on the fictional world of J.K. Rowling's Harry Potter novels, users could read books, which were represented as actual books in an actual book library in the fictional world.

The second practice has been called "Barely Games" (Davies 2009): often artistic augmented reality works that layer themed elements of a fictional world into the everyday. Davies (2009) for instance created the *Situated Audio Platform*.

This smartphone "browser for geo-tagged audio files" produces movement- and place-appropriate sounds from an alternate fictional world (such as movement and door sounds from the video game *Half Life 2*) as the user walks through a city, and triggers additional audio files when the user moves into the connected GPS coordinates.

Storification

If theming manifests make-believe entities in space here and now, *storification* extends their existence in a meaningful form across time (Akkerman et al. 2009). It means creating and communicating a narrative that explains the past of the make-believe entities and/or guides their (inter)action from the first point of user contact on. While theming and storification are analytically separable, in practice, like make-believe and narrative, they tend to entail each other. "Fitting" stories complete, enrich, and reinforce the fictional world conveyed by theming. In turn, while the main way of communicating narrative is through written or spoken text, video, and enactment, themed environments often partake in the process through "environmental storytelling", particularly "embedded narrative" (Jenkins 2004): the environment entails clues that the user can puzzle together to deduce their origin story.

The desirable effects of storification have been studied and explored more extensively than theming, particularly in game-based learning. Since narrative is a fundamental structure in which humans make sense of and memorize the world (Bruner 1990), presenting a subject matter in story form facilitates comprehension and learning (Dickey 2011; Murmann and Avraamidou 2014a). A well-composed dramatic story arc sparks suspense and curiosity, motivating sustained engagement (Dickey 2006). Third, stories lend emotional significance to actors and events: we sympathize with the underdog we know has been treated unfairly in the past (Carpenter and Green 2012). By connecting to values and (fictional) persons we care about, stories can similarly increase the perceived relevance of goals and tasks a system suggests to the user. Fourth, good stories can engender "transportation": the audience becomes attentively, cognitively, and emotionally absorbed in the events of the story, disregarding the outside world and the unreality of the narrated events. Transported individuals are more susceptible to persuasion: they are more likely to adopt the beliefs and attitudes proposed in the narrative (ibid.). There is evidence across a number of learning interventions that well-designed narrative drives motivation, enjoyment, and learning through these routes (e.g. Paulus et al. 2006; Dickey 2011; Carpenter and Green 2012; Murmann and Avraamidou 2014b).

Several authors have suggested that adding (fictional) stories to a design is an important dimension of gameful or playful design to drive engagement (Dickey 2006; Reeves and Read 2009; Langer et al. 2013; Sakamoto and Nakajima 2014). One relatively common genre are tourism-focused mixed reality applications like *REXplorer* (Ballagas et al. 2008) or *Voices of Oakland* (Dow et al. 2005). These typically consist of smartphone applications or dedicated devices that deliver audio files telling the story of historical sights in a city the user stands in front of, bound together by a larger, overarching, and usually fictional narrative, such as the ghost of a recently deceased guiding tourists through a cemetery and its stories.

Unfortunately, there are again relatively few effect studies on storification per se. Flatla et al. (2011) gamified several software calibration tasks, including a targeting task with a bare-bones fictional backstory about the universe being attacked by evil aliens; they found that gamification increased reported enjoyment. Halan et al. (2010) found that adding backstory, leaderboards, and deadlines to an application prompting medical students to interact with a virtual patient to train the underlying conversation model increased the participation rate. Downes-Le Guin et al. (2012) created a gamified version of an online questionnaire including a fictional fantasy theme and backstory, finding no significant effects. Chen et al. (2012) achieved increased user enjoyment and goal pursuit by wrapping math learning in a Tamagotchi-like pet nurturing game. Individual learning tasks were delivered as quests presented by fictional characters from the game world, complete with a narrative backstory motivating the task. Recently, Prestopnik and Tang (2015) compared player experience in two citizen science platforms that motivate players to solve scientific tasks, one with a fictional theme and story, the other with progress feedback (points, scores), and found that players significantly preferred the story-based platform. But really, research on the effects of storification in isolation is severely lacking.

Scripting, Ruling, and Framing

Both theming and storification are potentially passive forms of adding make-believe: they only require that the user expose herself to the themed space or narrative. In contrast, *scripting* and *ruling* turn the user into an active co-creator: rule or instruction sets guide the user to perform certain actions that result in generating a make-believe layer for herself (and potentially, initiated observers). These serve as and go hand in hand with social signals or meta-communications that *frame* the activity as e.g. play – frame here being understood with Goffman (1986) as a socially shared type of situation with particular norms, understandings, and socio-material organizations. Following Goffman (ibid, pp. 40–82), make-believe is not a frame, but a set of secondary frames ("keyings") that include daydreaming, theatre, movies, playing, and gaming. This set shares an ethos of voluntary, autotelic engagement and attentive absorption; the understanding of the situation being "as if"; muted social and physical consequence; and as a result of that, a practical and social license to temporarily engage in behaviours that in their non-keyed form would be physically dangerous and/or socially deviant (Deterding 2014).

Consequently, one positive effect of scripting, ruling, and framing highlighted in the literature is the exploration of new, alternative behaviours and experiences. Framing an activity as e.g., pretend play temporarily loosens whatever social norms prevail for the pre-existing situation, and replaces them with the norm to "play along," opening users up for new, potentially transformative experiences (Flanagan 2009; Stenros 2015).

Second, a rich strain in the sociology of labour has studied how factory workers spontaneously reframe work as a game, leading to increased perceived self-determination and positive affect (see Mollick and Rothbard 2014, for a review). Csikszentmihalyi (1975) likewise observed that workers approaching work as play were more likely to have optimal or flow experiences at work. Several studies have found that verbally or visually framing an activity as "game", "play", or "fun" (vs. "work" or "obligation") positively affects motivation and performance, moderated by personality factors like self-control, gender, and age (Webster and Martocchio 1993; Littleton et al. 1999; Laran and Janiszewski 2011; Lieberoth 2015). Two main theoretical explanations are proposed: stereotype threat – performance anxiety based on the negative stereotype that they are "bad" at games lowers the actual performance of e.g., women or older people (Inzlicht 2011); and autonomy support: framing an activity as (conventionally autonomous, voluntary) play cues participants to construe the activity as autonomous, which constitutes part of intrinsic motivation (Deci and Ryan 2012).

Direct precursors of this practice are Situationist and Fluxus art pieces (Flanagan 2009) as well as pervasive games like *Assassins* (Montola et al. 2009). Like their Situationist and Fluxus precursors, contemporary make-believe scripting, ruling, and framing is chiefly artistic. One example are so-called subtlemobs, created by the art group Circumstance. As the group explains its piece *Our Broken Voice* (Child et al. 2010):

> A subtlemob is an invisible flashmob, it integrates with the beauty of the everyday world, so only its participants are aware of it. It's like walking through a film. It is experienced on headphones, and it is performed by you and hundreds of strangers. Armed with only an mp3 player this subtlemob takes you on a cinematic experience of twists and turns. A mixture of narrative and richly textured music fills your ears. Different MP3 files are distributed to different audience groups, so while some perform simple actions, the others hear stories about these actions, so that everywhere they look the stories come alive in the world around them. The roles swap back and forth, sometimes you'll just be watching, sometimes you'll be following instructions.

In the case of *Our Broken Voice*, participants are cast into the roles of either persecuted or persecutors in an ambiguous Orwellian surveillance state, instructed to act inconspicuously while trying to identify their target or persecutors, running away or persecuting a runner, etc.

Where *Our Broken Voice* works with scripts, *Massively Multiplayer Soba* (Flanagan 2010) chiefly employs rules: Teams are instructed to procure ingredients and stories about them for a shared noodle soup from residents of a local diverse neighbourhood – ingredients whose names are written in different foreign languages. Thus, the game rules and materials prompt participants to talk to strangers from other cultures about food, while the framing as a game provides the social license or alibi to do so.

A final example is the *Drift Deck* by Bleecker and Lozzi (2008). Picking up on the Situationist art practice of *dérive*, letting oneself drift through a city guided by its geographical and architectural cues to discover new, unbeaten paths and experiences, it presents cards with intentionally ambiguous instructions such as "Some Bit of Unevenness. Confirm this with a passerby. Then turn and run." Participants are instructed to make sense of these instructions in their context, follow them, to then draw new cards.

In summary, scripting, ruling, and framing can be seen to afford an open-ended form of pretend and rule play that engages people in novel behaviours and experiences. These have an interesting relation to make-believe: Some interventions directly instruct participants to generate make-believe. Others constitute alternative meanings and functions in the same way games do: moving a pawn-sized black piece of wood on a chequered slate of wood has no meaning outside the game of Chess. A third group uses the alternative frame of art or play expressly to prompt participants to engage in activities that *also* already have function and meaning in their surrounding everyday life context, e.g. paying compliments to strangers in a park as a means to 'assassinate' them within the frame of the game (McGonigal 2011, pp. 191–197). That is, they intentionally use scripting and ruling to drive desired activities – not so much (or not only) by organizing the activities to be more motivating, but by changing the perceived governing norms of the situation.

Role-Playing

Following the distinction between pretend and role play in developmental psychology, *role-playing* can be seen as theming, ruling, and scripting with "social content", that is, enacting alternative actors and roles. While role-playing in and beyond simulation and gaming has been connected to a wealth of desirable effects (see Schrier forthcoming), we here focus on those particularly salient with make-believe social actors in HCI, which can be roughly split into two groups: the system interacting with the user through a make-believe avatar, and users themselves taking on make-believe roles.

Casting interactive systems or system components in the form of an avatar has a long tradition in HCI and playful design, with famous examples like the Microsoft Office help dialogue rendered as "Clippy", the talking paper clip, or the Nabaztag, an ambient information console shaped as a cartoony white rabbit. The rationale behind this strategy is what Reeves and Nass (1996) called "the media equation": people tend to relate to machines and virtual agents as if they were real human actors, including liking, emotional bonding, and responding positively to their praise. This emotional relating to systems can be increased through avatar representations and game design patterns like making the well-being of the avatar dependent on the user's actions (Dormann et al. 2013). A recent example is "Freddie Von Chimpenheimer IV", the cartoon mailman-meets-chimpanzee mascot of e-mail marketing software Mailchimp. Intentionally designed to evoke emotion (Walter 2011), the mascot personally greets logged-in users with their name and some new irreverent joke each day, and gives them a congratulatory "high-five" when they successfully send an e-mail campaign.

Moving on to users enacting make-believe actors, one can name at least six different desirable effects. The first is self-efficacy through vicarious experience (see Liebermann 2006, for a survey): By playing the make-believe "nano-bot" character ROXXI shooting down cancer cells in the first-person shooter game *Re-Mission*, teen cancer patients increased their beliefs in their own capacity to change reality (self-efficacy), specifically that they were able to fight their own cancer through medication (Kato et al. 2008). A related potentially desirable outcome is the so-called Proteus effect (Yee and Bailenson 2007): people's behaviour conforms to their (digital) self-representation, even after they stopped interacting through it. That is, users who act through a highly attractive avatar will later act as if they themselves were more attractive. Third, role-playing can allow users to enact their desired ideal selves, an experience that generates positive affect and intrinsic motivation (Przybylski et al. 2012). Fourth, creating and customizing one's make-believe avatar is a self-expressive activity that offers motivating autonomy experiences (Turkay and Adinolf 2015). Fifth, like scripting and ruling, role-playing can give participants an alibi and rationale to explore new identities, experiences and behaviours they wouldn't otherwise (Turkle 1995). Sixth and finally, playing the role of another person or group of people can be a visceral form of perspective-taking, increasing empathy and understanding for the embodied person or group (Bachen et al. 2012).

Given this rich tapestry of desirable effects, it is all the more saddening that role-playing is rarely discussed in gameful and playful design. Instead, the literature has chiefly focused *avatars* as sensory representations of social actors (see above). Now representational props ("this strange business of masks and disguises", Huizinga 1949, p. 13) are indeed a crucial tool for role-playing: masks, costumes (Fron et al. 2007), and avatars allow a user to dissociate from their social identities and take on new ones. Yet the avatars discussed in gameful design are mainly representations of users' everyday selves, and deployed for the informational purposes of displaying (presumed-engaging) progress feedback and status markers to the avatar owner and (presumed trust and coordination-facilitating) reputation information to other users (Reeves and Read 2009).

Unified Experiences

Although theming, storification, scripting, ruling, framing, and role-playing do function and sometimes appear in isolation, they can complement and reinforce each other, and often occur together in one integrated design. While frequently labelled as playful or gameful design in media and research, such unified make-believe experiences are formally hard to distinguish from pervasive games (Montola et al. 2009), alternate reality games (ibid.; McGonigal 2011), live-action role-playing games (Harviainen et al. forthcoming), or mixed reality performances (Benford and Giannachi 2011). They represent the most sophisticated and compelling make-believe designs across application domains. For instance, in education, we find multi-player classrooms (Sheldon 2011), practo-mimetic learning (Travis 2011), or role-immersion games (Carnes 2014), which organize whole college courses as role-playing games set in a world fitting the educational topic, and use backstory and plot to engage students in their roles and motivate their learning tasks. As public education, the website campaign *World Without Oil* (Eklund et al. 2007) encouraged people across the world to join in the creation of the fictional first 32 days of a global oil crisis, with participants sending in fictional videos, blog posts, images etc. imagining the effects in their local community.

To illustrate how unified experiences make use of all dimensions of make-believe design, one may look at one much-publicized example in health and fitness, *Zombies, Run!* (Six to Start and Alderman 2015). *Zombies, Run!* is a smartphone application that encourages running by tracking the user's location and speed and blending a fictional world on top of it. In the initial fiction, users embody the sole survivor of a helicopter crash in a zombie apocalypse future that joins a fortified village of survivors as a "runner": somebody who runs into the world outside to recover resources while avoiding (and fleeing from) zombies. The app uses labels, visuals, and sound to evoke the *theme* of a zombie apocalypse, mainly interfacing with the user through headphone audio and the user's movement. It *rules and scripts* individual runs by setting target lengths and speeds to reach and including a sprint-inducing mechanic: at set but unknown points in time, a zombie horde is stirred up, meaning the user has to run at a higher speed for a certain period of time to escape them. Every run is wrapped in a motivating *story*, and continued engagement is motivated by the overall background story of the world being slowly told run by run. The user is given a clear *role* within the fictional world, and engages with established fictional characters that she builds up emotional relations with over time.

7.4   Conclusions

As the preceding pages have shown, make-believe – the constitution of fictional, as if functions and meanings – is a potent 'active ingredient' of play and games. Make-believe can stoke curiosity and arousal through surprising theming and suspenseful narrative. It can facilitate understanding and learning through organizing knowledge in experientially grounded metaphor and story. It can make us like and care about faceless systems as if they were real people, and lend tasks and goals relevance by linking them to values and (fictional) people we care about. It can open and motivate us to explore new identities, behaviours and experiences that lie outside our normal social roles. It can absorb and focus our attention, cognition, and emotion, making us more susceptible to persuasion. It can allow us to express and then follow in the footsteps of our own better selves, and enable us to see the world through the eyes of others.

Yet as the preceding pages also demonstrated, make-believe has remained somewhat at the fringe of applied games and play. Its desirable effects and their underlying affordances are different from those typically targeted in gameful design and gamification. True to Roger Caillois' contention, most current examples of make-believe are more readily classifiable as playful design, which is secondary in public, industry, and research attention to both gamification and serious games (Deterding 2015b). And whereas the latter aim at commercial mass markets, the make-believe designs we encountered are usually artistic, bespoke, one-time installations. Make-believe on a mass-market scale is – today – found mostly in theme parks.

This may be partially due to the particular affordances and requirements of make-believe – theming and framing through labelling and art direction; storification through texts and environmental storytelling; scripting and ruling through instruction sets; role-playing through scripts and representational props. The main draw of theme and narrative consists in their novelty, which rapidly diminishes with every engagement (cf. Koivisto and Hamari 2014). Common solutions to this are either designs of such scope and complexity that they allow for many revisits (cf. the immersive theatre experiences of Punchdrunk), or regularly producing new content – both of which aren't very scalable. Make-believe via scripting, ruling, framing and role-playing typically requires and invites a great amount of openness, emergence, ambiguity, and multiplicity of meanings and actions. While humans routinely make sense of novel and ambiguous actions, this capacity still proves elusive for computers (Suchman 2007). That puts another damper on the (computational) scalability of make-believe designs, and is a likely reason why existing computational make-believe designs typically rely on some "human in the loop".

Besides limited scalability, we observed two further potential downsides to make-believe designs – increased cognitive load and stereotype threat – which again diverge from the common critiques of gamification around issues like coercion or privacy.

Another point of interesting divergence is the underlying technology. Most serious games are audio-visual experiences players interact with through standard computer screens and controllers, with some underlying computational model that assesses the player's growing competencies based on their in-game actions. Most gameful design likewise captures user behaviour through sensors or in-application tracking, and audio-visually responds to the user through screens. Many of the make-believe interventions we encountered – *Situated Audio Platform*, *Voices of Oakland*, *Our Broken Voices*, *You Are Not Here*, *Zombies, Run!* – in contrast rely on sound via headphones as the interface output, and time and location as inputs. One reason for headphone sound as the output channel is that it affords a non-embarrassing, unobtrusive individual layering of additional meanings on top of everyday life: Wearing headphones in public is a socially accepted, normal behaviour, and sound via headphones usually doesn't reach nor disturb uninitiated bystanders. Indeed, the thrill and community sense of participating in the "secret" (Huizinga 1949) of a play society in plain sight is one of the explicit design goals of subtlemobs (Child et al. 2010). The use of time and location inputs in turn may link to the fact that make-believe typically needs to be *coherent* to achieve involvement and transportation. Since both sense-making and dramatic effects rely on the chronological sequence in which information is disclosed, and since users in make-believe designs often encounter information by traversing a space, make-believe designs often require the spatio-temporal choreographing of user *trajectories* through them (Benford and Giannachi 2011).

Yet there are also points of convergence. Like 'mainstream' serious games and gamification, there is a world of difference between most research studies testing the bare-bones addition of one line of flavour text to a cursor pointing task and real-world designs like *Zombies, Run!*, with multiple seasons of continuing and intertwining storylines produced by seasoned writers, expert voice acting and sound design, continually iterated interfaces and rules. This puts a question mark behind the ecological validity of most existing experimental studies, and may be one reason why some have actually found adverse effects of 'adding' make-believe (see Squire 2011, for a similar argument). A second shared shortcoming is that most designs and studies involve multiple interventions at once: progress feedback *and* goal-setting *and* story *and* avatars. From a design perspective, this often makes sense. From a research perspective, however, this makes it hard to draw conclusions and advance the systematic theorization of what the 'active ingredients' of make-believe are, and how design can reliably afford them. It also reproduces the casual conflation of concepts like make-believe, fiction, narrative, theme, and role-play prevalent in the current literature.

All of this doesn't make make-believe any less viable or appealing as a design strategy or research topic. If anything, it suggests that make-believe remains an unlifted treasure of gameful and playful design, to which the present chapter may serve as a first map and compass.

References

Aarseth E (2012) A narrative theory of games. In: Proceedings of the International Conference on the Foundations of Digital Games – FDG'12. ACM Press, New York, pp 129–133. doi:10.1145/2282338.2282365

Abbott HP (2014) Narrativity. In: Hühn P, Meister JC, Pier J, Schmid W (eds) The living handbook of narratology. Hamburg University, Hamburg. Retrieved from http://www.lhn.uni-hamburg.de/article/narrativity

Akkerman S, Admiraal W, Huizenga J (2009) Storification in history education: a mobile game in and about medieval Amsterdam. Comput Educ 52(2):449–459. doi:10.1016/j.compedu.2008.09.014

Bachen CM, Hernández-Ramos PF, Raphael C (2012) Simulating REAL LIVES: promoting global empathy and interest in learning through simulation games. Simul Gaming 43(4):437–460. doi:10.1177/1046878111432108

Ballagas R, Kuntze A, Walz SP (2008) Gaming tourism: lessons from evaluating REXplorer, a pervasive game for tourists. In: Indulska J (ed) Pervasive 2008. Springer, Berlin, pp 244–261

Bareis A (2014) Fiktionen als make-believe. In: Klauk T, Köppe T (eds) Fiktionalität. Ein interdisziplinäres Handbuch. De Gruyter, Berlin, pp 50–67

Barr P (2007) Video game values: play as human-computer interaction. Victoria University of Wellington. Retrieved from http://pippinbarr.com/videogamevalues/?page_id=7

Bateman C (2011) Imaginary games. Zero Books, Winchester

Bateman C (2015) Fiction denial and the liberation of games. In: DiGRA 2015 Ab extra. DiGRA, Lüneburg

Benford S, Giannachi G (2011) Performing mixed reality. MIT Press, Cambridge, MA

Berger PL, Luckmann T (1967) The social construction of reality: a treatise in the sociology of knowledge. Penguin, London

Birk MV, Mandryk RL, Bowey J, Buttlar B (2015) The effects of adding premise and backstory to psychological tasks. In: CHI 2015 workshop on researching gamification: strategies, opportunities, challenges, ethics, Seoul

Bleecker J, Lizzi D (2008) Drift deck. Near future laboratory. Retrieved from http://blog.nearfuturelaboratory.com/2008/09/02/drift-deck/

Blythe MA, Overbeeke K, Monk AF, Wright PC (eds) (2004) Funology: from usability to enjoyment. Kluwer Academic Publishers, Norwell

Bruner J (1990) Acts of meaning. Harvard University Press, Cambridge, MA

Burghardt GM (2005) The genesis of animal play: testing the limits. MIT Press, Cambridge, MA

Caillois R (2001) Man, play, and games. University of Illinois Press, Urbana

Carnes MC (2014) Minds on fire: how role-immersion games transform college. Harvard University Press, Cambridge, MA

Carpenter JM, Green MC (2012) Flying with Icarus: narrative transportation and the persuasiveness of entertainment. In: Shrum LJ (ed) Psychology of entertainment media, 2nd edn. Routledge, Florence, pp 169–194

Carroll JM (1982) The adventure of getting to know a computer. Computer 15(11):49–58. doi:10.1109/MC.1982.1653888

Carroll JM, Thomas JC (1982) Metaphor and the cognitive representation of computing systems. IEEE Trans Syst Man Cybern 12(2):107–116

Carroll JM, Thomas JC (1988) Fun. ACM SIGCHI Bull 19(3):21–24. doi:10.1145/49108.1045604

Chen Z-H, Liao CCY, Cheng HNH, Yeh CYC, Chan T-W (2012) Influence of game quests on pupils' enjoyment and goal-pursuing in math learning. J Educ Technol Soc 15(2):317–327

Child L, Grenier E, Speakman D, Anderson S, Stevens T (2010) Our broken voice. Retrieved from http://wearecircumstance.com/project/our-broken-voice/

Cohn D (1990) Signposts of fictionality: a narratological perspective. Poet Today 11(4):775–804. doi:10.2307/1773077

Csikszentmihalyi M (1975) Beyond boredom and anxiety: the experience of play in work and games. Jossey-Bass Publishers, San Francisco

Davies R (2009) Playful. In: This is playful 2009. London. Retrieved from http://russelldavies.typepad.com/planning/2009/11/playful.html

Deci EL, Ryan RM (2012) Motivation, personality, and development within embedded social contexts: an overview of self-determination theory. In: Ryan RM (ed) The oxford handbook of human motivation. Oxford University Press, New York, pp 85–107

Deterding S (2009) Fiction as play: reassessing the relation of games, play, and fiction. In: Sageng JR (ed) Philosophy of computer games 2009. University of Oslo, Oslo, pp 1–18. Retrieved from http://proceedings2009.gamephilosophy.org

Deterding S (2011) Situated motivational affordances of game elements: a conceptual model. In: CHI 2011 workshop "Gamification." Vancouver. Retrieved from http://gamification-research.org/chi2011/papers

Deterding S (2014) Modes of play: a frame analytic account of video game play. Hamburg University. Retrieved from http://ediss.sub.uni-hamburg.de/volltexte/2014/6863/

Deterding S (2015a) The lens of intrinsic skill atoms: a method for gameful design. Hum Comput Interact 30(3–4):294–335. doi:10.1080/07370024.2014.993471

Deterding S (2015b) The ambiguity of games: histories, and discourses of a gameful world. In: Walz SP, Deterding S (eds) The gameful world: approaches, issues, applications. MIT Press, Cambridge, MA, pp 23–64

Deterding S, Zagal JP (eds) (forthcoming) Role-playing game studies transmedia foundations. Routledge, New York

Deterding S, Dixon D, Khaled R, Nacke LE (2011) From game design elements to gamefulness: defining "Gamification." In: MindTrek'11. ACM Press, New York, pp 9–15

Dickey MD (2006) Game design narrative for learning: appropriating adventure game design narrative devices and techniques for the design of interactive learning environments. Educ Technol Res Dev 54(3):245–263. doi:10.1007/s11423-006-8806-y

Dickey MD (2011) Murder on Grimm Isle: the impact of game narrative design in an educational game-based learning environment. Br J Educ Technol 42(3):456–469. doi:10.1111/j.1467-8535.2009.01032.x

Disselkoen D (2015) Man-eater: An intervention in the tram. Retrieved from http://danieldisselkoen.nl/man-eater/

Dormann C, Whitson JR, Neuvians M (2013) Once more with feeling: game design patterns for learning in the affective domain. Games Cult 8(4):215–237. doi:10.1177/1555412013496892

Dow S, Lee J, Oezbek C, Macintyre B, Bolter JD, Gandy M (2005) Exploring spatial narratives and mixed reality experiences in Oakland cemetery. In: ACE'05. ACM Press, New York, pp 51–60

Downes-Le Guin T, Baker R, Mechling J, Ruylea E (2012) Myths and realities of respondent engagement in online surveys. Int J Mark Res 54(5):1–21. doi:10.2501/IJMR-54-5-000-000

Eklund K, McGonigal J, Bracewell M, Cook D, Senderhauf M, Lamb M (2007) World without oil. Retrieved from http://worldwithoutoil.org/metaabout.htm

Fagerholt E, Lorentzon M (2009) Beyond the HUD. User interfaces for increased player immersion in FPS games. Chalmers University of Technology, Göteborg

Fernaeus Y, Höök K, Holopainen J, Ivarsson K, Karlsson A, Lindley S, Norlin C (eds) (2012) Plei-Plei! PPP, Hongkong. Retrieved from http://playfulness.info

Fillmore CJ, Baker C (2009) A frames approach to semantic analysis. In: Heine B, Narrog H (eds) The oxford handbook of linguistic analysis. Oxford University Press, Oxford, pp 313–340

Flanagan M (2009) Critical play: radical game design. MIT Press, Cambridge, MA

Flanagan M (2010) Creating critical play. In: Catlow R, Garrettm M, Morgana C (eds) Artists re: thinking games. Liverpool University Press, Liverpool, pp 49–53

Flatla DR, Gutwin C, Nacke LE, Bateman S, Mandryk RL (2011) Calibration games: making calibration tasks enjoyable by adding motivating game elements. In: UIST'11. ACM Press, Santa Barbara, pp 403–412

Frasca G (2003) Ludologists love stories, too: notes from a debate that never took place. In: Copier M, Raessens J (eds) DiGRA 2003. Utrecht University, Utrecht, pp 92–99

Fron J, Fullerton T, Morie JF, Pearce C (2007) Playing dress-up: costumes, roleplay and imagination. In: Philosophy of computer games 2007. Modena

Gee J-P (2003) What video games have to teach us about learning and literacy. Palgrave Macmillan, New York

Goffman E (1986) Frame analysis: an essay on the organization of experience. Northeastern University Press, Boston

Gottdiener M (2001) The theming of America: dreams, media fantasies, and themed environments, 2nd edn. Westview Press, Boulder

Gray D, Brown S, Macanufo J (2010) Gamestorming: a playbook for innovators, rulebreakers, and changemakers. O'Reilly, Sebastopol

Grove SJ, Fisk RP (1992) The service experience as theater. In: Sherry JF, Sternthal B (eds) Advances in consumer research, vol. 19. Association for Consumer Research, Provo, pp. 455–461

Habgood MPJ, Ainsworth SE (2011) Motivating children to learn effectively: exploring the value of intrinsic integration in educational games. Journal of the Learning Sciences 20(2):169–206. doi:10.1080/10508406.2010.508029

Halan S, Rossen B, Cendan J, Lok B (2010) High score! – motivation strategies for user participation in virtual human development. In: Allbeck J (ed) IVA 2010. Springer, Berlin, pp 482–488. doi: 10.1007/978-3-642-15892-6_52

Halter E (2006) From Sun Tzu to Xbox: war and videogames. Thunder's Mouth Press, New York

Hamari J, Koivisto J, Sarsa H (2014) Does gamification work? – A literature review of empirical
    studies on gamification. In: HICSS'14. IEEE Computer Society Press, Waikoloa, pp 3025–3034
Harviainen JT, Simkins D, Stenros J, MacCallum-Stewart E, Hitchens D (forthcoming) Live-action
    role-playing games. In: Deterding S, Zagal JP (eds) Role-playing game studies: transmedia
    foundations. Routledge, London
Henricks TS (2015) Play and the human condition. University of Illinois Press, Champaign
Hocking C (2007) Ludonarrative dissonance in bioshock: the problem of what the game is
    about. Click Nothing. Retrieved from http://clicknothing.typepad.com/click_nothing/2007/10/
    ludonarrative-d.html
Huizinga J (1949) Homo ludens: a study of the play-element in culture. Routledge & Kegan Paul,
    London
Huotari K, Hamari J (2012) Defining gamification – a service marketing perspective. In: Proceed-
    ings of the 16th international academic Mindtrek conference. ACM Press, Tampere, pp 17–22
Imaz M, Benyon D (2007) Designing with blends: conceptual foundations of human-computer
    interaction and software engineering. MIT Press, Cambridge, MA/London
Inzlicht M (2011) Stereotype threat: theory, process, and application. Oxford University Press,
    Oxford
Jenkins H (2004) Game design as narrative architecture. In: Wardrip-Fruin N, Harrigan P (eds)
    First person: new media as story, performance, and game. MIT Press, Cambridge, MA, pp
    118–130
Jenkins H (2006) Convergence culture: where old and new media collide. New York University
    Press, New York
Jordan PW (2002) Designing pleasurable products. An introduction to the new human factors.
    Taylor & Francis, London
Juul J (2005) Half-real: video games between real rules and fictional worlds. MIT Press,
    Cambridge, MA
Kato PM, Cole SW, Bradlyn AS, Pollock BH (2008) A video game improves behavioral outcomes
    in adolescents and young adults with cancer: a randomized trial. Pediatrics 122(2):e305–e317.
    doi:10.1542/peds.2007-3134
Kim AJ (2011) Smart gamification. Slideshare.net. Retrieved from http://www.slideshare.net/
    amyjokim/smart-gamification
Koivisto J, Hamari J (2014) Demographic differences in perceived benefits from gamification.
    Comput Hum Behav 35:179–188. doi:10.1016/j.chb.2014.03.007
Korhonen H, Montola M, Arrasvuori J (2009) Understanding playful user experiences through
    digital games. In: Proceedings of the 4th international conference on Designing Pleasurable
    Products and Interfaces, DPPI 2009. Université de Technologie de Compiègne, pp 274–285
Krentz A (1998) Play and education in Plato's republic. In: Olson AM (ed) Twentieth
    world congress of philosophy. Boston. Retrieved from https://www.bu.edu/wcp/Papers/Educ/
    EducKren.htm
Lamarque P, Olsen SH (1994) Truth, fiction, and literature: a philosophical perspective. Clarendon,
    Oxford
Langer R, Hancock M, West AH, Randall N (2013) Applications as stories. CHI 2013 workshop
    on gamification – designing gamification: creating gameful and playful experiences
Laran J, Janiszewski C (2011) Work or fun? How task construal and completion influence
    regulatory behavior. J Consum Res 37(6):967–983. doi:10.1086/656576
Lieberman DA (2006) What can we learn from playing interactive games? In: Vorderer P, Bryant
    J (eds) Playing video games: motives, responses, and consequences. Lawrence Erlbaum,
    Mahwah, pp 379–397
Lieberoth A (2015) Shallow gamification: testing psychological effects of framing an activity as a
    game. Games Cult 10(3):229–248. doi:10.1177/1555412014559978
Lillard AS (2014) The development of play. In: Liben L, Mueller U (eds) Handbook of
    child psychology and developmental science, vol 2. Wiley-Blackwell, New York, pp 1–44.
    doi:10.2307/1131255

Lillard A, Pinkham AM, Smith E (2011) Pretend play and cognitive development. In: Goswami U (ed) The Wiley-Blackwell handbook of childhood cognitive development, 2nd edn. Blackwell, Oxford, pp 285–311

Linderoth J (2012) The effort of being in a fictional world: upkeyings and laminated frames in MMORPGs. Symb Interact 35(4):474–492. doi:10.1002/SYMB.39

Littleton K, Ashman H, Light P, Artis J, Roberts T, Oosterwegel A (1999) Gender, task contexts, and children's performance on a computer-based task. Eur J Psychol Educ 14(1):129–139. doi:10.1007/BF03173115

Lukas SA (2013) The immersive worlds handbook: designing theme parks and consumer spaces. Focal Press, New York/London

Malone T (1982) Heuristics for designing enjoyable user interfaces: lessons from computer games. In: Proceedings of the 1982 conference on Human factors in computing systems. ACM, New York, pp 63–68

Mäyrä F, Kultima A, Alha K, Tyni H (2013) Slide to work: the playful office. In: Physical and digital in games and play seminar: 9th Game Research Lab Spring Seminar. Tampere

McGonigal J (2011) Reality is broken: why games make us better and how they can change the world. Penguin, London

Mollick E, Rothbard N (2014) Mandatory fun: consent, gamification and the impact of games at work. Retrieved from http://ssrn.com/abstract=2277103

Montola M, Stenros J, Waern A (2009) Pervasive games: theory and design. Experiences on the boundary between life and play. Morgan Kaufmann, Amsterdam

Murmann M, Avraamidou L (2014a) Narrative as a learning tool in science centers: potentials, possibilities and merits. J Sci Commun 13(02):1–16

Murmann M, Avraamidou L (2014b) Animals, emperors, senses: exploring a story-based learning design in a museum setting. Int J Sci Educ B Commun Publ Engagement 4(1):66–91. doi:10.1080/21548455.2012.694490

Paharia R (2013) Loyalty 3.0: how to revolutionize customer and employee engagement with big data and gamification. McGraw-Hill, New York

Paulus T, Horvitz B, Shi M (2006) 'Isn't it just like our situation?' Engagement and learning in an online story-based environment. Educ Technol Res Dev 54(4):355–385

Pellegrini AD (2009) The role of play in human development. Oxford University Press, New York

Pine BJ, Gilmore JH (2011) The experience economy, updated edition, 2nd edn. Harvard Business Review Press, Boston

Prestopnik NR, Tang J (2015) Points, stories, worlds, and diegesis: comparing player experiences in two citizen science games. Comput Hum Behav 52:492–506. doi:10.1016/j.chb.2015.05.051

Przybylski AK, Weinstein N, Murayama K, Lynch MF, Ryan RM (2012) The ideal self at play: the appeal of video games that let you be all you can be. Psychol Sci 23(1):69–76. doi:10.1177/0956797611418676

Reeves B, Nass C (1996) The media equation: how people treat computers, television, and new media like real people and places. Cambridge University Press, Cambridge

Reeves B, Read JL (2009) Total engagement: using games and virtual worlds to change the way people work and businesses compete. Harvard Business School Press, Boston

Ritzer G (2009) Enchanting in a disenchanted world: continuity and change in the cathedrals of consumption, 3rd edn. Sage, Los Angeles/London/New Delhi/Singapore

Rucinska Z (2014) Pretend play as a basis of cultural games and norms. In: Enacting culture: embodiment, interaction and the development of human culture. Heidelberg

Ryan M-L (2008) Fiction. In: Donsbach W (ed) The international encyclopedia of communication. Wiley-Blackwell, Oxford

Ryan M-L (2014) Space. In: Hühn P, Meister JC, Pier J, Schmid W (eds) The living handbook of narratology. University of Hamburg, Hamburg. Retrieved from http://www.lhn.uni-hamburg.de/article/space

Sakamoto M, Nakajima T (2014) Gamifying intelligent daily environments through introducing fictionality. Int J Hybrid Inf Technol 7(4):259–276

Salen K, Zimmerman E (2004) Rules of play: game design fundamentals. MIT Press, Cambridge, MA

Schier K (forthcoming) Education. In: Deterding S, Zagal J-P (eds) Role-playing game studies: transmedia foundations. Routledge, New York

Seaborn K, Fels DI (2015) Gamification in theory and action: a survey. Int J Hum-Comput Stud 74(2):14–31. doi:10.1016/j.ijhcs.2014.09.006

Searle JR (1975) The logical status of fictional discourse. N Lit Hist 6(2):319–332

Searle J (1995) The construction of social reality. Free Press, New York

Sheldon L (2011) The multiplayer classroom: designing coursework as a game. Cengage Learning, Boston

Silvia PJ (2006) Exploring the psychology of interest. Oxford University Press, Oxford

Six to Start, Alderman N (2015) Zombies, run! Six to Start, London. Retrieved from https://zombiesrungame.com

Squire K (2011) Video games and learning: teaching and participatory culture in the digital age. Teachers College Press, New York

Stenros J (2015) Behind games: playful mindset as basis for ludic transformative practice. In: Walz SP, Deterding S (eds) The gameful world: approaches, issues, applications. MIT Press, Cambridge, MA, pp 201–222

Stenros J (forthcoming) The game definition game: a review of the meanings of "Game." Games and culture

Suchman L (2007) Human-machine reconfigurations: plans and situated actions, 2nd edn. Cambridge University Press, Cambridge

Sutton-Smith B (1997) The ambiguity of play. Harvard University Press, Cambridge, MA

Travis R (2011) Practomimetic learning in the classics classroom: a game-based learning method from ancient epic and philosophy. N Engl Class J 38(1):25–42

Turkay S, Adinolf S (2015) The effects of customization on motivation in an extended study with a massively multiplayer online roleplaying game. Cyberpsychol: J Psychosoc Res Cyberspace 9(3). doi:10.5817/CP2015-3-2

Turkle S (1995) Life on the screen: identity in the age of the internet. Simon & Schuster, New York

Walter A (2011) Designing for emotion. A Book Apart, New York

Walton KL (1990) Mimesis as make-believe: on the foundations of the representational arts. Harvard University Press, Cambridge, MA

Warfield Rawls A (2009) An essay on two conceptions of social order: constitutive orders of action, objects and identities vs aggregated orders of individual action. J Class Sociol 9(4):500–520. doi:10.1177/1468795X09344376

Webster J, Martocchio JJ (1993) Turning work into play: implications for microcomputer software training. J Manag 19(1):127–146

Werbach K, Hunter D (2012) For the win: how game thinking can revolutionize your business. Wharton Digital Press, Philadelphia

Yee N, Bailenson J (2007) The proteus effect: the effect of transformed self-representation on behavior. Hum Commun Res 33(3):271–290. doi:10.1111/j.1468-2958.2007.00299.x

Zichermann G, Cunningham C (2011) Gamification by design: implementing game mechanics in web and mobile apps. O'Reilly, Sebastopol

Zipfel F (2001) Fiktion, Fiktivität, Fiktionalität. Analysen zur Fiktion in der Literatur und zum Fiktionsbegriff in der Literaturwissenschaft. Erich Schmidt, Berlin

Chapter 8
The Role of Make-Believe in Foley

Lindsey Carruthers and Phil Turner

8.1 Introduction

Pretending is almost exclusively studied in the context of child development, where it is often treated as a synonym for pretend play. Pretend play (and play more generally) merits this attention because it is recognised to be essential to a child's cognitive, affective, and social development (e.g. Seja and Russ 1999; Russ 2004; Jent et al. 2011), but our interest here is in pretending alone. Children begin to pretend, quite spontaneously, early in life. Nakayama (2013), for example, has presented evidence that children as young as 7 months old are able to pretend to cry as a means of obtaining attention. So, surprisingly, children can pretend before they have learned to speak, walk, or feed themselves.

Earlier work by Leslie (1987, p.412) informs us that pretending can be observed at "the very beginning of childhood", while Harris (2000) agrees but argues that it appears later, and equates it with the development of language.

While the appearance of pretending remains a matter of some debate, its purpose is astonishing. Garvey (1990) writes that pretend play is the "voluntary transformation of the here and now, the you and me, and the this or that, along with any potential action that these components of a situation might have". Harris (ibid) writes, "Children's pretend play is [...] an initial exploration of possible worlds", and others suggest that pretend play is "acting as if something is when it is not" (Rutherford et al. 2007, p.1025). We can but echo Leslie's questions (which we paraphrase); if children are still learning about the complexities of the world and

L. Carruthers (✉)
School of Life, Sport, and Social Sciences, Edinburgh Napier University, Edinburgh, UK
e-mail: L.Carruthers@napier.ac.uk

P. Turner
School of Computing, Edinburgh Napier University, Edinburgh, UK
e-mail: p.turner@napier.ac.uk

© Springer International Publishing Switzerland 2016
P. Turner, J.T. Harviainen (eds.), *Digital Make-Believe*,
Human–Computer Interaction Series, DOI 10.1007/978-3-319-29553-4_8

are still well short of cognitive maturity, why are they engaged in the "voluntary transformation of the here and now", the creation of "possible worlds" and acting as though "something is when it is not". If all of this is in the service of cognitive development, is it fair to assume that it is discarded in adulthood?

We distinguish pretending/pretend play from make-believe by observing that the latter is typically associated with a prop (Walton 1990, 1993) of some kind and for this reason it is more structured (e.g., a pirate's costume will tend to constrain make-believe to the piratical). These props might include an established story and roles, which we might describe as "psychological tools" to borrow Vygotsky's term (1930), or they may include costumes, "swords", "magic wands", and other toys that extend into the physical world.

It is of note that pretending and make-believe have tended to be treated as the province of small children alone as there appears to be little or no reported work on adults engaging in these behaviours. Yet we all pretend. We pretend to like, believe, or feel (and so forth) one thing while actually liking, believing, or feeling another so as to avoid an argument, disappointing someone, to play along with a scheme, or while playing with a child. We all regularly make-believe when envisioning whether a new item of furniture will fit into our living room for example, and we may even pretend to sit on it. People will hold up an item of clothing against themselves and pretend they are wearing it. The entertaining World Air Guitar Championships that are held annually involve people pretending to play guitars that are not there, and to make-believe a rock star persona. These simply would not exist if people were unprepared to spend time practicing with thin air, nor would Star Trek™ conventions with their array of visiting aliens in their homemade costumes.

But more than this, considering the statistics reported by McGonigal (2011), 50 % of the UK population play video games and many of these have spent upwards of 10,000 h engaged in gaming by the age of 21 years. Without engaging in a discussion of the psychology of game playing we can conclude by saying, that is a lot of adult make-believe.

So How Does Pretending Work?

At present, there are a number of accounts of how pretending works. Again this has been directed at explaining the behaviour of children but, as we shall see, there is little reason to suppose why they cannot be extended to adults. We begin with a consideration of the oldest of these, which is based on meta-representation.

Leslie (1987) began by supposing that the child is able to create a representation of the world that is accurate and faithful. This he calls the primary representation and this has a direct semantic relation with the world. For pretending to occur, he tells us that the child makes a copy of this representation and changes it. This copy is decoupled from the world, becoming a copy of a copy. This copy of a copy is a meta-representation, and it is this that forms the basis of our ability to pretend. Of course, children also need to be able to distinguish between acting and believing in the real world, and pretending in a make-believe world. This is achieved by quarantining the meta-representation from the real copy (of the world).

Further and unlike other accounts, Leslie recognises that pretending is a process with identifiable stages. He proposes three stages or forms of pretending: immediate, planned, and remembered. Interestingly, this mirrors some of the current thinking in user experience that recognises a number of quite discrete forms of experience with technology. The key to Leslie's account is the de-coupler which has three main components: perceptual processes, cognitive systems, and the de-coupler itself. The perceptual processes feed representations of the current situation to the central cognitive systems, which comprise general knowledge, the ability to plan, and so forth. The de-coupler in turn comprises, a further three elements, namely, the expression raiser, the manipulator, and the interpreter, which are responsible for making a copy of the primary representation and its subsequent manipulation and quarantining. It should be noted that this model is speculative and is based on a number of additional, significant assumptions, not least of that there is a common representational code governing the whole process (cf. Prinz 1984). This model of pretending has had a measure of both support and criticism.

The next model, based on the conception of a "possible world box", has been developed by Nichols and Stitch (2005) and has proved to be influential. This cognitive model of pretending is based on a modification to what they describe as the "widely accepted account of cognition as adopted by people working in this field". Nichols and Stitch make it clear that they do not believe that their account is necessarily complete or definitive but that they do think they have, in contrast to other researchers, described pretending quite fully. Their most frequent criticism of other accounts is that they are "under-described". They begin by noting that the mind (sic) contains two quite different kinds of representational states, namely, belief and desires, which operate differently. Beliefs are what we know, true and false, about the world. Desires are what we want, and Nichols and Stitch implicate the bodily systems of being the source of them. To pretend is to create another "world" in a "possible world box" (or partition) created by our cognition. They tell us that pretending begins with a premise (say, "let's have a tea party") that, if adopted by the pretender, forms the basis for subsequent inference and embellishment. They also recognise that the premise may be bound or constrained by schematic structures, writing: "clusters or packets of representations whose contents constitute 'scripts' or paradigms detailing the way in which certain situations typically unfold" (p. 34). These they describe as "soft constraints". This idea has been developed more fully by Turner et al. (2015). The contents of these possible world boxes have full access to our beliefs, and from there, to our practical reasoning faculties. An updater mechanism keeps us informed as to the status of the pretend episode. These possible world boxes are populated with representation tokens, which are different from those found in the beliefs and desires boxes. These tokens do not represent the world as it is or what we would like it to be, but rather represent what the world "would be like given some set of assumptions that we neither believe to be true (that is, we believe to be the case) or want to be true" (Nichols and Stitch, ibid p. 29). As for the precise nature of this possible world box it is a little under-described, though it does appear to function in a manner that is logically very similar to Leslie's meta-representation account. Again, this model of pretending has had a measure of both support and criticism.

Finally, between these two accounts (at least chronologically) lies Lillard's (2001) "Twin Earth" proposal. She rejects the meta-representation account of pretending and offers the "Twin Earth" model in its place. The "Twin Earth" model has its origins with Putnam's Twin Earth thought experiment, which asks us to believe (pretend) that elsewhere in the universe there is a planet exactly like Earth in virtually all respects, referred to as "Twin Earth". Having said "virtually all respects", Putnam goes on to propose some differences between the two for the purpose of philosophical discourse and exploring the nature of semantics. Lillard writes that pretend play for children is similar to this Twin Earth thought experiment. She tells us that when children pretend, they create another world that shares many of the characteristics of the real world. While much remains the same, there are, of course, significant changes, such as the "child becomes the mother [and] ... sand becomes apple pie" (p. 22). Then, not unlike a philosopher, the child reasons about the constituent parts of this twin world. Many of the relationships are unchanged, for example, while the child may pretend to be the mother, this (twin) mother treats her children just like the real world version. Lillard notes that both pretend play and Twin Earth are quarantined worlds that are decoupled from the real world. She also adds that children engaged in playing signal to each other that they are pretending, that is, they make it explicit that they are making believe. Lillard also proposes her own model of pretending. She notes (twice) that pretending is "mental" for which we might read "cognitive".

While all three authors are proposing solutions to the same set of observed behaviours their solutions, it might be said, differ only as matters of implementation. They recognise the need for the pretender to have access to the real world and to be able to distinguish between their make-believe and it; they recognise the need for rule, or more specifically, schematic behaviour, and all require a de-coupler. Finally, whatever the mechanism, all three accounts result in what has been described as "cognitive decoupling" – a temporary, partial dislocation from the here-and-now, to the world of make-believe we have created.

8.2   A Study of Adult Pretending

So where might we find evidence of adult pretending? Any such investigation poses significant methodological issues: whereas childhood pretending occurs naturally in the course of day-to-day activity, and may therefore be explored in a relatively naturalistic fashion even in controlled settings, this is not the case in ordinary adult life. However, there are situations where make-believe, and pretending might reasonably be considered to have a central role. Goldstein and Bloom (2011) suggest that we take to the stage. They suggest that acting might be a promising candidate were it not for the convincing argument that (a) acting describes pretence as entailing a degree of exaggeration in the expression of the qualities assumed, which (b) characterises historic acting styles but not the more naturalistic performances of contemporary theatre. In similar vein, Cook (2007) equates "pretending" with "imitating", arguing that actors do not imitate actions, but perform them, the effect of such performance being to activate mirror neurons in members of the audience. Hence, she suggests, "it is the power and pervasiveness of audience imitation that is central to theatre" (p. 591).

8.3   Foley

A related role, and one much closer to the concept of make-believe as proposed above, is that of the Foley artist, and this chapter describes the result of a series of interviews with professional Foley artists talking about their work. A Foley artist is someone who recreates sounds in movies, television, radio, or theatre. On a film or television set, the only sound recorded is the dialogue. Other sounds, such as footsteps, the placing of a glass on a table, fiddling with a pen or pencil, and all other prop noises are added post-production. Thus every noise heard whilst watching a movie or show that is not a voice (although voices can be edited afterwards too) has been recorded after filming. It is the job of a Foley artist to add these sounds to a scene, and they do so by using props and their own bodies to recreate the sound in synchronisation with the picture. It was our belief that these artists were likely to engage in pretending and make-believing as part of their work to reproduce or recreate these sounds. Sound effects, as such, the "roar of a dinosaur" are not within the remit of a Foley artist, and are not considered here.

The job title derives from Jack Foley, who was one of the first to create post-production sounds in this way in the 1920s/1930s. Perhaps the most familiar example is the use of coconut shells to sound like horses' hooves. Somewhat surprisingly, this is not apocryphal, but a technique still used by Foley artists today, although alternatives have been developed. Foley presents a potentially rich domain for the exploration of adult pretending: the practice, as will be seen from the data reported below, involves (at least) a dual layer of pretence. Not only do Foley artists, for example, perform the bodily actions of actors in the filmed story, but such behaviour generally requires an extra layer of pretence, since the physical environment of the Foley studio is not that of the film-set.

Research Aim

We emphasize that this was an informal investigation that aimed to get a sense of the world of the Foley artist. This was an investigation of the artists' professional practice rather than a laboratory study. In short, we were interested in what they did, in their own words.

Method

The project used a qualitative approach, with the use of semi-structured interviews that aimed to elicit rich, detailed, personal data from flexible discussion with the target group of practitioners. The study was granted ethical approval by the Edinburgh Napier University Faculty Research Integrity Committee.

Participants

Ten Foley artists were involved in the study, five male and five female. Each participant identified themselves as a Foley artist, although many also had experience as sound editors or Foley recordists. The participants were recruited via email. Their contact details were found on the professional persons social media site LinkedIn (www.linkedin.com), using the simple search term "Foley Artist". A general email was originally sent to potential participants, explaining that the project was taking place, and requesting a reply if they were interesting in contributing. Many of the people contacted were keen to take part, and from there the details of the consent and interview process were specified.

Materials

As we have indicated, the study aimed to investigate the processes of pretending and make-believe in Foley artists. Determining the phrasing of questions to be asked was a difficult process, the biggest challenge being the avoidance of leading questions. We wanted the artists to discuss these concepts spontaneously, without a cue from the interviewer, yet finding ways of inducing a discussion about make-believe and pretending, without using those terms, is near impossible. Therefore, the terms occasionally appear in the questions.

The process of creating the questions involved multiple iterations. After the production of version one, a pilot interview was conducted with a sound design academic, who has experience in Foley. At that point, several inappropriate questions were removed as they referred to the job within a special effects department, and not a Foley artist, for example: "Where do you start for sounds that are make-believe? For example, mythical creatures or animals, lasers, space crafts, and so on". Furthermore, this first version contained only 12 questions, which proved to be over-generic and unproductive of discussion. Subsequently the questions were refined several more times with version six being the final form. This version contained 22 questions, some referring explicitly to the way participants performed, their mind-sets and strategies, and their acting processes.

Although the interviews were principally concerned with investigating the cognitive processes in Foley artistry, we added some practical, descriptive items designed to be easy to answer. While the main purpose of these questions was to set participants at ease, they also elicited material that was useful for our study. The list of questions is provided in Table 8.1.

Table 8.1 The list of interview questions

1.	For how long have you worked as a Foley artist?
2.	What do you do to prepare for a recording session? Do you rehearse?
3.	Do you think there is a state of mind or mood you have to get yourself into before you perform?
4.	Can you describe how you perform?
5.	When performing, do you wish to take on the role of the character? If yes: How important do you think it is to take on the role of the character? How do you do this?
6.	Is there an element of acting in your job?
7.	Do you use your body when you perform? Do you make gestures and movements?
8.	Are your performances real, or are they an act of make-believe?
9.	Tell me about your props, how do you know what will work for the scene or the audience?
10.	Are you able to watch a film and enjoy it without paying full attention to the sound? Or are you susceptible to the same effects as the audience?
11.	How do you come up with new sounds? What is your process?
12.	Do you ever get time to experiment?
13.	Do you find yourself discovering new sounds or techniques when you're off the clock?
14.	Do you think there is a specific mind-set or ability that one must have to successfully work in Foley?
15.	What is the single most important skill a Foley artist must have?
16.	Are there one or two scenes that stand out in your memory for being particularly difficult or unusual?
17.	Have you learnt anything important from other Foley artists?
18.	Are there any misconceptions about Foley?
19.	As a Foley artist, what are your three biggest obstacles to a successful performance?
20.	If we were to grant you three wishes to make your job easier / better / more effective, what would they be and why?
21.	Do any scenes spring to mind that were particularly fun for you to create?
22.	What have I forgotten to ask in terms of Foley?

Questions three to eight were of particular interest, as they relate directly to the aims of the study. If by the end of the interview, the participant had not mentioned the concepts of pretending, make-believe, and imagination, the interviewer asked directly if they were important aspects to the individual and to their job.

Procedure

After the initial contact with each participant, the information sheet and consent form were sent to sign and return. Each of our ten participants returned their form and agreed to allow us to acknowledge their contribution to the study within any publications. Thereafter, the interview arrangements were made at a time to suit the participant.

The interviews were conducted by the first author using online video calling, and lasted between 20 and 55 min, depending on the depth of the participant's answers. With the participant's permission, each conversation was recorded to allow for later transcription and analysis. After a brief introduction on both parts, the interviewer began asking the questions above. Additional, ad hoc questions were added when appropriate, and if single sentence answers were provided by the participants, they were encouraged to expand if possible. Furthermore, some questions had to be reworded if those with a first language other than English struggled with the terminology, although this only happened rarely. The questions were not always asked in the same order, but were guided by the flow of the discussion. Upon the completion of the session, the participants were asked if there was anything they would like to add, and were provided with the opportunity to ask any questions of their own. Finally, they were thanked for their time.

Adopting common practice in qualitative analysis, the transcribed data was reduced, then displayed, and conclusions were drawn (Miles et al. 2014). Each interview was played back several times and the answers from questions three to eight, along with any other discussion relevant to the study, were manually transcribed, according to the question asked. This top-down analysis was complemented by interrogating the data for emergent ideas and themes that were not predicted by accounts of childhood pretending. All of the transcriptions were read and re-read, after which an exploratory analysis was conducted that involved selecting key terms, phrases, and themes. These were generally found to be in accordance with the overall proposition that pretending remains available to adults, and more specifically to the aspects of childhood pretending, identified in the earlier sections of this paper.

The interview data obtained are presented below, in the form of participants' answers to a number of the questions posed. We illustrate this with direct, extended quotations from participants, having removed identity indicators, hesitations, and non-verbal vocalisations. The use of extended quotations is in keeping with the reporting recommendations of Pollio et al. (1997).

Findings

No one really knows the amount of effort that goes into producing a soundtrack. [...] No one can believe that all the feet they hear in the movie aren't even made by the real characters on the screen. I say 'No, that's all me'. All those feet and all those hands, and all those sips, and all those kisses, all of those bits and pieces, none of them are the actor, that's all me.

What Is Foley?

All of the Foley artists we interviewed noted that their work was little understood and peppered with misunderstandings. For example:

There's a misconception that it's all tricks, they'll say 'Do a trick! Do the sound of a dragon now!' as if you could do it with anything. It's not tricks, it's a slow, laborious process. [. . .] That's a misconception, that we're sonic magicians that can make the sound of anything out of anything.

Not tricks but a reproduction of the behaviour of the onscreen actors.

Sometimes, people [think that] you invent sound effects. [This is] a completely different situation. We are doing the movements of the actors, and some particular sounds, but we are not able to invent an airplane landing or other sounds from the effects part. They are other kinds of sounds.

And . . .

Some people think it's fake, which I think is a misconception. It is not really faking it, it is recreating sound that isn't there. If they could record all of this stuff on location they would use it. The physical reality is they can't do that. [. . .] I feel it's much more a crafted recreation of a soundtrack rather than faking it or trying to fool the public in any way.

As we have already noted, Foley artists are primarily concerned with recreating the sounds that one would expect to hear from the image or scene a viewer is watching. This is different from a special effects team, who work with sound libraries and other instruments to create non-replicable and somewhat fantastical, or novel sounds. However Foley artists can add to the work of special effects editors.

There might be a car crash. So they'll [the special effects editors] add the tyre skids and the main impact, but I'll add some real little creaks, and some scrapes, and glass tinkling on the ground, and maybe the hubcap sound falling and doing a spin. So Foley is a real detail adder, and brightens things up.

Foley artists' work is "not as fun and easy as people imagine". The main obstacles they face are a lack of time, budget, and studio space. The work they do allows us, the audience, to enjoy television shows and films. Foley effects are indispensable to film and television, without them, the sense of reality would diminish, along with the quality and enjoyment of the film. While this is perceived as under-appreciated and undervalued by audiences, it is testament to just how seamless the Foley performances are. As most of the interviewees stated, only poor Foley effects are noticeable.

It feels very uncomfortable as a viewer to have something that's filling your screen and not being able to hear anything that sounds like its natural movement.

The thing with Foley is, if it is done well, you don't notice it. [. . .] If I do my job well, you shouldn't notice it.

You shouldn't really be aware of sound. You should be sucked up in the experience and you shouldn't be focusing on the sounds per se. [. . .] If it is a bad sound or a wrong sound, that's where you spot it. But if it's [the Foley] been done well, you can just sit back and enjoy the ride.

If the Foley stands out because it is out of sync or bad, then I will notice it.

[When watching a film] "I try not to listen to the sound. Sometimes what happens is the sound, and usually if it is unsuccessful, it will jar me out if the movie."

Having established how important Foley is and the evident pride these professionals take in their work we now consider a little of the detail involved in this.

All those interviewed described building sounds, one layer at a time. For example, they may perform all of the footsteps, followed by all of the clothing sounds, and then they will add the sounds of additional props in the scene. A day or two spent performing only footsteps and cloth scenes can be very physically demanding. Each character's footsteps will be recorded separately, with a pair of shoes that suit the image, be it a high heel or a heavy boot. Furthermore, the surface on which the footsteps take place is also matched to the scene, and will be recreated in the studio on concrete, gravel, wood, or whatever is appropriate. The speed and weight of the footsteps will also match the scene, as well as the rhythm and pace.

So you're watching how the little character moves around, [. . .] he's got big flappy feet and he walks a bit funny so you've really got to watch how he goes and try and walk [that way]. He's meant to be light you can't have as much weight as a normal person, but you've got to be careful that you can hear him, so that's his character, [he] sort of sneaks around a bit. And then you've got the bigger fellas, [. . .] the big guy which eats all the time, [. . .] you almost sort of blow up a bit like a big fish and sort of plonk around and try to get as much weight down, and we over emphasise his feet a lot to make him stand out from everybody else.

The clothing sounds will then be recorded for each main character, involving the manipulation of several pieces of fabric or garments that are the same texture, weight, and type as those seen in the film. Thereafter, anything the actor touches, or any other 'visible' sounds in the scene will be recreated.

When the Foley artists are in the studio, they are usually accompanied by a recordist, and they physically perform the sounds required. Many have a background in music, dance, acting, or sound editing; such past experience is considered as a valuable foundation for the job. Most Foley artists do not simply sit at a table surrounded by props, grabbing the most appropriate one as they follow the scene, unless for a live recording. It is an active role that requires physical fitness, stamina, and rhythm. They tell us:

Quite often it is not fun. It's painful, it's exhausting . . .

You have to be able to come up with stupid sounds on the spur of the moment, its essential.

You have to have a good sense of rhythm, but not be locked into it . . . [Musicians] work to a very tight, constant beat, but people don't walk like that. Sync wise you can be bang on to begin with, but then the pace will alter, and I wouldn't catch it, and I would stick to my rhythm. [. . .] So you need to have a good sense of rhythm but be flexible with it.

. . . anybody coming into doing Foley, you need basic skills such as good coordination and really good timing, and be able to pick up on rhythms.

Confidence is necessary to produce a convincing performance, with some participants stating that if they are not confident or happy with a sound they produce, they may revisit it at a later time. Another key skill that contributes to a successful performance is the ability to concentrate.

> [One of the most important skills a Foley artist must have is] "the ability to focus and the ability to listen. You just have to listen. [. . .] The focus is difficult, it takes a lot of practice and you have to really want to focus. [. . .] Focusing that hard all of the time is difficult, but you have to find a way to get through it."

Are You Acting?

In response to the question, "Is there an element of acting in your job?" for a number of the artists, the answer was that there was:

> I think the ability to act, it's the difference between being an average Foley artist and a super Foley artist.

> Absolutely, this is all about acting. [. . .] Yes, I think that it's like 70 % acting, and 30 % about being a sound generator.

> Oh yes absolutely, because you're giving the subject life. So you have to take into account the context of the film, and what's going on with the film, and you're basically trying to give somebody character through sound.

> Yes, you become each character and each movement. [. . .] It really is acting, I really feel that you take on the character and the mood. [. . .] Each effect has to be acted . . . we can change or enhance all of the sounds that can communicate. So acting is a very big part of it, although not in the traditional way.

> Yes. I would say so. But it is acting that is not acting with your feet, or acting with your energy, or it is not in how we dress, mostly I'm alone when I do it, nobody sees me, so I am just play acting maybe.

So, do they act? It would appear so, for perhaps 70 % of the task, but not in a traditional way, more a case what they describe as "play acting" or as we might put it, pretend acting rather than the form that is associated with delivering a soliloquy.

Are the Performances Real, or Are They Just Pretend?

We asked the artists if their performances were real or were they just pretending. We recognise that this is a leading question but we encouraged our participants to offer more than a simple affirmation or denial.

One artist thought that it is all pretending, another thought that it was real, while many others thought they are a bit of both.

> Eh, well I guess it's all pretend isn't it. Because nothing I do is real, it's the industry's real, we're just making a noise and we try and make it believable I guess, that's the main thing, so people think that the noise I make is coming from the actor on the screen, that's the main job really, is to make it, people think it is actually happening.

> I would say they were real. Because you are very much constrained by your environment really because you're in a studio, and you have other people there, and a monitor and a

microphone, you have to make sure that you're not going off mic[rophone]. That's why I think they are real. You can't get too involved in it because you'll end up just not being, the recording side of it just won't be as good.

It is a mix between those things because sometimes you're doing the same situation that the actors made, and you can have to decide if it sounds good. But sometimes, if you're doing the same, you have to change it a little bit to make it a better sound.

Eh, they would be both, because when they are real, I work within the confines of the screen. There is something happening on the screen, I have to match it I have to follow it, but how I get there comes from my imagination. But I actually don't think too hard about it, I've done it long enough it just flows out of me.

Bit of both. Sometimes you come across stuff, certainly if you do a lot of animation, there's stuff that you've never seen before, and will probably never see again. I did a sequence where there was a chicken suspended from a cable car, and his chicken friend had to rescue him but he was also tied up, so the only way they could get out was to swing, grab with his teeth, swing the other one, and that one grabbed with his teeth, he released, and they carried on down the cable. So in cases like that you have to imagine 'what's that going to sound like', then try and come up with something that's going to work. But for something a lot more straightforward, like you know, straight drama or straight natural history, it's purely about trying to recreate what's going on in front of you, so you play it quite straight.

I have to do my pretending synced to a picture, whereas an actor doesn't. An actor creates it then I do it synced to the actor. That may make it less pretending. Somehow I feel like it is less pretending because I have to do what they want me to do. Even with animation once I've got my sound, I have to move how the picture moves. I have to follow the picture. I can't make it up how she's going to move, or when she touches her face.

When asked the direct question as to whether or not these artists regarded their performances were real or pretending we received a mixture of replies, but we have found our evidence of adult pretending.

Evidence of Make-Believe

It will be recalled that we define make-believe as, effectively, pretending with a prop. The artists told us that the job calls for creativity, confidence, and as we have seen, a degree of acting. Another important part of being a Foley artist is the ability to select the right prop for the sound. When the sound is unusual or novel, or if the film is animated, the artist may be required to create the sound using their own ingenuity and initiative. Creativity also influences the way in which the artist chooses to layer their sounds, the manner in which they move to produce sounds, and their attempts to add life and emphasis to characters.

... you have to interpret other people's ideas and make something up from nothing with the few props that you've got.

Things you wouldn't normally hear on a film as well, for instance women's jewellery and earrings, it is not something you'd think about. But suddenly when you add a little tiny tinkle on it, it really brings the character out forward.

As an example, when you're doing the glass scene, if the actor is putting the glass like a stiff move (i.e., straight onto a table), you have to fake it a little bit to sound like a 'cinema glass on table sound', and it has to be like 'tap tap', two times, so that is where you are playing with the realness and the "flakiness", I don't know how to explain it. First of all ok, you have to do the same movement as the actor made and everything, but it has to sound good, so sometimes you have to forget about what the actor is doing and use another prop to get a better sound.

One artist continued,

When you do real films like live action films, you're just trying to reproduce the real [. . .]. You know when I'm trying to have the sound of the real wine glass on a real table, it's really, looking for the right props, and acting. And it's your acting that will get you through whether that wine glass sounds like the same wine glass as the actor put down. And to do big things like car doors and crashes and stuff like that you have to separate the sounds into different tracks so that you can come up with the one final sound. Like in a car crash we might have a car door in the studio and you might smash on that then you might add some glass breaking, and then a screech of metal and I guess those three tracks take some know how.

One point of interest here. Another layer of make-believe is occasionally in play, namely, the difference between animation and live action.

Well definitely when I am asked to do the moves of a wax character, that is, made of wax, and she becomes soft when it's warm and hard when it's cold that is very imaginative. We're all day long thinking about what to do, her hair moves and its made of wax and its different gloves and pieces of wax, I didn't want it to be too hard so I didn't want to use candles, so that was an imagination, the imagination is a big part of it at that point.

This is a nice example of Walton's props forming a seed around which a make-believe episode can be formed. There is evidence of make-believe here in the regular reference to the use of props.

Explicit Evidence of Decoupling?

Unsurprisingly, none of our informants volunteered that they had consciously practiced cognitive decoupling when performing but one did distinguish between what he called "reality" (i.e., the finished film he is working on, which he treats as immutable) and what he does, which lies between this and his imagination.

. . . if you call a film "reality", that's the picture set in stone, that's the reality, and it is up to me to come up with a sound which I think best fits that image. . . . I have different scales of high heels, so if it was quite a sassy young lady with sexy heels, I've sharp heels for that, or if it is a sort of middle-aged woman who sort of clumps in I've got some old blocky heels. So it's up to me to think, right I think she should have, it would fit her to have this sounding shoe or this sounding dress. Or a guy comes in and he's a violent, heavy guy, he might have a big, heavy boot, so you've got to read it. I've gotten quite good I've been doing it for 11/12 years. I guess it meets in the middle of imagination and reality.

We see how an artist describes how "film reality" is created using sexy heels, blocky heels and big heavy boots – which, of course, are never seen.

8.4 Discussion

The research reported here reflects our interest in the work of what we hoped would be professional make-believers.

The interviews revealed abundant evidence of these professional Foley artists engaging in pretending, making-believe, acting, play acting, and being imaginatively creative. Firstly, we do not argue with the artists' use of "imagination" or "play acting" as we wanted their words, but we are happy to suggest that our definitions of pretending and make-believe seem to have a good measure of support in the transcripts. There is some, though more scant, evidence of what they are engaged in being recognised as not being real.

Secondly, there are frequent and occasional oblique references to creativity and imagination in conjunction with their use of props. This suggests that make-believe may function as, or be in the service of, improvised cognition. Cosmides and Tooby (2000), writing from the perspective of evolutionary psychology, argue that our ability to pretend is the result of making use of contingent information and the artefacts that embody that information. They write, "Arguably, one central and distinguishing innovation in human evolution has been the dramatic increase in the use of contingent information for the regulation of improvised behaviour" (p. 53). This ability they describe as "cognitive de-coupling". From this reading, pretending is revealed as improvised behaviour that exploits external artefacts and representations that are, to use Heidegger's term, ready-to-hand.

Cosmides and Tooby suggest that this ability to decouple from the "here-and-now" and to engage with the "what-if" as offering significant advantages over "hardwired" forms of problem solving. They write, "The benefits of successful improvisation are clear [. . .] what 10 years of ordinary battle on the plains of Troy could not accomplish, one Trojan Horse could".

Further empirical evidence of this kind of improvised behaviour has been reported by Dalton et al. (2012) when they describe their "nomadic TUI [tangible user interface] that takes advantage of the fact that the world is full of potential tangibles and that people appear to be comfortable in improvising with them". In a field trial they found that people readily appropriated a range of available objects (including teabags, mobile phones, jewellery, and drinks containers) to act as tangible tokens to be used within their interactive system. These acts of appropriation reflect our immediate needs and the range of artefacts that are ready-to-hand. This also serves to cast pretending/make believe as a form of what Clark (2008) would call "external cognition".

Finally, the artists' many references to acting (and its variants) suggest that pretending is embodied, that is, it reflects the opportunities, capabilities, and restrictions afforded by their bodies. This comes as no surprise. When children pretend, it is often a whole hearted endeavour with little holding back. Witness the sheer exuberant energy of a school ground at mid-morning break. It is interesting to note that pretending may not have been wholly internalised as Vygotsky suggests, and that any account of pretending/make believe needs a place for embodiment.

Acknowledgements Considering how busy the artists are, and the small time frames they have to complete projects, we were delighted and very grateful that they enthusiastically took time out of their schedules to speak to us. Thank you to Julie Ankerson, Céline Bernard, Ronni Brown, Mauricio Castañeda, Richard Hinton, Carlos de la Madrid Valencia, Maureen Murphy, John Simpson, Barnaby Smyth, and Lise Wedlock.

We recognise and are grateful for the financial support from Edinburgh Napier University for a summer internship. Thanks also to Iain McGregor for his technical support.

References

Clark A (2008) Supersizing the mind. Oxford University Press, Oxford

Cook A (2007) Interplay: the method and potential of a cognitive scientific approach to theatre. Theatr J 59:579–594

Cosmides L, Tooby J (2000) Consider the source: the evolution of adaptations for decoupling and metarepresentation. In: Sperber D (ed) Metarepresentations: a multidisciplinary perspective. Oxford University Press, Oxford

Dalton N, MacKay G, Holland S (2012) Kolab: appropriation & improvisation in mobile tangible collaborative interaction. DIS 2012, June 11–15, 2012, Newcastle, UK, pp 21–24

Garvey C (1990) Play. Harvard University Press, Cambridge

Goldstein TR, Bloom P (2011) The mind on stage: why cognitive scientists should study acting. Trends Cogn Sci 15(4):141–142

Harris P (2000) The work of the imagination. Blackwell, London

Jent JF, Niec LN, Baker SE (2011) Play and interpersonal processes. In: Russ SW, Niec LN (eds) Play in clinical practice: evidence-based approaches. Guilford Press, New York

Leslie AM (1987) Pretense and representation: the origins of "theory of mind". Psychol Rev 94:412–426

Lillard AS (2001) Pretend play as twin earth: a social cognitive analysis. Dev Rev 21:495–531

McGonigal J (2011) Reality is broken. Jonathan Cape, London

Miles MB, Huberman AM, Saldana J (2014) Qualitative data analysis: a methods sourcebook. Sage Publications Inc., California

Nakayama H (2013) Changes in the affect of infants before and after episodes of crying. Infant Behav Dev 36(4):507–512

Nichols S, Stich S (2005) Mindreading: a cognitive theory of pretense. Oxford University Press, Oxford

Pollio HR, Henley TB, Thompson CJ (1997) The phenomenology of everyday life. Cambridge University Press, Cambridge

Prinz W (1984) Modes of linkage between perception and action. In: Prinz W, Sanders A-F (eds) Cognition and motor processes. Springer, Berlin, pp 185–193

Russ SW (2004) Play in child development and psychotherapy. Erlbaum, Mahwah

Rutherford MD, Young GS, Hepburn S, Rogers SJ (2007) A longitudinal study of pretend play in autism. J Autism Dev Disord 37(6):1024–1039

Seja AL, Russ SW (1999) Children's fantasy play and emotional understanding. J Clin Child Psychol 28:269–277

Turner P, Hetherington R, Turner S, Kosek M (2015) The limits of make-believe. Digital Creativity

Vygotsky LS (1930) The instrumental method in psychology. Available from https://www.marxists.org/archive/vygotsky/works/1930/instrumental.htm. Last retrieved 3 July 2015

Walton KL (1990) Mimesis as make-believe: on the foundations of the representational arts. Harvard University Press, Cambridge

Walton KL (1993) Metaphor and prop oriented make-believe. Eur J Philos 1(1):39–57

Chapter 9
Enactive Mechanism of Make-Belief Games

Zuzanna Rucińska

9.1 Introduction

Make-belief games, such as pretend play games, are typically considered to require mental representations. Mental representations are considered indispensable to explain how one can 'act as if' one thing was another. Mental representations, in turn, are features of cognitivist approaches to make-believe, and cognitivists (Leslie 1987; Nichols and Stich 2000, 2003) propose a mechanistic explanation of pretence. This chapter shows that pretence can be re-described in enactivist terms without the use of mental representations. It uses a particular conception of affordances from ecological psychology (Turvey 1992) to show how else might it be possible to explain pretending that one thing is another. The chapter further shows that with the conception of affordances, we can consider pretence affordances to be present possibilities for play (instead of absent entities that need to be represented). Finally, the chapter argues that even enactivist explanation of pretence is compatible with a type of mechanistic explanation: wide and situated mechanism (Bechtel 2009; Zednik 2011).

The chapter considers what is involved in the best explanation of pretence. It unfolds in the following way. Section 9.2 showcases the two popular explanatory mechanisms of pretence as proposed by cognitivists Leslie (1987) and Nichols and Stich (2000, 2003). It sets the stage for questioning the need to posit mental representations in explaining certain aspects of pretence, and opens up the room for alternative structures that do not posit mental representations in the best explanation of pretence. Section 9.3 proposes approaching pretence from the enactivist perspective. It suggests that a particular conception of affordances as dispositional

Z. Rucińska (✉)
Leiden University, Leiden, Netherlands
e-mail: z.a.rucinska@phil.leidenuniv.nl; z.rucinska@hotmail.com

© Springer International Publishing Switzerland 2016
P. Turner, J.T. Harviainen (eds.), *Digital Make-Believe*,
Human–Computer Interaction Series, DOI 10.1007/978-3-319-29553-4_9

properties of the environment can make affordances explanatorily useful. Section 9.4 explains what an enactive mechanism of pretence might look like, showing how environmental affordances (and corresponding animal effectivities) can form the wide and situated mechanism of pretence. The chapter is a first step towards reconsidering the conceptual bases of make-belief interactions, and has potential to contribute to the search for new models of human-computer interaction. It concludes with suggestions for potential applicability of the affordance-based explanations to virtual environments.

9.2   Cognitive Mechanisms of Pretence

To date, there are at least two developed and interestingly different theoretical accounts of pretence in the literature: *metarepresentational* (Leslie 1987) and *behaviourist* (Perner 1991; Harris and Kavanaugh 1993; Lillard 1994; Nichols and Stich 2000, 2003). These accounts form the standard frameworks for understanding pretence and what best explains it (see Liao and Gendler 2010). They can be considered as explanatory models of pretence, as they feature both a theory about what pretence is (the models assume some pretence characteristics), and propose mechanisms to explain how pretence comes about. These models further attribute specific functions to mental representations, which explain why they were posited in the first place. This section will mainly focus on the mechanisms that the cognitivist models of pretence posit in explaining how make-belief gets achieved. Such exemplar mechanisms are Leslie's (1987) Decoupling Mechanism and Nichols and Stich's (2000) Inference Mechanism. These will be briefly discussed in turn.

A caveat is in order with regard to how the term 'mechanism' will be used in this chapter. Firstly, the pretence scholars often speak of mechanisms on what can only be described as the 'algorithmic level of explanation' on Marr's (1982) scale. This means that they propose mechanisms that explain cognitive phenomena like pretence through representations, targeting how the system does the pretending, without explaining how the mental representations work on the physical level. They do not provide causal explanations on the physical level explanation of how the unorthodox pretence representations get selected. One may have to go deeper into the workings of the human body, including the human brain, to propose explanations of pretence that physically cause the pretence. My explanation will target the same level of explanation as the one proposed by cognitivists, but instead of representations, the explanatory tools will be of affordances. Should a further explanation of the 'deeper' causes of pretence on the physical level explanation be necessary, my account is also open to accommodate a variety of neuroscientific findings.[1]

---

[1] For example, Bruineberg and Rietveld (2014) propose to explain how affordances that invite action 'move' us through a story involving action readiness potentials of the human brain.

To explain pretence phenomena, Leslie (1987) has posited *metarepresenting*. To metarepresent is to represent oneself as the actor who engages in representing the banana as a phone. This requires possession and exercise of the concept 'PRETEND'. The function of metarepresentation is to enable the side-by-side coexistence of the two kinds of representations: primary and pretence representations. Leslie proposed that acts of pretending are best explained by manipulation of representations of how things are pretended to be (*pretence representations*), which are distinct from representations of the real world (*primary representations*).[2] The problem occurs when Leslie tries to explain how perception of a real banana can invoke a "this is a phone" representation, in such a way that the latter is not taken seriously. The primary representations fail to explain how children can engage in symbolic play like the banana-phone play. Here, the pretender is at risk of *representational abuse*. This is the danger of applying the signifier ("banana") and another signifier ("phone") to the very same object in a way that makes no sense. According to Leslie, unless these representations are somehow kept apart (what he calls 'cognitive quarantine'), the pretenders would be at risk of confusing the banana and its properties with those of a phone. Of course, pretenders do not make this sort of mistake. For this reason, Leslie concluded that there must be a *decoupling mechanism* present in the cognitive architecture of those capable of pretence. The decoupling mechanism marks (or makes a copy of) the primary representation ('this is a banana') and decouples it into a pretence representation ('this is a banana'*). According to Leslie, manipulations on the pretence representation can now be made (such as transforming 'this is a banana'* to 'this banana is a telephone') without losing the original representation. Decoupling allows 'normal semantics' to be suspended, and the pretence representation to be treated as a purely formal object (1987, p. 417). As it is part of a metarepresentational model, Leslie's decoupling mechanism requires a *manipulator* (sequence 'I PRETEND'), which manipulates the expression ('this is a banana'*), thereby, allowing for manipulation of the content that is cut free from literal connotations. Moreover, an *interpreter* allows the decoupled expressions to be anchored to parts of primary representations and, thereby, not refer to actual objects (*idem*, p. 418). Finally, *inference rules* are part of the decoupling mechanism. It makes inferences on the already decoupled input (for example, an inference from "this is a phone" to "this can be used to call with"). While Leslie's model has been heavily criticized (see, for example, Harris 1994), his proposal that cognitive quarantine is needed has been influential.

Another proposal of how to explain pretence was elaborated on by Nichols and Stich (2000, 2003). They are the 'behaviourists' of pretence, though they share

---

[2]Primary representations, on Leslie's model, feature in everyday perception and cognition. Their main job is to provide a "literal and sober" account of the world and to represent accurately. For example, the current perceptual situation (there being a banana) is represented by a token "this is a banana."

little to nothing with behaviourism as such.[3] The 'behaviourist' model of pretence emerged as a direct response to Leslie's model; it redefined pretence from 'thinking as if' to 'behaving as if' (hence the name). Its representatives (i.e. Perner 1991; Harris and Kavanaugh 1993; Lillard 1994; Nichols and Stich 2000, 2003) all agree that entertaining a concept 'pretend' and engaging in metarepresenting need not be invoked in order to explain pretence. The behaviourists in the debate on pretence share the assumption that what is required to pretend is simply to be behaving appropriately as if the situation was real. The central claim of this account is that pretenders need only behave 'as-if' a scenario obtained by having beliefs and desires about how to do so appropriately. This does not require the pretenders' beliefs about their own mental states (to metarepresent "I pretend . . ."), the concept 'PRETEND', or the need to conceptualise the mental states of others, in order to preserve the cognitive quarantine.

In some respects, however, the behaviourists are not different from the metarepresentationalists. They still consider pretending to be a cognitively demanding task. Offering a 'cognitive architecture underlying pretence' (p. 125), Nichols and Stich (2000) posit an inference mechanism that incorporates a cluster of smaller mechanisms (e.g., Possible World Box and UpDater). Unlike Leslie, they do not posit special 'pretence representations', or mental representations with pretend contents, to do the explanatory work. Instead, they only speak of 'initial premises', which are akin to Leslie's primary representations, but what takes care of the representational abuse is the special structure of the cognitive mechanism called 'Possible World Box' (henceforth: PWB). The initial premise is an assumption that *decides what is to be pretended*, e.g., that the child is going "to make a phone call with the banana", or in a restaurant play context, "that one person is a waiter and one a customer". The content of the initial premise specifies the impending pretence play episode. The premise is a proposition, which represents a specific situation and which can be evaluated. Initial premises form scripts (hypothetical scenarios or event representations), which detail the way in which certain situations typically unfold. Scripts have plans that guide action or sets of rules of what to do. According to Nichols and Stich, scripts "play an important role in guiding and constraining the description of a possible world which gets elaborated in the course of a pretense episode" (2003, pp. 126–127). They provide general structure to pretence episodes, but need not be themselves accurate descriptions of the world. Moreover, on Nichols and Stich's account, pretence involves a distinct type of attitude: supposing (alongside believing and desiring). The token primary representations, which form initial premises, are what the pretender supposes about what the world would be like. Then, the pretender's "cognitive system must start generating thoughts and actions that would be appropriate if the pretense premise were true" (Nichols and Stich

---

[3]While these accounts are called 'behaviourist', they share little to nothing with psychological behaviourism (Pavlov, Skinner) or logical behaviourism (Ryle). They still represent cognitivist frameworks of explanatory account, referring to beliefs and desires in their theories of cognition and using mental representations in their cognitive explanations.

2000, p. 119). The initial premises enter the PWB, leaving the Belief Box with the true beliefs (e.g. "this is really a banana") and the Desire Box (really wanting to play banana-phone) intact.[4] The PWB contains tokens of primary representations, whose function is "not to represent the world as it is [which is the domain of the Belief Box] or as we'd like it to be [which is the domain of the Desire Box], but rather to represent what the world would be like given some set of assumptions that we may neither believe to be true nor want to be true" (2000, p. 122). In addition, Nichols and Stich posit an "Up-Dater" component of the overall mechanism, whose function is to ensure that the beliefs that go into the PWB remain fresh and intact. Thus, the PWB plays the same role as Leslie's decoupling mechanism, which is to quarantine the pretence-initiating representations, and thereby avoid representational abuse and conceptual confusion (Nichols and Stich 2000, p. 136). This account is said to be simpler than Leslie's as it does not require additional metarepresentational structures, and it provides a clear place for storing intact primary representations (Belief Box). Only the relevant token primary representations that form the initial premise have to be manipulated.

To summarise, it is clear that the main explanatory proposals of pretence posit (mainly mechanistic) structures with mental representations, whose contents are said to do the required explanatory work. Across the models we mainly find contents that are formed of propositions and have conditions of satisfaction.[5] For example, the banana-phone play would not count as pretend play without the child being able to think counterfactual thoughts like 'there is an imaginary voice coming out of this banana', regardless of whether additional metarepresenting is required or not. As is especially clear in the models of Leslie or Nichols and Stich, mental representational contents and cognitive mechanisms are important in explaining *how* pretence occurs. As summarised by Varga (2011), Leslie's account explains the following aspects of pretence: *object substitution* (using an object as if it is something else, e.g., using a banana as a phone); *attribution of false properties* (ascribing a pretend property to something, e.g., pretending that the doll's dry hair is wet); and *making a reference to an absent object* (the invention of an imaginary object, e.g., feeding the doll invisible cake, and referring to it as if it were present). According to Leslie, the primary representations manipulated in the decoupling mechanism explain these capacities, which to Leslie is the having of 'pretence representations' that allows *thinking* as if one thing were another. According to Nichols and Stich, the initial premises manipulated in the PWB component of the overall inference mechanism explain pretence, which they see as *behaving* as if one

---

[4]By a 'box', Nichols and Stich refer to a metaphor, or a "notational device for distinguishing representations that have systematically different functional or computational properties." (2000, p. 136).

[5]Other models of pretence propose the contents to be image-based or formed of motor plans (see, for example, 'Active Imagination Thesis' by van Leeuwen 2011). Whether these contents form mental representations of the necessary kind is, however, debated (see Rucinska 2014b).

thing were another. Whether their explanatory proposals are satisfactory or not will not be assessed in this chapter, although there are reasons to be sceptical of them.[6]

Overall, while there are two distinct models of pretence in the literature, they are similar in at least one interesting way. They commit to some form of mental representationalism, where mental representations are the underlying enablers of the assumed mental abilities, playing various explanatory roles in each model of pretence. However, that is not necessary, as other non-representational structures can be introduced to allow for some of the same functions to be performed, implementing them in a different way. While to date, there is no explanatory model of pretence that is based on the enactive framework, it is possible to seek non-mental representational structures to explain how children play in an imaginative way (Rucinska 2014a) or to explain what guides pretend play (Rucinska 2014b). What is at stake in this chapter is to show what an alternative explanatory mechanism of pretence could look like on the enactive framework. This will be proposed in Sect. 9.4 of this chapter. However, before that, it is important to clarify the tools that the enactivists could use in their explanatory work. Certain conception of Gibsonian affordances can be introduced to the enactivist explanatory model. This will be addressed in the next section.

9.3   Enactivist Model of Pretence: Making Use of Affordances

The term 'affordance' has been used in multiple ways in the ecological, embodied and enactive cognition literature (incl. Gibson (1979/1986, 1982), Turvey (1992), Reed (1996), Chemero (2003, 2009), Noë (2004), Withagen et al. (2012), and Rietveld and Kiverstein (2014)). The concept has been predominant in Gestalt psychology and phenomenology. There is even mention of affordances in the HCI literature, but they are often considered as having limited relevance to HCI due to their vague meaning (see, for example, Kaptelinin and Nardi 2012). This section attempts to mediate this worry, showing how affordances should be conceived of so that they are useful explanatory tools of make-belief.

The only consensus with respect to affordances is that they are possibilities for action. With respect to what they are (properties or relations), where they are

---

[6]For example, it is debatable whether Nichols and Stich's model can claim to be superior to Leslie's model in its economic value and simplicity. Nichols and Stich do not explain why these and not other primary representations form the initial premise, or where the PWB come from. It is also intriguing how the PWB could hold a detailed description of the entire world in which a banana would be a phone; there are presumably close to infinite descriptions that would fit the bill. In addition, this model fails to capture the sense in which the pretence is not serious (for example, it does not explain why children do *not*, in reality, expect someone to pick up on the other side of the 'banana'), unless more descriptions of the relevant kind are added. So as it stands, it is unclear whether there is a benefit in appropriating the cognitivist explanations even of the weak version; there are reasons to believe both models fail in their explanatory role.

located (in the environment or cutting between the environment-animal dichotomy), or how do they work (whether they invite actions or not) is a matter of great debate. I propose that the most fruitful way of thinking about affordances for the purposes of explaining pretence is to conceive of affordances as dispositional properties of the environment (*ala* Turvey 1992).[7] This conception might best serve the explanatory function of affordance-based account of pretence, as it divides the explanatory burden equally between the animal and the environment. Thinking of affordances as dispositional properties of the environment relative to the animal asks for something else to act as the dispositional properties of the animal, relative to the environment. Introducing effectivities (below) as animal-relative counterparts of affordances makes room for the dynamic relationship between the environment and the animal.

The coining of the notion of affordance has been attributed to ecological psychologist James Gibson. Gibson (1979/1986) emphasised the relational nature of affordances, as existing in the environment for the animals. As Gibson famously writes, "The affordances of the environment are what it offers the animal, what it provides or furnishes, either for good or ill" (1979/1986, p. 127). On one interpretation, affordances are to be placed in the environment. They might be thought of as properties of the environment. Chemero (2003) clarifies that to Gibson, "an affordance (. . .) is a resource that the environment offers any animal that has the capabilities to perceive and use it. (. . .) Thus, affordances are properties of the environment but taken relative to an animal" (p. 182). Hence, affordances seem to be properties of the environment, which exist not completely independent of the animal (they 'refer' to the animal), but are mind-independent, or independent of the animal's perceiving of them in the broad sense. However, on another interpretation, Gibson's affordances are not clearly properties of the environment; some quotes suggest that affordances have a peculiar ontological status. For example, in Gibson's own words, "An affordance is neither an objective property nor a subjective property; or it is both if you like. (. . .) It is equally a fact of the environment and a fact of behaviour. It is both physical and psychical, yet neither. An affordance points both ways, to the environment and to the observer" (1979/1986, p. 129). On this description, affordances seem to go beyond mere animal-environment coupling; they occupy an ontological space of their own; perhaps they can be considered as a relation. Also, if it is a 'fact of behaviour' of the animal, it is difficult to understand how they are 'mind-independent'. The seeming inconsistency has sparked a great discussion, and many interpretations of what is the nature of Gibsonian affordances, including how best to think of them, have been proposed since Turvey (1992), Reed (1996), Chemero (2003), Noë (2004), Withagen et al. (2012) or Rietveld and Kiverstein (2014). It is beyond the scope of this chapter to explain how each of these positions differs from each other. What is to be noted, however, is the fact that each of these positions takes a slightly different

---

[7]One may consider these to be relational dispositions of the environment, such as the disposition to elicit certain actions from certain agents in certain circumstances.

stance on what role the environment and the animal play in shaping affordances, which in turn makes a difference on what explanatory role affordances can play.

On the one hand, Reed's conception of affordances would have to commit to the view that the 'phoneness' affordance of the banana exists in the banana, completely independent of any subjects. Reed would further have to commit to saying that, as long as affordances can be used to explain pretence, even 'phoneness' affordance of a banana influenced the types of animals that evolved (human beings), with the capacities to respond to such affordances in phone-like ways. His position is most animal-independent. On the other hand, Varela et al. (1991) disagree that the affordances do not depend in any way upon the perceptually guided activity of the animal (p. 203). If we follow Varela et al., affordances should be understood as dependent on how the animal perceives the world. They seem to place more focus on the capacities of the animal than on the properties of the environment in securing affordances.[8] Hence, Varela et al. promote that affordances only come into existence when there is a self-sustaining organism present; on their view we can only speak of the world affording action when it shows up for animals. To take yet another example, Rietveld and Kiverstein (2014) speak of capacities that could be found in a whole set of animals, or forms of life; the 'phoneness' of a banana would then be found in the *landscape* of affordances. This means that we do not look at dispositions of a particular animal, but look at practices of types of animals. In the case of pretence, they would have to say that there is a practice of playing 'phone' that is part of our 'human' form of life. The practice shapes the landscape of affordances, where cultural niches such as 'phone play' practices exist. On this story, the particular animal is not as important as the animal's socio-cultural context that forms the landscape of affordances. The way of using bananas as phones is independent of the individual, but not independent of the society the individual is part of.

I propose to follow another conception of affordances, inspired by Turvey (1992). His story depicts a dynamic relationship between the objects in the environment and animals, where the object is just as important as the animal that it interacts with. Turvey introduces effectivities, or dispositions of the animals. Effectivities are based on the animal's interaction history with the object. They shape the object to have a disposition that is essentially connected to that animal. Turvey's notion of effectivities can be extended to involve capacities of animals, capabilities, as well as moods, all shaped by histories of interactions. On this story, the banana affords 'phoneness' only if there is a subject with the capacity to play 'phone' with a banana (dispositions that could be shaped by, e.g., the history of interactions with phones) and if there are objects with right dispositions to be like phones (bananas due to their shape and size). It is not a view about emergence of phone qualities

---

[8]Several things they say come close to suggesting this; for example, "the meaning of this or that interaction for a living system is not prescribed from outside but is the result of the organization and history of the system itself (*idem*, p. 157).

in the direct manipulation by the animal of the banana; rather, the idea is that the 'phoneness' affordance, or possibility for action, is residing in the banana only in so far as it is matched with an individual agent who has latent dispositions (prior to the interaction) to manipulate the banana in relevant phone-like ways. The animal does not have to act upon the affordance, but the affordance is there in the virtue of there being an animal that can interact with it. This means that the affordance is in the environment even when the animal is not interacting with the environment; it is there in the sense of being disposed to be taken up by a particular animal should that animal be present.[9] In short, the story can be cast in terms of animal-environment mutuality: just as the objects we shape have a pull on us with respect to how to engage with them (Malafouris 2013), so the affordances of the environment can invite specific behaviours when the right effectivities are in place.

However, Turvey's account appropriated to pretence does not yet explain why we pretend. After all, an object has many affordances and just as many effectivities. What explains which affordance-effectivity pair is actualised that would lead to action? Turvey (1992, p. 180) suggests a right actualising context: "Let Wpq (e.g., a person-climbing-stairs system) $= j(Xp, Zq)$ be composed of different things Z (person) and X (stairs). Let p be a property of X and q be a property of Z. Then p is said to be an affordance of X and q the effectivity of Z (i.e., the complement of p), if and only if there is a third property r such that (i) $Wpq = j(Xp, Zq)$ possesses r; (ii) $Wpq = j(Xp, Zq)$ possesses neither p nor q; (iii) Neither Z nor X possesses r. Thus, a person cannot execute locomotion in the highly particular manner of stair climbing unless a sloped surface is underfoot composed of adjacent steps with suitable dimensions (of rise and horizontal extent). When it is, then the disposition to locomote in this highly particular way is actualised.

To clarify, something can actualise an affordance-effectivity pair if and only if there is a third property given by the context. One such property can be a sloped surface. Applying Turvey's conception of affordances to pretence context, we can explain the banana-phone pretend play using a similar structure. Let Wpq (a child pretend playing that banana is a phone) be composed of different things Z (the child) and X (the banana). Let p (phoneness) be a property of X (banana). Let q ('capacity to play phone with') be a property of Z (the child). Then p (phoneness) is said to be an affordance of X (banana) and the q (capacity to play phone) the effectivity of Z (the child). The effectivity is a complement of the affordance, hence, we can conceive of the effectivity as the flexibility to play 'phone' with, history of interactions with the phone, know-how to use phones, etc. Then, what actualises this affordance-effectivity pair is the right circumstance, such as being in a playful context, which is shaped by the presence of toys, other people playing, or narrative contexts (see Rucinska 2014a). The third property can also be another

---

[9]This is similar to Chemero's (2003) conception of affordances being 'lovely': "Affordances, which are the glue that holds the animal and environment together, exist only in virtue of selection pressure exerted on animals by the normal physical environment. They arise along with the abilities of animals to perceive and take advantage of them" (p. 190).

agent. For example, one is strongly disposed to play phone with the banana when the circumstances are inviting, and such a disposition is brought forth by mere presence of other people who create playful contexts.[10] Once the right context is in play, these factors can invite action.

Turvey's account of affordances is a good candidate for the best conception of affordance to explain pretence, for the following reasons. It allows us to find affordances in the environment, and treat them as real properties of the environment, and as dispositions of the environment relative to the animal. As real properties, pretence affordances are simply present possibilities for action. Instead of absent entities that need to be represented (as 'phones'), the child is simply switching between affordances (from non-pretence ones like eating the banana, to pretence ones like playing phone with it), triggered by the right contextual factors. Hence, cognitive quarantining or decoupling from the 'real' or 'primary' affordance does not need to take place, as there is no 'real' or 'primary' affordance to begin with; the possibilities for action are all equal. However, even if some affordances invite more strongly as they are part of the typical engagements with objects (such as 'canonical' affordances of Costall 2012), and so even if eating the banana invites more strongly, there is no reason to assume that any representational decoupling of the relevant sense is needed to step away from the 'eating' practice to the 'pretend phone' practice; the switching of practices is triggered directly by the context.

Moreover, if we speak of affordances as properties of the environment, and effectivities as properties of animals, we have clear component parts to provide a wide-and-situated mechanistic explanation of pretence. As such, affordances can form explanatory mechanisms that can serve as alternative explanatory mechanisms to the cognitivist ones. For these reasons, it is fruitful to conceive of affordances as dispositional properties of the environment. What such alternative mechanism would look like will be proposed below.

9.4   Introducing Wide and Situated Mechanism

By now, it should be clear that the philosophical frameworks of cognitivism and enactivism make use of very different conceptual tools: mental representations and affordances, respectively. This has implications for what methods of explanation of cognitive phenomena these positions typically rely on: mechanistic explanations vs. covering law explanations, respectively. To secure the claim that possible non-representational explanation of pretence can provide a genuine counter proposal to representational explanation of pretence, it could be shown that enactivists actually use the same explanatory method as cognitivists, which is providing a mechanistic explanation of pretence. To show this, we first have to understand what are the criteria of mechanistic explanations. The section shows that affordance-based

---

[10]See McKitrick (2003) on 'extrinsic dispositions'.

explanations of enactivists, while dynamical, are actually compatible with mechanistic explanations understood in a certain way, but in which there is no reason to think that mental representations figure as proper parts. Such explanatory structure is a *wide and situated mechanism*, which incorporates both the relevant animal-pertaining and environment-pertaining factors as components of its explanatory mechanism, where none of these factors must be mental representations.

Enactivism contrasts cognitivism not only on its theoretical commitments to positing mental representations, but to methodological strategies to studying cognition as well. Many E-theorists, such as radical enactivists, do not seek to explain cognition at all, but re-describe it (see Hutto and Myin 2013). Other E-theorists such as embodied cognition theorists and ecological psychologists, who do attempt to explain cognitive phenomena, rely not on mechanistic explanations, but on providing covering law explanations (Varela et al. 1991; Chemero 2009). The target of this section is to showcase methodological commitments of enactivists in light of the ones of cognitivists, examples of whose methods we have seen in Sect. 9.2.[11]

Enactivists have entirely different approach to studying cognitive phenomena than cognitivists, with whom they disagree on several points. Two of them will be mentioned below. Firstly, according to enactivists, cognition is not first and foremost representation, with respect to both the essence of cognition and its implementation. As Varela et al. (1991) claim, "(Enactivism) questions the centrality of the notion that cognition is fundamentally representation. Behind this notion stand three fundamental assumptions. The first is that we inhabit a world with particular properties, such as length, color, movement, sound, etc. The second is that we pick up or recover these properties by internally representing them. (. . .) We propose as a name the term *enactive* to emphasize the growing conviction that cognition is not the representation of a pregiven world by a pregiven mind but is rather the enactment of a world and a mind on the basis of a history of the variety of actions that a being in the world performs (p. 9)."

Secondly, enactivism proposes the study of living organisms, and describes autopoietic systems in their environments (Varela et al. 1991; De Jaegher and Di Paolo 2007). In this respect, enactivism is modelled on ecology, and ecological approaches stress the dynamic relation between organisms and their environments. That is a sharp methodological contrast to the cognitivist approaches, which focus on manipulation of mental representations or representational mapping in implementation of cognition. Enactivism also stresses the activity of the animals in their

---

[11]For the purposes the argument in this chapter, the distinction between enactivists, radical enactivists, radical embodied cognition scientists and ecological psychologists need not be made, as they all importantly contrast cognitivists in the same way. For example, as Chemero (2009) clarifies, "Ecological psychology's core concepts—perception for action, direct perception, affordances, environmental information—form the core of the embodied cognition movement" (p. 86), and he defines "radical embodied cognitive science as the scientific study of perception, cognition, and action as necessarily embodied phenomenon, using explanatory tools that do not posit mental representations" (pp. 28–29). Hence, for simplicity sake, I will refer to all e-theorists as 'enactivists', as they share lack of positing mental representations.

environments (Hutto and Myin 2013). It considers the animal in its context, focusing on the role of the objects and other animals in this context in shaping the animal cognition (Froese et al. 2013; De Jaegher and Di Paolo 2007). The outcome of taking an enactive approach to cognition is that it finds mentality in the interactions between organisms and environments, not in encapsulated mental representations. It can be concluded that enactivist explanations of cognitive engagements will not posit mental representations, but rather will focus on interactions of the animals with their environments, which dynamically shape their cognition.

In general, enactivists do not provide mechanistic explanations because living things are importantly unlike mechanisms. Instead, they propose covering law explanations. Covering law explanation (Kelso 1995) "relies on a lawlike regularity to deduce properties of the target phenomenon" (Zednik 2011, p. 242). In *The Embodied Mind*, Varela et al. claim that "(...) the overall concern of the enactive approach to perception is not to determine how some perceiver-independent world is to be recovered; it is, rather, to determine the common principles or lawful linkages between sensory and motor systems that explain how action can be perceptually guided in a perceiver-dependent world" (*idem*, p. 173). An example of covering law explanation outside philosophy and other studies of cognition is law of gravity. It provides us with a principle of why objects fall to the ground, explaining this phenomenon without having to posit an underlying mechanism in the object. Dynamical explanation is just a special case of covering-law explanation. Therefore, it may seem that mechanistic explanations are not compatible with dynamical explanations.

Clearly, there seems to be two different kinds of explanatory projects occurring. This is a slight problem for a non-representational alternative explanation of pretence, as it can be argued that enactivists and cognitivists are engaging in different work, hence, they need not be in each other's way (see Aizawa 2014). However, that conclusion also seems principally unfitting the strong contrast between theoretical and methodological commitments provided by both accounts that motivated enactivists to counter cognitivists. Clearly, enactivists should not want to just provide a different explanation to cognitivists, but one that substantially rivals it. This motivates the question: could enactivists propose a mechanistic alternative explanation of cognition? I will argue that they can, but first, it is imperative to clarify what actually is meant by a mechanistic explanation.

It is useful to begin with the most influential conception of a mechanism in contemporary philosophy of science. "A mechanism is a structure performing a function in virtue of its component parts, component operations, and their organization. The orchestrated functioning of the mechanism, manifested in patterns of change over time in properties of its parts and operations, is responsible for one or more phenomena (Bechtel and Abrahamsen 2010, p. 323; see also Machamer et al. 2000; Bechtel and Abrahamsen 2005; Craver 2007)" (in Zednik 2011). Mechanisms have typically two explanatory heuristics: decomposition and location (Bechtel and Richardson 1993; Craver 2007; Zednik 2011). Location refers to the idea that mechanisms typically occupy some space in time. Decomposition can be structural and functional. "Structural decomposition involves breaking a complex system down into a collection of simpler subsystems or parts. (...) Functional decomposition involves re-describing the behavioral phenomenon as a series or organized collection of simpler behaviors or operations" (Zednik 2011, pp. 240–241). Those operations are working parts of the system and are realised in the system from which the target phenomenon arises. This shapes what is to be considered as a mechanistic explanation. According to Zednik (2011), "mechanistic explanation consists of describing the particular organized collection of parts and operations that is responsible for the behavioral regularity being explained" (p. 240). Furthermore, mechanistic explanation is "a form of reductive explanation; phenomena manifested at one level of organization are explained in terms of component parts and operations at lower level(s) of organization (Machamer et al. 2000; Craver 2007; Bechtel 2008)" (p. 261).[12]

Considering these characteristics, it may be clear why speaking of mechanisms and mechanistic explanations have been applied to philosophy by cognitivists. Decomposability seems to fit with cognitivist explanatory strategies, which break down the phenomena they study (e.g., cognition) into smaller component parts (e.g., mental representational structures).[13] Cognitivists also appeal to the location heuristic of the mechanism. The idea is that the cognitive mechanism reflects some sort of internal processing, which is often said to be located in the brain. It would look like mechanistic explanations have a good fit with cognitivist types of explanations. There are two ways to challenge this apparent fit. First is to note Ramsey's (2007) caution against considering mechanistic explanations of cognitive phenomena as necessarily representational. Mere correlations between internal states and inputs do not suffice to amount to a satisfying notion of mental representation as held by cognitivists. Ramsey's argument opens the door for mechanistic explanations to be applied to non-mental representational explanations as well. Hence, second way to challenge the fit between mechanistic explanations and cognitivist explanations is to show that enactivists could also rely on mechanistic explanations.

There are clear reasons why relying on mechanistic explanations have not been popular in enactivism. On the surface, both heuristics of mechanisms do not seem to fit the enactivist framework, making mechanistic explanations unlikely to be appropriated by enactivists at face value. With regard to the decomposability heuristic, enactivists would not study cognition by breaking it down to component

---

[12]Other, yet similar, definitions include Bechtel's (2009): "mechanism is understood as an organized set of parts that perform different operations which are orchestrated so as to realize in the appropriate context the phenomenon in question. The explanation itself consists of representing the mechanism and showing how it realizes the phenomenon (often by simulating its functioning)" (p. 544).

[13]This seems to follow Marr, but that is confused. Marr suggested that his levels of classification are to be treated as independent of one another. What should follow is that, for example, the structure of the mechanism of the algorithmic level should not make a difference to the description of the phenomenon on the highest computational level. However, this is the one key point that many decide *not* to follow Marr on, assuming that the findings about one level will make a difference on the findings about the other (see, for example, Nichols and Stich 2000, p. 11).

parts in virtue of following the principle of Gestalt psychology, namely, that the properties of the parts are not properties of the wholes. As enactivists are interested in studying cognition holistically through a dynamic interaction of the animal in its environment, they would argue against the method of singling out properties of cognition and studying those independently of cognition as a whole.

There is also a clear worry with the location heuristic. If there is a specific location of the cognitive process, it is natural to locate it in the brain. For example, computational models "specify the component operations of a mechanism that are then (in ideal cases) localized in neurobiological component parts" (Zednik 2011, p. 241). Location may imply internalisation of the cognitive processes, such as by encapsulation of the cognitive process in a representational structure, most often found in the brain and realised by neural structures alone. As location of the mechanism suggests its internalisation (and, possibly, representationalism), it is not compatible with non-representationalism and worldly interactionism of the enactive accounts. Finally, another worry might be that mechanistic explanations posit chains of causes and effects, whereas dynamical systems explanations do not, which is why enactive explanations are not mechanistic. The worry has to do with positing inputs and outputs that mechanisms usually mediate. It is the cognitivist approach to understanding cognition that pertains to an input-output relation between the mind and behaviour, whereas the ecological approach as appropriated by enactivists stresses the dynamic relation between the organism and its environment.

However, these heuristics are actually not problematic for potential enactive explanations. The structural decomposition can be made to (minimally) two working parts: animal and environment (see Beer 2003).[14] These components could form a wide-mechanism (to be explained shortly). Also, location is not threatening. As Clark and Chalmers (1998) argued, the mind can extend beyond skin and skull into the world and its objects, such as notebooks. Many enactivists endorse this idea, taking it even further; for example, they argue that the cognitive processes are already *extensive*, or reaching wide into the world (Myin and Zahidi 2015). Hence, make-belief could also be located in the world. Finally, the worry about positing inputs and outputs can be adhered to with the notion of wide and situated mechanism. The wide and situated mechanism has non-hierarchical components that engage in continuous reciprocal causation, and its location is extended, in the sense that the components are distributed in the world. Furthermore, continuous reciprocal causation is how the component parts stand in relation to each other, without proposing that a particular component is the 'input', where the 'output' is the behaviour.

Hence, adhering to wide and situated mechanism is not a worry for an enactive explanation of pretence that has, for instance, affordances in its explanatory toolkit.

---

[14]Beer (2003) relies on the explanatory heuristic of structural decomposition to identify two working parts—the embodied brain on the one hand and the environment on the other (. . .). Then, he provides a detailed dynamical analysis to describe the operations associated with each part (see Zednik 2011, p. 254).

It is possible to understand enactivist claims as compatible with mechanistic explanations, when mechanism is understood in a certain way, as wide (Zednik 2011), and situated (Bechtel 2009). Firstly, Zednik (2011) argues that dynamical explanations "may be uniquely able to describe mechanisms whose components are engaged in complex relationships of continuous reciprocal causation (p. 239), and that dynamical explanations "actually resemble mechanistic explanations rather than covering-law explanations" (p. 245).[15] He argues that dynamical explanations "are well suited for describing extended mechanisms whose components are distributed across brain, body, and the environment" (p. 239). The structural decomposition can be made to (minimally) two working parts: animal and environment (see Beer 2003).[16] Applied to enactivism, the enactive mechanism could involve taking the environment and taking the animal as a single thing, with no representing. For example, animal's know-how can be said to be a component located 'in the body', and the affordance could be said to be located 'in the environment'. Moreover, "insofar as it makes sense to talk of body and environment as the components of a (minimally) cognitive mechanism, that mechanism is extended; its components are distributed across brain, body, and environment" (Zednik 2011, p. 256). The parts and operations of the mechanism are distributed. Additionally, it could include social structures and cultural environment. Moreover, Zednik argues that continuous reciprocal causation implies that the interacting parts do not have static inputs and outputs. This takes care of the problem of input-output structure of traditionally understood mechanisms. The continuous reciprocal causation can be thought of as a form of coupling between the components. As he clarifies, "Coupling is a technical term that applies whenever two or more dynamical systems mutually influence one another's change over time. In the philosophical literature, such mutual influence is more commonly known as continuous reciprocal causation (. . .). Systems B and E are engaged in a relationship of continuous reciprocal causation because each system's behavior is at all times determining, as well as being determined by, the other's" (p. 258). Hence, a wide and situated mechanism does not posit chains of causes and effects, but speaks of dynamical reciprocal causation. This is not a problem for affordance-based explanations. Even understood as components of a wide and situated mechanism, they can causally interact with effectivities and other affordances as part of the mechanism, without being causes of behaviour in the sense of providing inputs, where the outputs are pretencebehaviours. Affordances

---

[15]"Therefore, [he claims] a closer look at dynamical cognitive science will reveal that the extant philosophical conception of mechanistic explanation may have underestimated practicing scientists' willingness and ability to describe increasingly complex and distributed cognitive mechanisms" (p. 239).

[16]Beer (2003) relies on the explanatory heuristic of structural decomposition to identify two working parts—the embodied brain on the one hand and the environment on the other (. . .). Then, he provides a detailed dynamical analysis to describe the operations associated with each part (in Zednik 2011, p. 254).

and can be said to form components of a continuously reciprocating causal system. Thus, what is clear is that affordance-based explanation is compatible with a type of a mechanistic explanation.

Secondly, I propose to follow Bechtel's (2009) notion of a mechanism, whose components interact in complex ways, and which is situated in a wider context. As Bechtel claims, "Accounts of mechanistic explanation have emphasized the importance of looking down—decomposing a mechanism into its parts and operations. (. . .) But once multiple components of a mechanism have been identified, researchers also need to figure out how it is organized—they must look around and determine how to recompose the mechanism. (. . .) Researchers also need to look up—situate a mechanism in its context, which may be a larger mechanism that modulates its behavior. When looking down is combined with looking around and up, mechanistic research results in an integrated, multi-level perspective" (p. 543). By 'looking around and up', Bechtel emphasizes both the organisation of a mechanism and its situatedness in a wider context ('larger mechanism'), where external factors further affect the behaviour of the mechanism. For example, by the original mechanism he refers to the visual system, claiming that it cannot be best understood without also situating it in a context where the animal, or object in the environment, is moving. To explain the mechanism of perception, the movement of the perceiver and objects in the environment should be appealed to, as it impacts what information is received by the visual system. Bechtel claims that is in line with Gibson's notion of "optic flow, the manner in which the visual scene changes as a result of the relative movement of the perceiver and objects in the environment" (Bechtel 2009, p. 558). Thus, he concludes that the mechanism is always situated.[17]

Such understanding of a mechanism (as wide and situated) is compatible with the explanations proposed by enactivists thus far. For instance, Varela et al. (1991) look for 'common principles' or 'lawful linkages' that can be generalised to all perception to explain what colour experience is. However, they look also at the relation of the sensory-motor systems to the external world, one that is perceiver-dependent. Their explanation of colour experience includes the description of the physiognomy of the human eye as well as the influence of the colour concepts of our culture on perception. In that respect, it could be considered as a wide and situated mechanistic explanation. Similarly, Chemero (2009) speaks of component parts of the dynamical system.[18] He looks for a unified model to explain the coupling of brain-body-environment systems and interpersonal (social) coupling, looking for

---

[17]"The behavior of mechanisms is highly dependent on conditions in their environments, including any regularities that occur there. But these are not discovered by looking inside the mechanism to the parts and operations or how these are organized. They must be discovered by examining the environment in which the mechanism operates and employing tools appropriate for such inquiry" (*idem*, p. 559).

[18]"In dynamical explanations, the behavior of a system is typically explained in terms of collective variables (. . .). A collective variable describes the emergent, coordinated activity of the parts that compose a dynamical system, and in some cases this collective variable is causally responsible for the component parts" (p. 199).

models to be applied to data that are "widely applicable and easily extensible" (p. 100). Again, such models could be interpreted in the line of a wide and situated mechanism.

It is clear that neither Varela et al. nor Chemero speak of mechanisms, but provide their explanations as covering law explanations. If that is the case, why is it a good idea to think of them as providing explanations that are compatible with wide and situated mechanistic explanations? Aside securing the claim that enactivists can give genuine alternative explanations of pretence that contrast in relevant ways the cognitivist explanations, speaking of a mechanistic explanation is better for explaining pretence or make-belief than providing a covering law explanation. The reason is that mechanistic explanations are not general, but specific, whereas covering law explanations generalise. Dynamical models understood as providing covering law explanations describe general principles, and thus, account for wide range of cognitive phenomena.[19] Hence, their explanations are not restricted to any particular system. This may be why providing covering law explanations is not most applicable to pretence, because there may not be a unique phenomenon of pretending that would pertain to such a law: pretence comes in various forms (object-substitution, role-play, playing with an imaginary friend, acting, etc.). Since there is no one unitary account of what can be covered by the phenomenon of pretence, it may be difficult to establish whether what we are trying to explain can have one law. Moreover, what follows from generalisation is decontextualisation. Giving laws of pretence would also imply de-contextualizing pretence, so that the component parts of a functioning mechanism would always hold for any pretence case. The worry is that perhaps the phenomenon of pretence is so varied that we can only at best speak of exemplars, or specific tokens of pretence acts. However, we don't have that worry when speaking of a wide and situated mechanism. The mechanism can be multiply realisable, in the sense that different environmental affordances and different animal effectivities, actualised in different contexts, can form the wide and situated mechanistic structures of individual pretence acts, explaining individual pretence acts and accounting for their variety.

To conclude this section, I have shown that there is nothing about the definition of 'mechanism' that is incompatible with enactivist explanations and that if enactivists take on a liberal notion of mechanisms that is wide and situated, their explanations are not different in kind from the explanations of cognitivists. What this results in is that enactivist explanations could be considered as genuine rival explanations to cognitivist explanations in the sense that both could propose a kind of explanation that is scientifically respectable.[20]

---

[19]As Chemero claims, "This would allow scientists to predict that other, similar behaviors would fall under the same covering laws, and then test that prediction" (2009, p. 85).

[20]However, should dynamical explanations be not mechanical in the end, and it turns out that affordance-based alternative is right, then it would have meant that mechanistic explanations are not appropriate to target cognitive phenomena like pretence. Given any outcome of the debate, proposing affordance-based explanations is a valuable contribution.

9.5   Conclusion and Application to HCI

This chapter clarifies what type of explanation of make-believe an enactivist may provide in response to the explanations provided by cognitivists. Many think it is necessary to give an explanation of pretence that posits mental representations. In this chapter I have shown that this is not the only option. I have suggested what an enactivist explanation can look like. It can appropriate a certain notion of affordances found in the literature (Turvey 1992) to show how environmental affordances and animal effectivities can form component parts of a wide and situated mechanism of make-believe. While more work is required to spell out how the component parts interact with each other (for example, to explain exactly how the affordance-effectivity pairs are actualised, or what triggers the right pretence affordances to 'come forward' and invite specific behaviours in the play context), this account sets the stage for developing the affordance-based explanatory structure and applying it to explaining specific pretence cases. While the enactive explanation of pretence will be complex and multi-faceted, it is clear that it need not posit mental representational structures, but it still should be considered a genuine alternative explanation of pretence that stands in sharp contrast to explanations proposed by cognitivists.

Establishing the possibility of conceiving of wide and situated mechanism of pretence could form a nontrivial contribution to various fields studying pretence, such as redefining the possibilities for human-computer interaction in make-believe. Next I suggest some possible implications for the way we theorise the experience of virtual environments. Virtual environments are 'as if' environments, which agents experience as real. This could be explained by the fact that the degree to which agents experience an environment as real depends on the degree to which they are inclined to act in this world, including interacting with the computer.[21] Various forms of interactions with the computer (hence, not just passively receiving visual stimuli, but acting with the features of the computer, such as using a joystick, gaming tools or moving in the virtual environment while wearing the 'gaming glasses') could bring out and intensify the make-belief experience. As Turner (this issue) claims, "the experience of presence or immersion in a movie, game or virtual environment is not automatic but is the product of our deliberate engagement with (. . .) the world" (p. 1). However, decoupling understood as 'stepping away' from the world by representing it 'as pretend' is no longer necessary with the affordance-based account of a wide and situated mechanism of pretence. One is simply attuned to the different possibilities for action (including make-believe possibilities) when one is directly engaging with the computer, and the virtual environment forms the right actualising context. Moreover, the wide and situated mechanism approach to make-believe is compatible with situated accounts of HCI.Acknowledging that the

---

[21]Thanks to Marc Slors for suggesting this point.

environment is more than a context in which gaming occurs, but active component of the gaming experience, supports the need to look for ways to adapt the computer to the user.[22]

References

Aizawa K (2014) The enactivist revolution. Avant 5(2):19–42

Bechtel W (2008) Mental mechanisms: philosophical perspectives on cognitive neuroscience. Routledge, London

Bechtel W (2009) Explanation: mechanism, modularity, and situated cognition. In: Robbins P, Aydede M (eds) Cambridge handbook of situated cognition. Cambridge University Press, Cambridge, MA, pp 155–170

Bechtel W, Richardson RC (1993) Discovering complexity: decomposition and localization as strategies in scientific research. Princeton University Press, Princeton

Bechtel W, Abrahamsen A (2005) Explanation: a mechanist alternative. Studies in history and philosophy of biological and biomedical sciences 36:421–441

Bechtel W, Abrahamsen A (2010) Dynamic mechanistic explanation: computational modeling of Circadian rhythms as an exemplar for cognitive science. Studies in History and Philosophy of Science A 1:321–333

Beer RD (2003) The dynamics of active categorical perception in an evolved model agent. Adaptive Behavior 11(4):209–243

Bruineberg J, Rietveld E (2014) Self-organization, free energy minimization, and optimal grip on a field of affordances. Front Hum Neurosci. doi:10.3389/fnhum.2014.00599

Chemero A (2003) An outline of a theory of affordances. Ecol Psychol 15(2):181–195

Chemero A (2009) Radical embodied cognitive science. MIT Press, Cambridge, MA

Clark A, Chalmers D (1998) The extended mind. Analysis 58(1):7–19

Costall A (2012) Canonical affordances in context. AVANT 3(2):85–93

Craver C (2007) Explaining the brain. Oxford University Press, Oxford

De Jaegher H, Di Paolo E (2007) Participatory sense-making: an enactive approach to social cognition. Phenomenol Cogn Sci 6(4):485–507

Froese T, Gershenson C, Rosenblueth DA (2013) The dynamically extended mind. In: Evolutionary computation (CEC), 2013 IEEE congress on IEEE, pp 1419–1426

Gibson JJ (1979/1986) The ecological approach to visual perception. Houghton Mifflin, Boston

Harris PL (1994) Understanding pretense. In: Lewis C, Mitchell P (eds) Children's early understanding of mind: origins and development. Lawrence Erlbaum Associates, Hillsdale, pp 235–259

Harris PL, Kavanaugh RD (1993) Young children's understanding of pretense. Monogr Soc Res Child Dev 58:1

Hutto DD, Myin E (2013) Radicalizing enactivism: basic minds without content. MIT Press, Cambridge

Kaptelinin V, Nardi B (2012) Affordances in HCI: toward a mediated action perspective. In: Proceedings of the SIGCHI conference on human factors in computing systems. ACM, pp 967–976

Kelso JAS (1995) Dynamic patterns: the self-organization of brain and behavior. MIT Press, Cambridge, MA

---

[22] As Mills and Scholtz (2002) propose, "researchers must find a means to endow cyberspace with a better understanding of the physical and logical world in which people live and work" (p. 4).

Leslie A (1987) Pretense and representation: the origins of "theory of mind". Psychol Rev 94: 412–426

Liao S, Gendler T (2010) Pretence and imagination. Wiley Interdiscip Rev Cogn Sci 2(1):79–94

Lillard A (1994) Making sense of pretense. In: Lewis C, Mitchell P (eds) Children's early understanding of mind: origins and development. Lawrence Erlbaum Associates, Hillsdale, pp 211–234

Machamer P, Darden L, Craver C (2000) Thinking about mechanisms. Philos Sci 67:1–25

Malafouris L (2013) How things shape the mind. MIT Press, Cambridge, MA

Marr D (1982) Vision. Holt, New York

McKitrick J (2003) A case for extrinsic dispositions. Australas J Philos 81(2):155–174

Mills KL, Scholtz, J (2002) Situated computing: the next frontier for HCI research. National Institute of Standards and Technology Gaithersburg MD Information Technology Laboratory

Myin E, Zahidi K (2015) The extent of memory: from extended to extensive mind. In:Moyal-Sharrock D, Munz V, Coliva A (eds) Mind, language & action, proceedings of the 36th international Wittgenstein symposium. Ontos Verlag, Berlin, Germany

Nichols S, Stich S (2000) A cognitive theory of pretense. Cognition 74:115–147

Nichols S, Stich S (2003) Mindreading: an integrated account of pretence, self-awareness and understanding of other minds. Oxford University Press, Oxford

Noë A (2004) Action in perception. MIT Press, Cambridge, MA

Perner J (1991) Understanding the representational mind. MIT Press, Cambridge, MA

Ramsey WM (2007) Representation reconsidered. Cambridge University Press, New York

Reed ES (1996) Encountering the world. Oxford University Press, New York

Rietveld E, Kiverstein J (2014) A rich landscape of affordances. Ecol Psychol 26(4):325–352

Rucińska Z (2014a) Basic pretending as sensorimotor engagement? Lessons from sensorimotor theory for the debate on pretence. In: Bishop JM, Martin AO (eds) Contemporary sensorimotor theory: studies in applied philosophy, epistemology and rational ethics 15. Springer, Cham/New York, pp 175–187

Rucińska Z (2014b) What guides pretence? Towards the interactive and the narrative approaches. Phenomenol Cogn Sci 13(3):1–17

Turvey MT (1992) Affordances and prospective control: an outline of the ontology. Ecol Psychol 4(3):173–187

Van Leeuwen N (2011) Imagination is where the action is. J Philos 108(2):55–77

Varela FJ, Thompson E, Rosch E (1991) The embodied mind: cognitive science and human experience. MIT Press, Cambridge, MA

Varga S (2011) Pretence, social cognition and self-knowledge in autism. Psychopathology 44:46–52

Withagen R, de Poel HJ, Arauja D, Pepping G (2012) Affordances can invite behaviour: reconsidering the relationship between affordances and agency. New Ideas Psychol 30: 250–258

Zednik C (2011) The nature of dynamical explanation*. Philos Sci 78(2):238–263

Chapter 10
Immanent Story Worlds: The Making of Punchdrunk's *The Drowned Man: A Hollywood Fable*

Carina Westling

Coyne's critique of the rationalist modernist perspective in information technology proposes the relevance of a postmodernist perspective, drawing on Derrida's deconstruction of the metaphysical and logocentrism (Coyne 1995: 102–104). Derrida's contemporaries Deleuze and Lyotard also sought to deconstruct the metaphysical as the undeclared totalising principle of liberal humanism; Deleuze via establishing the dichotomy of the transcendental and immanence in his critique of the Cartesian subject-event relationship (Deleuze 2014: 203), and Lyotard in his discussion of narrative and scientific knowledge generation (Lyotard 1984). Twenty years after Coyne's critique, the postmodernist perspective on information technologies is still not fully established in the design and analysis of human-computer interaction, although media theorists in the interim period, e.g. Hayles (2002) and Galloway (2004), have addressed the subject in their critique of the totalising influence present within both cyber-Romanticism and distributed network protocols, respectively. In the interest of furthering a postmodern (or even post-digital) approach to the design of interactive storyworlds, this study aims to identify principles that counter or disable the facilitation of transcendental (totalising) structures and support an immanent subject-event relationship through analysis of the work of theatre company Punchdrunk, pioneers of immersive theatre as interactive systems in physical space. The enquiry was formed around an analysis of the conditions of making and experiencing storyworlds during and after the build and run of *The Drowned Man* (beginning in spring 2012 and finishing in the autumn of 2014), with part of the research occurring as a participant study within the design team, complemented with semi-structured interviews with members of the company ('Com') and audience ('Aud') participants. The objective of the research was to gather observational data from the making of and participation in

C. Westling (✉)
Media and Cultural Studies, University of Sussex, Brighton, UK
e-mail: C.E.I.Westling@sussex.ac.uk

© Springer International Publishing Switzerland 2016
P. Turner, J.T. Harviainen (eds.), *Digital Make-Believe*,
Human–Computer Interaction Series, DOI 10.1007/978-3-319-29553-4_10

161

live Punchdrunk productions. Further data was gathered on social media, followed by analyses of lay reviews on TripAdvisor and the Punchdrunk fandom discourses on Facebook and Tumblr. The concluding section of this chapter proposes three features of Punchdrunk's work that are key to immanence and can be implemented in digital interaction design, and applies the conclusion to the reported outcomes of Punchdrunk's digital R&D project with MIT (Digital R&D Fund For the Arts 2012).

10.1   The Punchdrunk Formula

The Punchdrunk productions referred to in this chapter are three-dimensional interactive sets housing a labyrinthine story world with story fragments embedded in the set detail and enacted by overt (performers) agents, supported by covert (Black Masks) agents. Participating audience members coming into this world are expected to assume agency in order to compose and complete 'their' story, with no guidance beyond recommendations to explore and follow what takes their interest. In 2013, Punchdrunk began building the production *The Drowned Man – A Hollywood Fable* in the old sorting offices at Paddington, London. The company had at that point been running *Sleep No More*, an adaptation of Shakespeare's *Macbeth*, in New York for 2 years. The story world of *Sleep No More* takes place in the fictional McKittrick's Hotel, which had been created in over 100 fully realised and interactive rooms over five floors in an old warehouse accommodating 400 audience members per night, but *The Drowned Man*, based on Büchner's *Woyzeck*, was to exceed this in scope, with 170 rooms distributed over four floors occupying 150,000 sq ft, accommodating 600 audience members every night.

The interactive sets constructed from a vast range of materials: furniture, books, cars, caravans, live trees and, in the case of *The Drowned Man*, 3.5 tonnes of sand. Story elements are encoded in layered metaphor and embedded into the sets from the level of architecture to set detail, including the way the space is shaped and furnished, with hidden references in books, drawers, purses and documents to be found throughout. Sufficiently inquisitive audience members who choose to engage with the sets will find a level of resolution that aims to be 'cinematic' but in reality exceeds that. Audiences do not have seats and roam the sets on the same level as the actors, free to explore set detail as closely as they would under any normal conditions outside of the performance space. Prior to the show, they are advised to be inquisitive and proactive, and to follow performers that interest them as the narrative is played out across the entire set, without indications of where and when participants can find scenes as they are acted. There are no raised or otherwise designated stages, and audiences and actors share the sets and the performance environment. Stagehands and stage managers known as Black Masks operate as mediators between the production and audiences; hidden within the set unless direction of participants is needed, when they emerge from the shadows to interact with audience members wordlessly, using specific techniques for interaction to preserve the integrity of the story world:

[. . .] the Black Mask workshops were often really interesting. And how easy you can move an audience member, or get them not to do something – just by shaking your head, making eye contact and shaking your head, and they'd put the prop back. And you couldn't talk to them either; it's all sign language [. . .] The main thing about moving an audience member is not to make them jump, so if you put your hand on their shoulder the likelihood is they'll do that, and then it'll pull them out of the show. Or you know, break that wall. So everything was sort of very in-motion (Com02).

Audience members must compose their own story from story elements embedded in the set and played out by actors/performer in no given order, under disorientation conditions created by labyrinthine floor plans in near darkness. The sets are so vast that audience members may find themselves completely alone at times, and without immediately discernible plot fragments to follow. They are free to interact with the set: open drawers, rifle through bags, books, rooms, and examine every object, as they may hold clues to the storyline. This repeats nightly during production runs of 1–4 years (and counting).

Punchdrunk audiences fall into two relatively well-defined groups: those who come away with extremely positive experiences, and those who find it an unsatisfactory experience. The latter (approximately 15 % of total audience numbers, based on an analysis of lay reviews online; $n = 708$) (Tripadvisor 2015a, b) tend to find the lack of central presentation and narrative overly demanding, and as there is no alternative option for participation without assuming agency and taking active pursuit, a traditional approach (expecting a centrally presented story arc) will result in disappointment. In spite of this, the company has gained a significant following and a reputation for creating extraordinary shows, and many fans travel the world to go to their shows. Some 'Superfans' visit the same show in excess of 100 times, and many visit dozens of times, documenting and cataloguing their experiences in online fandom communities.

Like *Sleep No More*, which at the time of writing is still playing in New York, *The Drowned Man* was 3 h long, with 12 h-long interwoven main story loops comprising 12 scenes, enacted across 12 story zones, repeating three times with slight variations. There were no intermissions or natural pauses, and audiences were on foot for the duration of the show, often running through the space and up and down stairs in pursuit of performers. The lighting was minimal, and the narratives were fragmented, layered and looping rather than linear. The 12 main character loops of *The Drowned Man* were sparingly scripted in regard of dialogue and relying primarily on physical acting. Due to the number of possible permutations, it was not possible to experience all of the story loops during one visit. Many 'Superfans' visited dozens of times and still could not individually exhaust the possibilities for experience and narrative combinations.

The structure of the formula used in these productions suggests the relevance of an analysis based on regarding them as not just theatre, but interactive systems. Behind the scenes, Punchdrunk productions are run like clockwork, as the cast and the Black Masks need to be in the right place at the right time, to enact physically demanding story loops that overlap and cross throughout the sets, with choreographic precision and quick connections while pursued by free-roaming groups of audience members. The sheer scale and ambition of the productions, as well as the volume of visitors (400/night for *Sleep No More*, 600/night for *The Drowned Man*), require the system to be robust and consistently delivering a high quality experience to the majority of the participating audiences, while accepting that a relatively stable percentage of audience members will find the experience strongly aversive.

10.2 Embodied Making

Punchdrunk have developed a sophisticated embodied methodology for 'thinking with things' and thinking with bodies. During the build, and even before the sets have taken shape, performers and designers refer to the production as 'the world' – held together by multimodal communication and infused with a shared aesthetic, emanating from the meta-narrative of the company itself. Felix Barrett and Maxine Doyle, joint creative directors of the company, work with a team of designers and choreographers who interpret and distribute creative directions throughout the larger team for implementation and further interpretation, with nested iterations proliferating throughout the process:

> The process necessitates for it to be constantly evolving and changing, which can be hugely frustrating, so you could be going down one thread and then it would change, but that allowance keeps it fresh and I think that's why it has the result it does on people, it's never kind of, nothing remains stagnant, because if your performer's got one, you know he developed some new story, then the whole thing's got room for manoeuvre, so it's . . . you . . . but that kind of working process, you're going back and forth and you know, it can take ten times as long (Com03).

Approximately 500 people were directly involved with the build and run of *The Drowned Man*; the majority contributing with skilled interpretation of the narrative in physical form through relayed communication, performing or making. This methodology for making encourages and depends on distributed agency, generating layered meaning through multi-step devising and a process intensity that embeds metaphor within the set to a depth that cannot be fully known even by directors of the company. The detail is realised to such a degree that it in some instances may go unnoticed, but is nevertheless regarded as essential to the substance of the experience:

> And there's always in the back of your minds that . . . you might be doing ten processes that no one is ever going to notice, but if it catches one persons attention then it's worth it, you know? And there's lot of stuff that we kind of design completely and it ends up being in the dark: it's something that you're . . . that without it you can kind of see, you know it's just like . . . there's something in the shadows, that you know is there, but that's kind of . . . [gesturing to indicate weight or heaviness] (Com03)

While the creative directors disseminate and inspire a shared aesthetic, the company employs a design methodology that hides the full extent of details from full view, thereby ensuring that the production is not fully known or controlled centrally or peripherally, only collectively, exemplifying distributed cognition. Even then, the stories are not fully formed until they are realised by participating audiences, who will combine and interpret story elements in ways that are unique to each participant, and therefore unknowable to the company as well as other audience members.

Punchdrunk are regarded as pioneers of immersive theatre, but their work is perhaps better termed immanent theatre: acentric principles pervade design processes, set architecture and narrative structure, and makers and audiences are positioned within the work and on the same level, disallowing the Cartesian relationship between subject and event that traditional theatre design, as well as much of interaction design, embodies. Devising is key to their design methodology, and continues throughout the run of the production, with adjustments made to both set and acting in response to how live audiences move and interact with the set. Actors and designers working in direct physical contact with the work and its performance are given significant freedom to express and develop the interface at close range. The emphasis on a close-range perspective during the making of and participation in the work emerges as a key element of the company's aesthetic and design methodology, and opens their work up for critical understanding according to the spatial theories of de Certeau and Deleuze, particularly in regard of how concepts of space reflect organisational principles and orders.

The importance of a close-range relation with the interface, and the detailed engagement with and articulation of the interface and interactions that results from it, is confirmed by it being mirrored on both sides of the interface, i.e. by both designers and participating audience members:

> And without feeling like "why am I here, and this feels like it's trying far too hard to kind of, live up to something that it doesn't." But when I got there it really did, I just loved it; I just thought it was great... I just left...I was forced to leave all my cynicism at the door. [. . .] The scale of how much detail and planning has gone into it was, I think, really apparent (Aud02).

Several of the interviewed participants in this study remarked on how their psychological immersion was a direct result of recognising how much work had been invested in the interface, as made evident by its aesthetic characteristics. Another participant commented in particular detail on the experience in terms that suggest a state of immanence, where critical distance has collapsed into elated psychological immersion:

> I know it's for entertainment, but it needed to exist. And it felt like this culmination of like so many different talents, and they must've been influenced by so many other different talents over the course of their careers, who were, you know again, going back. So it was like, it felt like, my tiny little pinpoint experience of it, it felt like it was such, I don't know, I just felt at the same time so miniscule, my little eyes looking at this thing, but so infinite at the same time. And then kind of...quite thankful? But also, it was probably just kind of like, joyful immersion, as well – like forced immersion. [. . .] if people can make you fall off the cliff face of consciousness, then you drop into this pool of like, eternal oneness. [. . .] (Aud05).

These remarks suggest that the process-intense design methodology of the company, where embodied cognition in the form of iterative devising is central, communicates across the interface layer and allows audiences to suspend disbelief and assume an immanent subject position in relation to the work: the collective imagining of the story world that guided its realisation throughout the design process was given sufficiently articulated form to fully immerse the participant. This would not have been possible without drawing on the interpretative templates, or narratives, that audiences bring into the space. The reflexive process, where the subject creates meaning from their experiences through narrative, and subsequently enact story worlds against the background of this meaning, is exemplified in the way story worlds emerge, merge and extend through being called-upon and named by the company; interpreted and embodied by designers and performers, and completed, re-interpreted and enacted by audience members.

10.3   In the Beginning Was the Story

In order to be engaging, story worlds require an appropriate balance between rules and possibilities. According to Caillois, all play falls somewhere on the *ludus-paidia* axis; some forms are more rule-based and tend toward *ludus*, others are more focused on unsettling the prevailing order, and are closer to *paidia* (Caillois 2001: 27). De Certeau's theory of space and place offers a more articulated theory that emphasises the importance of story to the making, maintenance and destabilisation of thought-worlds and that which emanates from, and is materialised through, thought-worlds. De Certeau (1988: 117) discusses place as a site or location that is an expression of order, regulation and control, and contrasts it with space, which is dynamically determined by actions; extending through exploration at close range. According to de Certeau's definition, place is defined by constructions or constructs (e.g. buildings, plans, hierarchies; imposing or implementing principles and order), while space is dynamically actualised by the "operations [...] of historical subjects" (Certeau 1988: 118).

De Certeau's treatment of these concepts follows from the meaning of the French *lieu* (place), and *espace* (space). *Lieu* is derived from the Latin *locus*; location in relation to a definition or characterisation, a subdivision of 'social space', perceived in relation to a specific purpose. It can refer to an occasion or a specific instance in a context, as in an appropriate (or inappropriate) moment for a particular action or statement, the situation of which is potentially both spatially and temporally bound. Place/*lieu* describes locations within hierarchies, situations, constructs that stabilise and establish positions and social order. The verb forms of 'place' and 'space' make the differentiation clearer: 'to place' means to position, to set, while 'to space' implies an act of extension. The French noun *espace* (space) is derived from the Latin *spatium*, and is close to the meaning of the English 'extent', as in 'extension of (time or space)'; a field of directions and dynamic properties such as movement and time. De Certeau specifies that space occurs as a function of dynamic time and location, and that space/*espace* only exists as it is performed, or practiced (Certeau 1988: 117).

The enactment of space is thus an act of negotiation: iterative or adaptive movement through a terrain that, in the course of progression, presents a succession of conditions, circumstances, limitations and affordances.

De Certeaus definitions and differentiation of space and place form around a discussion of narrative; storytelling as an act of practiced space; the creation, unfolding and extension of a storytime and –place: "Its discourse is characterized more by a way of *exercising itself* than by the thing it indicates." (Certeau 1988: 79, original emphasis). Walking, which can be expanded to include other spatial practices, is emphasised as a form of spatial discourse through which alternative narratives can overwrite the order presented by the city. Narratives, which are dependent on memory for their creation and interpretation, connect place and space, and transform one into the other; they "organise the play of changing relationships between places and spaces" (Certeau 1988: 118). In Punchdrunk's work, narrative is embodied in and produced by the set, performers and audience members through a collaborative process or negotiation:

> [...] you're sort of in it together, and it's a negotiation. I think a negotiation between audience and...the space and the performers, and everything that's going on. [...] and I think that the space does that as much as the performers (Com04).

According to de Certeau, both the making and the telling of stories are spatial practices; unfoldings or extensions of space that negotiate a terrain composed of places. In the course of doing so, story-journeys can both define and undo places. De Certeau's theory of place and space, and its implications for the founding, negotiation and unsettling of story worlds, thus underpins the way we understand the world through discursive practices, which can be embodied as well as told as stories of make-believe. In Punchdrunk's work, this positions the participant *as* an embodied story or nexus of storylines, in an unfolding process of meaning-making that negotiates between disorientation and embedded story elements through making physical and cognitive connections.

The concept of reality as discursively constructed and maintained supports early play theory, which suggests that law, war and judiciary processes originated in play behaviours, and that play underpins the formal patterns that are the foundations of civilisation (Huizinga 1955: 76, 100–101). What, then, is *not* make-believe, if that which we consider civilisation is founded on make-believe? The story of man as distinct from his domains and transcending our animal origin may be told in and through art, literature, science and technology, but it is no less a story. The posthuman discourses of Hayles (1999, 2002) and Braidotti (2013) touch, via their critique of man, on both Huizinga's (1955) and Sutton-Smith's (2001) work on play theory, as they insist on the ambiguity of the boundaries between us and not-us.

> [...] the human who inhabits the information-rich environments of contemporary technological societies knows that the dynamic and fluctuating boundaries of her embodied cognitions develop in relation to other cognizing agents embedded throughout the environment (Hayles 2002: 303)

The fundamental instability of identity, and its dependence of memory and narratives that unfold in co-relation with the environment of the subject, is not just revealed, but enacted in the acentric story worlds of Punchdrunk. Deeper investigation of the interlocking narratives in *The Drowned Man* reveal the doubling of the Wendy/William (for Woyzeck) Marshall/Mary (for Marie) character pair in *Woyzeck*, with genders switched to deprioritise individuality in favour of narrative. The main story is further supplemented with characters from *The Day of the Locust*, elements of news stories of the era in which the play takes place, and what the company calls 'superstitions', further undermining the concept of inviolable identity, and highlighting the capacity of narratives to weave through and in between stories, maintaining their coherence and meaning by travelling with individual and collective memory, as stowaways or known passengers. Through the embodied pursuit of meaning by walking, running, chasing, searching, examining and connecting narrative motifs, audience participants *become* stories unfolding in space.

The sublime fear of becoming-other (Braidotti 2013: 3) has enduring fascination in the world of stories and make-believe, and transformations are a key motif in our oldest stories from the Bible, through the Grimm fairy tales, to modern-day cyborgian fantasies. Hayles, Braidotti and Clarke draw on this motif in discussions of the posthuman not as a transhumanist machine fantasy that promises to liberate the purely rational man from the imperfect flesh, but as a fundamentally relational subject who's "cognition is a systemic activity distributed throughout the environment and actuated by a variety of actors, only some of which are human" (Hayles 2002: 303), and who is in a two-way relationship with their environment. While focusing on our relationship to technology, and in particular our interaction with information technology, the posthumanist discourse incorporates a post-anthropocentric perspective that challenges the *doxa* that separates man from animals and mind from body, suggesting that we de-polarise our constructs of nature and culture and rethink our existential locale as a "nature-culture continuum" (Braidotti 2013: 92) where technology is part of an environment we have always existed within in a mutually shaping relationship. Clarke writes of stories of metamorphosis that they "oscillate in the space between psychic constructions and social discourses" – a space where social and psychic systems interpenetrate (Clarke 2008: 158). Metamorphosis, then, emerges as a narrative motif we use to regulate, through story-play, transcendent longings and the fear of dissolution on this nature-culture continuum that no longer allows us to regard our identity, as a species and as individuals, as distinct from all else; exceptional and transcending the bounds of the animal body.

If metamorphosis is the play child of make-believe and the sublime fear of dissolution, normative reality is configured to reinforce the exceptionalist supremacy of man. Deleuze critiques the Cartesian perspective, and the *Cogito* on which it is based, as fundamentally flawed, as it relies on eight transcendental postulates (Deleuze 2014: 217), two of which being the formation of problems in relation to their solvability and the externalisation of fault. The dogmatic structure of thought that underpins the Cartesian perspective is thus reliant on the exclusion of uncertainty: an impossibility that reveals the make-believe origins of the Cartesian subject position expressed in the *Cogito*.

In place of the impossibility of a subject position outside the system in which we exist, Deleuze and the posthumanist discourse proposes immanence, embedding man within a culture-nature continuum, intrinsically complicit in the formation of reality as it is created. Perhaps, then, what makes us Man is the making of man, particularly our capacity for make-believe. In our world-building capacity, we might therefore be called *homo fabulans*, rather than *homo ludens*. If one accepts Deleuze's argument that the Cartesian perspective is fundamentally flawed and that we are telling ourselves transcendent stories of gods, animals, and the god-like man from within a plane of immanence, the telling of man, and the embodied story worlds that emanate from the telling of man, collapse into one creative act and one creative substance, extending across media and thought-worlds.

Metamorphosis invites art and science to negotiate the fear of becoming-other and differentiate from *doxa* in order to realise dynamic possibilities. Clarke, in his analysis of science fiction texts, and Hayles and Braidotti in their critique of the modernist cyborgian fantasy, emphasise ambiguity in their posthuman discourses, perhaps because ambiguity and uncertain definitions are so uncomfortable to so many. Deleuze, in his analysis of Artaud's work, states that difficulty is not "a de facto state of affairs, but *de jure* structure of thought" (Deleuze 2014: 192–193), suggesting that discomfort is an essential part of differential thought processes, abstract or embodied. The discomfort of ambiguity can be framed and interpreted as pleasurable: audience members who were interviewed for this study of Punchdrunk's work, and the ~80 % of highly positive lay reviews gathered from a much larger compound sample of visitors to *The Drowned Man* and *Sleep No More* on Tripadvisor, associate disorientation and challenge with positive arousal and exploratory strategies as well as ambiguous psychological states (including immersion and dreamlike states). The subset of Tripadvisor reviews that were highly negative (~15 %) used terms such as confusing, disorientating, alienating, disorganised, uncomfortable and tiring to describe their experiences (Tripadvisor 2015a, b), suggesting a polarised response to ambiguity and uncertainty, based on interpretative framing.

10.4   Complicity in Becoming-Other

The sublime in art, according to Lyotard, is a psychologically profound experience associated with the secondary privation of a threat. Secondary in that the soul is "deprived of the threat of being deprived of light, language, life" (Lyotard 1991: 99), otherwise commonly described as the dissolution of being. The nested deprivation described by Lyotard can be experienced in art, with the subject taking a position in relation to the event that, in traditionally presented art, is outside the frame of the depicted threat. In the work of Caspar David Friedrich, Turner and other painters of the Romantic sublime, the primary threat (of dissolution of being, or deprivation of "light, language, life") is often represented as man before vast and raging forms of nature; avalanches, storms at sea, or the plunging abyss of a gorge.

Nature, here, symbolises the unknowable beyond the meaning made by man, and the definitions of being associated with that meaning. The posthumanist discourse seeks to redefine human-being through accentuating relationality, ambiguity and opening towards becoming-other (Braidotti 2013: 3), which calls for a re-framing of the fear of dissolution.

The sublime experience, where fear is rendered pleasurable, depends on threat being twice removed: once through representation and the second time through framing or containment. In traditional theatre, television, cinema and screen-presented computer games, this framing is achieved in a similar fashion to painting, by physical (visual) containment, where the subject-event relationship remains mapped to the Cartesian concept where that which is observed can be regarded within a three-dimensional grid (albeit flattened within the frame): a transcendent subject position. In Punchdrunk shows this is disallowed, as the subject position is within the work, engulfed in a set designed to be disorientating which temporarily deprives the participant of light (the sets are very dark) and language (audiences are not permitted to speak within the performance space). The first privation, the sublimation of threat by representation, is already present: the experience is an artistic representation of an acentric system, presented as puzzle with missing pieces where the only meaning that can be extracted has to be produced through completion and deduction by participants, whether 'real' or 'imaginary'. The final threat defined by Lyotard is deprivation of life. While the company boldly deprive audiences of light and language, they are naturally not deprived of life, although they are temporarily deprived of their quotidian identity. Audiences are required to be masked during the performance, and are given a version of the Venetian *Bauta* mask, adapted by the company so as to be more androgynous and resembling the Grey Alien of science fiction lore, of undetermined gender and species. The effects of wearing a mask for long durations are well documented, and include the deprioritisation of the day-to-day identity of the wearer, as well as the licence associated with anonymity; a function of the partial dissolution of the social contract with which the quotidian identity is enmeshed.

The framing that the secondary privation of sublime experience calls for cannot be achieved traditionally with a subject position within the work. Instead, the containment of the experience that allows it to be rendered sublime has to be provided by the participant, in the form of entering a play state. The physical presentation of the work facilitates the establishment of a bounded zone for the play state or, using Huizinga's definition, a magic circle, as the experience is limited in time (3 h) and space (the story world is contained within a building). The assumption of a play frame of mind is an expression of agency in relation to an experience, which may go some way towards explaining why Punchdrunk's theatre polarises their audiences so sharply. The agency required to enter a play state, albeit encouraged and supported by the design of the experience, remains with the participant, and voluntariness lies within the nature of play. The play state allows the player to commit voluntarily to the situation while hiding their complicity to themselves in order to support make-believe:

It was very dreamlike…erm…it was dreamlike without being pretentious. Without kind of trying to be dreamlike. I genuinely felt, with the mask on, completely passive. That was a really new experience for me, feeling completely passive. Also, while walking around, and you know, like, your body is really active but you're not expected to intervene unless asked, and.. and I remember at one point I tried to cross a room while the actors were dancing, and…. You know, after being told "explore!" like this, I thought, "I will just cross the room", and I actually got stopped by one of the…kind of 'bouncers'… not bouncers but the kind of people, and physically stopped. They were like "you can't pass the room right now". Like there was all of these kind of, just kind of quite disconcerting experiences (Aud02)

The 'bouncers' referred to here were the Black Masks, acting as mediators between the interface (set and acting) and audience. Dressed and masked in black, their attire is designed to allow them to move unseen in the shadows of the set, only stepping forward to interact wordlessly with audience members in order to prevent disruption of performances if needed, and in the event of health and safety risks. While there were approximately 50 Black Masks working every night (stage managers and front of house staff combined), for the most part they were invisible and an audience member entering a room could have the sensation that they were completely alone, inviting the surreptitious licence one might experience if left alone in a department store or museum at night.

As the formation of meaning requires active participation in the composition of narrative fragments into a whole (although that will not be identical to another participant's version), agency and the assumption of contributory authorship remains central to 'successful' participation, meaning that it is entirely possible to fail by remaining passive. This is not exclusive to Punchdrunk's work; much of the performance art and performance theatre that has emerged from the Social Turn in live art relies on participatory practices that challenge, and even compromise the audience. This type of practice reflects the "de-centered and heterogeneous net that composes post-Fordist social co-operation" (Bishop 2012: 12), often with utopian themes of collective desires replacing neoliberal individualism. Representations of post-Fordist capitalism in the form of participatory systems in which it is possible to fail may serve the sublime experience in contemporary art practice in the same way that the abyss or void, by which the individual may be swallowed up, served the sublime experience in eighteenth and nineteenth century Romantic art.

Masks, apart from supporting the primary deprivation of Lyotard's formula for the sublime in art through deprioritisation of quotidian identity and reinforcement of the requested silence from audience participants, also contribute to secondary privation through simultaneously being a play boundary and a frame, as the mask has openings for the eyes. Some participants in this study reported that masks added to their experience of dreamlike states and a sense of dissolution of personal boundaries (Aud02, Aud03), but the recognition of how masks may contribute to their experience of the sublime through secondary privation is more elusive, as participants appear to become habituated to it. One participant articulated profound experiences characterised by a combination of licence and awe, both in part attributable to being masked, without recognising its influence, and only remarked on masks in the context of the behaviour of others (Aud05).

10.5 Posthuman Design Principles

The sublime in Punchdrunk's work, while supported by masking and the assumption of a play state of mind, rests on the instability of identity that represents the primary threat: dissolution of being. Anonymity and ambiguity are key devices for destabilisation of the quotidian identity of the participant, and also support the posthuman subject position. The incorporation or dissolution of individuals into interactive digital systems can be represented by the way their behaviour is recorded through data mining:

> 'Data-mining' includes profiling practices that identify different types of characteristics and highlights them as special strategic targets for capital investment. This kind of predictive analytics of the human amounts to 'Life-mining', with visibility, predictability and exportability as the key criteria (Braidotti 2013: 62).

Braidotti's critique of transcendence, as the principle underpinning the Cartesian subject position, includes a critique of data mining that highlights three criteria that signifies the transcendence of the practice; visibility, predictability and exportability. This analysis of Punchdrunk's work as posthuman interactive systems takes the opposites of these criteria into account as possible identifiers of immanence, allowing the posthuman to be a subject that understands itself from a position of embodied cognition in emergent relations to their environment (Hayles 2002: 303). The capacity for becoming-other that is supported by the immanent subject position serves the metamorphic narrative motif in embodied form, and contributes to the psychological immersion, dreamlike states and sublime experiences reported by participating audience members.

Wordless interaction by and with masked participants yields no information beyond that which is contained within the performance situation at the point of both entry and exit, and anonymity ensures that predictive modelling can only occur decoupled from user-specific information. Audience modelling is primarily based on observation of non-verbal behaviour, analysed in general terms without demographic profiling (Com01). In place of recording information about specific audience members or demographic profiles, in-system behaviours and micro-interactions are given keen attention. When moderation of behaviour is called for, it is based on observations of in-system behaviours, triggering in-system responses (normally by the Black Masks). Overly predictive instructions are avoided (Com04), and regulation of behaviours is designed as situation-specific responses, implemented by actors and Black Masks on the interface level (Com01, Com03). 'Records' of in-system audience behaviours are only preserved as iterations of the choreography and designed interactions.

Anonymity also supports ambiguity, which has further potential as a principle for consideration when designing systems and can be opened up through the concept of form as a two-sided construct; a proposed differentiation between an outside and an inside (Clarke 2008: 87–88). This redefines form as a conceptual boundary, drawing upon the cognitive narrative of the form-maker. Form has no meaning in a conceptual vacuum; it, like stories, draws on memory for meaning, and thus emanates from within the world order of its maker: imposed, through making, on the material at hand and in response to the imposition of the material on the hand. Form-as-boundary is a negotiation between maker and material, an emergent spatial practice. *Personified* form, according to Clarke, is a unity "created by holding the inside and the outside of distinctions together", allowing for metamorphosis (Clarke 2008: 88). The requirement for audiences to be masked at all times during Punchdrunk shows positions participants as personified form, an ambiguous state described by several interviewees as 'dreamlike' (Aud01, Aud02, Aud03, Aud04, Aud06). The two-sidedness of form is brought into acute focus during one-to-ones, when audience participants are invited into enclosed spaces by a performer, who proceeds to unmask them. The sudden exposure in close proximity to the performer is often experienced as unsettling, even unnerving, as the boundary between what has become the outside and the inside collapses, leaving only the instability of the situation: "I was like "no no no no no, I want it back, I want it back, I want it back; I feel safe with my mask on" (Com02).

Ambiguity also challenges ideological constructs that are embedded within systems through practices of classification. Categorisation of participants in interactive digital systems is an extension of the broader phenomenon of classification for use within administrative systems that inform "social and moral order" (Bowker and Star 2000: 5). Classification also underpins the discursive construction and maintenance of concepts of gender, race and species:

> In a brilliant mock taxonomy, Louis Borges classified animals into three groups: those we watch television with, those we eat, and those we are scared of. These exceptionally high levels of lived familiarity confine the human-animal interaction within classical parameters, namely, an oedipalized relationship (you and me on the same sofa); an instrumental (thou shall be consumed eventually) and a fantasmic one (exotic, extinct infotainment objects of titillation) (Braidotti 2013: 68).

Categorisation invites transcendent power relationships, with the 'observer' being the point of issue of the categories applied to that or those who are surveilled and categorised. This transcendent relation also allows the 'observer/categoriser' to remain uncategorised and unmarked, while defining the norm through occupying the only position that escapes scrutiny. As the Cartesian subject, transcending the animal state, is the liberal humanist definition of man, it follows that those observed may be positioned somewhere between not-quite-man and animal, according to Borges' classes of animals, i.e. those we watch television with, those we eat, and those we are scared of:

> [...] Deleuze insists that a 'minority' is not a question of numbers, but of the subordination of difference to a transcendent measure. Under majority rule, groups such as 'women, children, the South, the third world' (but also nonhuman animals) are, despite their numbers, constituted as subordinate minorities in relation to a standard measure: *the supposedly universal model of Man* (Cull 2012: 20, original emphasis)

Cull focuses on what Deleuze calls minor theatre; forms of non-traditional theatre that diverge from conventional narrative structure and representational techniques

(Cull 2012: 20). The use of the term 'minor' indicates, as in the case of Deleuze's definition of a minority, its relation to a transcendent measure, rather than an implicit value.

> [Deleuze] suggests that the revolutionary nature of a minor usage of theatre lies in its affirmation of the primacy of cross-categorical mutations, its emphasis on the tendency of life perpetually to differ from itself, alongside its tendency to congeal into recognizable or categorizable identities. (Cull 2012: 21)

In Punchdrunk's theatre, anonymity and ambiguity combine to produce alternative conditions for interaction and social organisation within a system. Classifications that are used within Punchdrunk systems are formed based on the particulars of interactive processes, reflecting immanence. The resulting conditions facilitate cross-categorical mutation, where the two sides of ambiguity, embodied in the interface layer, facilitate metamorphosis as dynamic instability.

A third condition in addition to anonymity and ambiguity is the information-rich (or high resolution) environment (Hayles 2002: 303). Audience participants report that their psychological immersion, or their decision to suspend disbelief, was supported and even made possible by the deeply layered and complex interface detail (Aud02, Aud03, Aud05). Process intensity in making is not tied to aesthetics similar to those in Punchdrunk productions, where every object is as 'real' as possible with a patinated and deeply detailed surface appeal; applied to digital materialities, process intensity might take a number of different expressions, including refined minimalism. Resolution can be regarded as a measure of the outcome of a more or less intense process, with more or fewer iterative steps, reflecting cognition in making. An artist working in oil would regard their process as extending over a lifetime of development, in addition to it being reified in individual paintings. Design is often more focused on products as objects in their own right, but good design is also the result of process intensity, usually involving many iterations, regardless of which particular aesthetic appeal the finished product bears. A minimalistic aesthetic can bear the marks of refinement, demanding a multi-step process of simplification rather than addition, and resulting in a product where lack of excessive detail reveals well-considered priorities with enhanced clarity. The meaning of the term resolution, in the context of the challenge or problematic presented by a particular design project or artistic exploration, can draw on its alternative meaning as an outcome of problem solving to clarify the importance of process intensity. Ideally, process intensity results in an outcome that is coherent and balanced in respect of aesthetic, semiotics, materials, technique, presentation, dynamic tension and audience appeal.

10.6   Implications for Digital Interactive Systems

Conclusions from this study include observations regarding the influence of immanent vs. transcendent subject-event relationships on the quality of experience in interactive systems. To facilitate psychological immersion in digital interactive systems designed according to posthumanist principles, this study identifies three signatures of immanence in particular for consideration when designing interactive storyworlds:

1. Process intensity, applied to the creation of semiotically rich interfaces with deeply encoded layers of meaning that encourage close-range engagement with the detail of interface and interactions.
2. Ambiguity, allowing participants a more fluid in-system identity, and careful consideration of how in-system actions are categorised to avoid over-instrumentalisation when not strictly necessary for the purpose of the interaction.
3. Anonymity, in order to preserve an immanent subject position, as longitudinal recording of in-system behaviours positions the in-system subject as event-object, with a transcendent observing subject that is external to the interaction.

Taken together, these indicate the direction for a paradigm shift in interactive system design, away from personalisation based on longitudinal tracking of participants and towards moment-by-moment responsiveness to the precise quality and detail of interactions. This could, for example, take the form of formulae that identify antisocial in-system behaviour and trigger previously scripted responses, an emerging concept in HCI (Cheng et al. 2015) and the design of online art interventions (Zero Trollerance 2015).

The identified principles can be employed as a framework for interpretation of the results of an R&D project undertaken by Punchdrunk in collaboration with MIT (Digital R&D Fund For the Arts 2012), and provides a hypothetical explanation for the reported lack of immersion experienced by many participants who participated in the project. The aim was to extend the experiential space of *Sleep No More* through the use of biometric sensors for real-time data gathering and mediated communication between the in-system participant and the external confederates, via portals embedded within the set. The external confederates also had access to the biometric data via screen presentation. The stated goal for participants was that they should be able to enter a playful mood, where they were "not directed by external goals", suggesting psychological immersion:

> This project intended to test whether an online interactive experience could be created that in some way matches the quality of the physical and visceral, live experience that is at the heart of immersive work. The experiment would attempt to join two audience members together to experience a coherent, shared storyline. One, physically present in the space of *Sleep No More*, one online, remotely on a laptop or other computer (Digital R&D Fund For the Arts 2012).

The external confederates, although they could interact with the in-system participant as if they were a game character, however generally failed to experience psychological immersion, with the exception of some external confederates who reported a stronger connection with the experience when working alone and at night in a one-to-one interaction with a performer. While the formal report on the MIT R&D project puts forth the conclusion that psychological immersion relies on induction into a liminal state through ritualistic story devices (including the masking and the imposed silence), the research discussed in this chapter proposes that ritualistic features are not necessarily sufficient on their own. For the profound sense of psychological immersion reported by a majority of live Punchdrunk audiences, experiential conditions created according to the signatures of immanence introduced above need to be in place.

As to the interface effect, the report suggests that digital screen presentation is not conducive to intrinsic motivation for behaviours, a conclusion that can be contested by the existence of autotelic digitally mediated, screen-presented experiences. The authors of the report furthermore conclude that there is a limit to scalability, due to the apparent need for this connection to be experienced as personal, with one in-system participant connected to one external confederate. They state that AI components in the system do not work in favour of immersion, and that a human co-participant is needed (Digital R&D Fund For the Arts 2012). This conclusion could be based on an incomplete analysis of the Punchdrunk format that does not take into account all relevant factors. While the importance of process intensity identified in this study supports part of the argument that scalability is limited, some aspects of interactive systems could be designed using carefully scripted AI agents. For example, the Black Masks are identified in audience interviews as key to the elicitation of dreamlike states of mind due to the effect of their interference with participant agency. In digital interactive systems, AI agents could serve the role of scripted moderators according to a template based on the function and design of the Black Mask interventions, translated and designed so as to be relevant to the particular material circumstances.

An analysis of the subject-event relationship, key in postmodern discourses, could reposition the observations made in the official report on the MIT project and suggest fertile directions for augmented reality and interaction design research. Several factors identified in the report are pertinent to the recognition of the transcendence-immanence dichotomy as crucial to psychological immersion, e.g. extrinsic vs. intrinsic motivation, AI vs. human participants, and the matter of scalability. The question of extrinsic motivation is key to a critique of the transcendent or metaphysical subject position in relation to the event, as it leaves the structure of the experience exposed to extrinsic motives. Furthermore, the argument that AI participants cannot be as effective as a human counterpart in a digital interactive system is incomplete without a detailed analysis of how the AI is scripted. The argument against scalability goes straight to the core of the issue of transcendence vs. immanence, and is complex. Scalability is an inherent feature of the transcendent subject-event relationship, and is generally encouraged in digital design to optimise the return on process intensity. When over-optimised or expressed as over-instrumentalisation, scalability impacts negatively on user experience; an observation that is often acknowledged in commercial interaction design. Several audience participants that were interviewed during the ethnographic research in this study associated the intensity of detail and deeply encoded layers of meaning designed into the interface with their psychological immersion and the collapse of critical distance in relation to their experiences (Aud02, Aud05, Aud06), supporting the hypothesis that the process intensity applied to the design and build of the production supports suspense of disbelief. But while constructed with extreme attention to detail, both *Sleep No More* and *The Drowned Man* are scaled experiences, built for large numbers of audience participants and long production runs. The shows are also constructed, built and run according to replicable design formulae that the company developed during previous productions, so scalability expressed as repetition is demonstrably not counterproductive to the artistic aims of the company, which specifically include inducing psychological immersion in participants. Replicable formulae that are designed with sufficient process intensity to yield a refined, information-rich, and high-resolution experience do not appear to counter the suspense of disbelief, suggesting that scalability, as a concept used in the commercial design environment, need to be further articulated to avoid the conflation of overly reductive design and replicability. Scalability in itself is not necessarily counterproductive to good or even excellent user experience, but we need an incisive critique of exactly what – or whom – is scaled, and in what manner, if we are to imagine and build story worlds that are posthuman, rather than inhuman.

The analysis of the MIT R&D project against the proposed design principles above suggests that it was not the digital mediation or screenic presentation per se that countered psychological immersion, but the conversion of an experience characterised by immanence into one that allowed the incursion of transcendence. In order to produce interactive storyworlds that are structurally supportive of deep psychological immersion and the suspension of disbelief, this research therefore proposes immanence as a condition, maintained through a design paradigm that includes anonymity, ambiguity and process intensity.

References

Bishop C (2012) Artificial hells, 1st edn. Verso Books, London

Bowker GC, Star SL (2000) Sorting things out: classification and its consequences. MIT, Cambridge, MA

Braidotti R (2013) The posthuman. Polity, London

Caillois R (2001) Man, play, and games, 1st edn. Free Press of Glencoe, New York

Cheng J, Danescu-Niculescu-Mizil C, Leskovec J (2015) Antisocial behavior in online discussion communities. *arXiv: 1504.00680 [cs.SI]*. Cornell University Library. [online] Available at: http://arxiv.org/abs/1504.00680. Accessed 13 Jul 2015

Clarke B (2008) Posthuman metamorphosis: narrative and systems. Fordham University Press, New York

Coyne R (1995) Designing information technology in the postmodern age. MIT Press, Cambridge, MA

Cull L (2012) Theatres of immanence. Palgrave Macmillan, Houndmills

de Certeau M (1988). The practice of everyday life. University of California Press, Berkeley

Deleuze G (2014) Difference and repetition. Bloomsbury, London

Digital R&D Fund For the Arts (2012) Between worlds: report for NESTA on MIT/Punchdrunk theatre sleep no more digital R&D project. University of Dundee, University of West England

Galloway A (2004) Protocol: how control exists after decentralization. MIT, Cambridge, MA

Hayles K (1999) How we became posthuman. University of Chicago Press, Chicago

Hayles K (2002) Flesh and metal: reconfiguring the mindbody in virtual environments. Configurations 2(2):297–320

Huizinga J (1955) Homo Ludens. Beacon, Boston

Lyotard J-F (1984). The postmodern condition: a reflection on knowledge. Manchester University Press, Manchester

Lyotard J-F (1991) The inhuman: reflections on time. Polity, Cambridge

Sutton-Smith B (2001) The ambiguity of play. Harvard University Press, Cambridge, MA

Tripadvisor (2015a) Sleep No More. [Online] Available at: http://www.tripadvisor.co.uk/Attraction_Review-g60763-d2631104-Reviews-Sleep_No_More-New_York_City_New_York.html. Accessed 4 Apr 2015

Tripadvisor (2015b). The Drowned Man: A Hollywood Fable. [Online] Available at: http://www.tripadvisor.co.uk/Attraction_Review-g186338-d4579588-Reviews-The_Drowned_Man_A_Hollywood_Fable-London_England.html#REVIEWS. Accessed 4 Apr 2015

Zero Trollerance (2015). Self-help for sexists in six simple steps. [Online] Available at: http://zerotrollerance.guru/. Accessed 13 July 2015